Disability and the Internet

Disability in Society

Ronald J. Berger, series editor

Disability and the Internet

Confronting a Digital Divide

Paul T. Jaeger

LYNNE
RIENNER
PUBLISHERS

BOULDER
LONDON

Published in the United States of America in 2012 by
Lynne Rienner Publishers, Inc.
1800 30th Street, Boulder, Colorado 80301
www.rienner.com

and in the United Kingdom by
Lynne Rienner Publishers, Inc.
3 Henrietta Street, Covent Garden, London WC2E 8LU

Library of Congress Cataloging-in-Publication Data
Jaeger, Paul T., 1974–
  Disability and the Internet : confronting a digital divide / Paul T. Jaeger.
    p. cm. — (Disability in society)
  Includes bibliographical references and index.
  ISBN 978-1-58826-828-0 (hbk. : alk. paper)
1. Computers and people with disabilities. 2. Digital divide. I. Title.
  HV1569.5.J34 2011
  362.4'0483—dc22

                                              2011016941

British Cataloguing in Publication Data
A Cataloguing in Publication record for this book
is available from the British Library.

Printed and bound in the United States of America

∞ The paper used in this publication meets the requirements
   of the American National Standard for Permanence of
   Paper for Printed Library Materials Z39.48-1992.

5 4 3 2 1

Contents

Preface

There has long been a need for a book that examines the social, cultural, and political intersections of disability and the Internet. This is especially so given the enormous potential benefits and looming barriers for persons with disabilities in using the Internet and its progeny like the World Wide Web and the now omnipresent Web-enabled mobile technologies that combine phones, computers, and media players into a single device.

The Internet has resulted in major changes in today's society, with considerable ramifications for all people. Equal access to the Internet is quickly becoming essential to education, employment, government, and many other forms of social interaction. A lack of access or limited access may soon equate to isolation from many aspects of society. For persons with disabilities, unless technological design and implementation meaningfully focus on inclusion, the Internet may become a new means of increased marginalization in society. Study after study has found extremely high levels of inaccessibility in commercial, educational, and government websites, often between 90 and 100 percent. This inaccessibility can be tied to the technologies used to access the Internet, the Internet connection, or the online content.

Because people with disabilities are the largest minority in the United States, constituting about one-sixth of the population, an inaccessible Internet affects a great many people. Barriers to equal access online threaten to promote societal isolation and to instill a sense of disconnect and disempowerment for this group. Common misconceptions and biases among developers of new technologies, along with giant loopholes in the law, facilitate the creation, implementation, and perpetuation of inaccessible technologies and content related to the Internet. Ironically, the pre-Web Internet—an environment in which content was mostly limited to electronically readable text—was more accessible to many users with disabilities than is the contemporary Web-enabled Internet.

In sharp contrast to the current limited levels of access, an accessible Internet has the potential to provide people with disabilities the opportunity to be more integrated into society than ever before. Online education and telework open the door to earning degrees and having a career without the hindrances that may accompany travel outside the home. As people with disabilities have far lower average levels of education and employment than the rest of society, these are extremely important avenues toward increased social inclusion.

E-commerce could alleviate similar challenges with shopping, and e-government opens up many new ways that people with disabilities could become more involved in politics and government. Online social interactions create opportunities for people with unique disabilities to talk with others who share the same condition, opportunities that may never exist in the physical world. For people with disabilities in general, online social interactions create innumerable new ways to share advice and friendship with others with disabilities and to meet people without disabilities in a manner that does not emphasize the disability. In fact, people with disabilities can use the Internet to build friendships with people who are not even aware of the disability.

Such opportunities for increased social inclusion depend on the Internet providing equal access to people with disabilities. Unfortunately, the general state of Internet accessibility has not improved greatly since the World Wide Web has existed, even with a range of laws intended to promote equal access online. Issues of Internet accessibility for people with disabilities receive surprisingly little attention in the media, the government, scholarship, and general public discourse. A vibrant—though not large—body of scholarly literature considers these issues. However, it is far beyond time for a book that focuses exclusively on the social, cultural, and political ramifications of disability and the Internet. Hopefully, this book will meet this extremely important need.

Acknowledgments

This book exists because Andrew Berzanskis, acquisitions editor at Lynne Rienner Publishers, and Ronald J. Berger, editor of the Disability in Society series, invited me to address the topic. Andrew and Ronald have proved to be bountiful sources of terrific insights into the organization and presentation of the ideas in the book. The anonymous reviewers also offered very helpful comments on an earlier version. Additionally, Lynne Rienner Publishers as a company deserves gratitude for investing their resources in a book series devoted to topics of disability in society.

I have been thinking about disability as long as I can remember, initially for purely practical reasons. And I have spent most of my adult life teaching, researching, and writing about issues of disability and technology. As a scholar and an educator, I regard my work related to disability as the most personally significant aspect of what I do. It was a tremendous experience to be able to collate a lifetime of reflection and a dozen years of professional endeavors into this book.

During my career, I have worked with a lot of people on various studies related to disability and broader considerations of diversity. I have learned an enormous amount from these collaborations and friendships, which of course significantly informed the thoughts in this book and its perspective, though any deficiencies in the text are purely my responsibility. I would like to express my warmest appreciation to John Carlo Bertot, Cynthia Ann Bowman, Gary Burnett, Kathleen Burnett, Renee E. Franklin Hill, Cassandra B. Jones,

Jonathan Lazar, Howard Rodriguez-Mori, John A. Shuler, Mega M. Subramaniam, Kim M. Thompson, and Brian Wentz.

I would also like to thank the staff members of the Information Policy and Access Center (iPAC) at the University of Maryland, who looked after things when I periodically wandered off to work on my manuscript: Simon Boyce, Stephanie Clarke-Graham, Elizabeth J. DeCoster, Kerry M. Dhakal, Leahkim Gannett, Natalie Greene, Justin M. Grimes, Ursula Groham-Oscilowski, Sarah M. Katz, Karen M. Kettnich, Christie M. Kodama, Lesley A. Langa, Elizabeth C. Larson, Erissa R. Mann, Abigail J. McDermott, James P. Neal III, Natalie L. Perkins, Katie Shanahan, Kathryn I. Sigler, Joyreeta Soibam, and Emily E. Wahl. I'm particularly grateful to Sarah Katz for finding some rather inexplicable typos and for wanting to read the book in the first place. I owe some fresh, new catnip toys to Rosa and Willow for being constant company while I was working on the book.

Finally, I would like to thank you, the readers, for taking the time to consider the ideas presented in this book and to express my hope that you find the experience valuable.

—*Paul T. Jaeger*

Disability and the Internet

1

Disability in the Internet Age

It is nearly impossible to live a life exclusively offline in today's world. In most cases, registering a student for school, filing taxes, applying for social benefits, banking, and performing numerous other tasks require use of the Internet. In many cases, these types of services are offered exclusively online. Additionally, many entertainment options and shopping resources only exist online. When there are physical and virtual equivalents, the online versions often offer lower prices, greater selection, home delivery, and other conveniences.

The devices powered by the Internet have created new means of interaction and information resources that were unthinkable even ten years ago. A portable device that simultaneously surfs the Web, stores digital media, works as a computer, stores and plays audio and video, takes digital pictures, works as a phone, provides navigation, and performs many other functions is still incredible, even though such devices have become extremely commonplace.

Since the development of the World Wide Web in the mid-1990s, the Internet has dramatically changed the ways we live. Yet, the opportunities the Web offers are not equally available to all. Information technology (IT) has been both a liberating tool that provides increased access to information as well as "a creator of new or additional barriers to accessing information and the benefits of an information society" (Stienstra, Watzke, and Birch, 2007, p. 151). Issues of socioeconomic status, education, geography, literacy, and other factors shape the availability of the Internet and the extent of the role it plays in an individual's life. "While the digital divide has definitely narrowed over the last decade or so, it's still wider than many would like it to be" (Rainey, 2011, p. 9). For most disadvantaged groups, however, gaps in Internet access can be overcome with the provision of computers, connections, and education. Many groups that were formerly severely disadvantaged in their access to the Internet are much less so now because public libraries across the country provide free public Internet access and training to their patrons, and Web-enabled mobile devices have become more affordable.

For persons with disabilities, the gaps in access and usage are much more complex. People with disabilities use the Internet and related technologies at levels approximately half of the rest of the population. The main reason for this is not a lack of interest or education or inclination, but the fact that the Internet is inherently unfriendly to many different kinds of disabilities. These barriers to access and usage vary by type and extent of disability.

Persons with visual impairments can face challenges in the lack of compatibility of content with screen readers, the failure to put text tags on graphics, the use of color schemes that negatively impact users with color blindness, and numerous other programming decisions that can shut out users with limited vision and no vision. For persons with mobility impairments, the barriers are created by incompatibility with alternate input devices, cluttered layout, buttons and links that are too small, and other important navigability considerations that can render entire sites and functions unusable. For persons with hearing impairments, the lack of textual equivalents of audio content can cut off large portions of the content of a site, and interactive webchats and other conferencing features may be impossible. People with speech and communication impairments can also be excluded from interactive webchats and other conferencing features. For persons with cognitive impairments, issues of design, layout, descriptive text, use of visual guides, alignment, and navigability are the difference between being able to use a site and not being able to use it. Persons with specific learning disabilities, depending on the nature of the disability, may face the same barriers as people with visual impairments or people with cognitive impairments. For people with seizure disorders, rates of flickering and flash can literally jeopardize their health.

Experiences with the Internet also frequently vary by type of disability. The same website often offers opportunities for one group and excludes another. Consider Web-based distance education. For a student who is a wheelchair user, being able to take courses online may make education much easier; if the course website is not designed to be accessible for students with impairments that limit mobility in the hands, however, participation in the course may be limited or impossible. Similarly, the Web-enabled mobile device with a touch screen may seem like a miracle to a user with a hearing impairment and a nightmare to a user with a visual impairment. As such, the Internet and related technologies present a complex set of problems for persons with disabilities, both as a larger population and as separate populations by type of disability.

Although the range of potential barriers to persons with disabilities in the online environment is great, there are ways to develop and implement technologies so that persons with disabilities are included. There are known and achievable means to address the problems previously mentioned. However, these solutions are frequently not considered in the process of design and implementation of websites and Web-enabled technologies.

Many developers of websites and related new technologies simply do not consider persons with disabilities when they create or update products. The reasons include lack of awareness of disability issues, active belief that persons with disabilities have little value as users of the website or technology, bigotry against persons with disabilities, and simple neglect of persons with disabilities as users. In many cases, the websites and technologies that result from this disregard of accessibility run afoul of federal civil rights laws for persons with disabilities. Yet, these laws are not even enough to spur an accessible Internet. For a decade, the websites of the US federal government and those receiving federal government funding have been required by law to be accessible to persons with disabilities. Unfortunately, studies of government website accessibility regularly find government agencies with extremely low levels of compliance.

In fact, many of the issues of inclusion and exclusion online for persons with disabilities have been considered in law and policy, but the conceptions of disability under the law, exemptions from compliance, limited enforcement, and the inability of law to keep pace with technological development all hinder the impact that the laws have had thus far. An organized disability rights movement focused on the Internet also has the potential to force changes in the level of access by working to have greater say in the development and enforcement of online accessibility. Although issues of online accessibility affect most persons with disabilities, there has not yet been large-scale coordination between populations with different disabilities—and between persons with disabilities and other underserved populations—to create a movement that campaigns for equal access online.

The neglectful and negative attitudes of developers would be shocking even if persons with disabilities represented a very small portion of the overall population. These attitudes are even more shocking in light of the fact that persons with disabilities are a large and growing population. Currently constituting about one-sixth of the US population, persons with disabilities will continue to increase as a portion of the population as the baby boom generation ages. There is a very sizable market for accessible websites and related technologies, but the demand far outstrips the supply.

Such a disjunction is not new to the Internet, however. It is part of a much larger trend. "The introduction of new technologies sees people with disabilities overlooked, omitted, neglected, and not considered" (Goggin and Newell, 2007, p. 160). The distance between writing and writing systems for persons with visual impairments can be measured in millennia. The gap between typeset printed books and Braille and talking books was nearly half a millennium. More recent developments, like TTD/TTY services and closed captioning to include people with hearing impairments, came decades after the mass production of the telephone and television. While it is not a new problem, unequal access to the Internet is a broader problem than these previous gaps in access due to the scope of the Internet in social, education, government, entertainment, communication, information seeking, and other functions.

Many new Web products are developed and launched seemingly with the intent to be openly discriminatory against persons with disabilities. For example, although portable e-book readers can easily be built with the capability to verbalize the text of the e-books, they often are not. Amazon's Kindle reader has the capability, but, when it was launched, the speech function was blocked in most of the titles available for the reader, and the navigation options were limited for users with visual and mobility impairments. Later versions of the reader were improved so that the Kindle 3 enabled the speech functions on the device and had improved enlargement features so that users with visual impairments had far more access to Kindle texts. However, when the Kindle 3 was launched, it was still the only e-book reader that had such accessibility features.

Perhaps more distressing, the lack of consideration for disability in the design of information technologies often is replicated in the adoption of information technologies. When the Kindle was introduced, a number of major universities planned to start using it for textbooks, and that number continues to grow (Sadon, 2010), but without consideration of the implications for students and faculty with visual and mobility impairments. Threats of lawsuits from nine disability rights groups were required to change the attitudes of Amazon and the universities, though persons with disabilities were widely mocked on technology blogs and websites—and on Amazon's site—for fighting for equal access to the Kindle. Educational institutions were even more enthusiastic to adopt the Blackboard online course software, which was primarily inaccessible when it was launched and only became disability-friendly ten years later. Nevertheless, Blackboard software was used at most universities in the country.

In spite of all of these barriers, the Internet has been justifiably viewed as having enormous potential for promoting social inclusion for persons with disabilities. In 2000, people with disabilities who were able to access and use the Internet were already reporting notably larger benefits from the Internet in some areas than the general population. Adults with disabilities in 2000 were already more likely to believe the Internet improved the quality of their lives (48 percent of people with disabilities vs. 27 percent of the general population), made them better informed about the world (52 vs. 39 percent), helped them meet people with similar interests and experiences (42 vs. 30 percent), and gave them more connections to the world (44 vs. 38 percent) than the general population (Taylor, 2000).

More than a decade later, the potential benefits of the Internet have increased exponentially, but the equality of access has not improved meaningfully. In 2011, 54 percent of adults with disabilities used the Internet, whereas 81 percent of other adults did (Fox, 2011a, 2011b). People with disabilities who regularly use the Internet also lag behind in quality of access, with 41 percent of adults with disabilities having broadband access at home, in contrast to 69 percent of the rest of the population. A 2010 study similarly found that broadband adoption by persons with disabilities was two-thirds that of the national average and that people with disabilities who have broadband engage in a much smaller range of online activities as a result of accessibility issues (Horrigan, 2010).

Given the importance of the Internet in education and employment, such differences in access have serious ramifications for the opportunities available to people with disabilities. The 2011 study found 46 percent of adults with disabilities living in a household with

$30,000 or less in annual income, compared with only 26 percent of the rest of the population (Fox, 2011a). Similarly, 61 percent of adults with a disability had a high school education or less, while only 40 percent of other adults did.

Currently, some Internet technologies are a significant benefit to people with specific types of disabilities, while other Internet technologies offer potential opportunities to all persons with disabilities. Smartphones, although they exclude many other persons with disabilities, have been a boon for persons with hearing, speech, or other types of communication impairments, who can now use the phones to communicate face-to-face much more efficiently than they previously could. Similarly, with video chat, these same individuals can now carry on conversations over the phone in new ways. People with certain cognitive impairments that inhibit the formation of speech or short-term memories—such as Down syndrome and amnesia—also benefit enormously from the capacity of the portable technologies to provide instant communication through text. For the broader populations of people with disabilities, the Internet has a great deal of potential to create new means of communication and interaction through online communities devoted to particular types of disabilities. People who might never encounter someone with a similar disability in their physical environment can now interact directly with people with similar conditions worldwide. For people whose disabilities limit their ability to leave their homes, the Internet has the potential to provide a far greater world of interaction. People with disabilities even have the option to choose to live their online lives as people without disabilities.

Beyond the clear potential socialization and communication benefits, the Internet offers an enormous array of new ways to pursue education and employment. For people who might find it very difficult or even impossible to travel to a building for work or school, the Internet provides the ability to work or take classes from home. These potential benefits might be the greatest benefits in the long term for promoting social inclusion of persons with disabilities, as the current levels of employment and education for persons with disabilities are catastrophically low in comparison with the rest of the population. In this book I examine this tremendous ball of complexities that surrounds the intersections between disability and the Internet.

Exploring issues of society, technology, law and policy, communication, information, interaction, education, employment, and social participation, I analyze the complex and often contradictory relationships between persons with disabilities and the Internet. Though a respectable amount of scholarship has been created about issues of disability and the Internet, such work is spread across many disciplines and is rarely considered as a whole. This diffuse approach also often results in a fragmented current picture of disability in society. For example, this text uses the most recent statistics related to disability available, but the limited attention to these issues often results in measures that are not frequently updated. Drawing upon this research from a wide range of disciplines, I identify the social issues of disability and the Internet, analyzes relevant research from across related disciplines, synthesize the implications of these issues and research, and consider future approaches that could promote online opportunities for persons with disabilities and address online inequalities they face.

For persons with disabilities, the Internet has enormous potential to increase social inclusion, but thus far it has offered only limited opportunities for equal participation as a result of issues of technological design and development, policy, and even overt discrimination. Despite laws intended to promote equal access online for persons with disabilities, access remains limited due to inaccessible design and implementation of websites and other technologies, incompatibility with assistive technologies, and widely used exemptions to the laws. Yet, the Internet also has provided significant benefits to some individuals with disabilities, ranging from allowing people with rare conditions to meet others with similar conditions online, to enabling speakers of sign language to converse over great distances. New online communities foster social interactions between different groups invested in disability issues, and not only do they allow persons with disabilities to discuss emotional and physical experiences of disability, but they also enable their parents, spouses, and friends to find information and support. Simultaneously, the Internet is helping to shape new social perceptions of disability—both good and bad—through the content about disability and persons with disabilities that is appearing online.

As Internet access becomes increasingly central to education, employment, government, communication, and social interaction, it is vital to understand the role of the Internet as an aspect of disability in society. By examining these issues across the research from diverse academic disciplines and from cross-national perspectives, this book is intended to provide a full portrait of disability and the Internet, and through this portrayal, illuminate means by which the Internet can ultimately serve to make society more inclusive of persons with disabilities.

Drawing upon scholarship related to disability and the Internet from a number of different disciplines, the book embraces related insights from information studies, sociology, education, computer science, law, public policy, communication, media studies, history, anthropology, and disability studies. With the intent of trying to thoroughly examine the social, cultural, and political dimensions of access to the Internet for persons with disabilities, I have written the book to be of interest to teachers, scholars, and students from any discipline. It is scholarly in nature but written at a level intended to make it useful and accessible to all of these readers. The discussions are not technical in nature; this is to ensure that they are understandable to readers of all levels of technological literacy. Additionally, discussions of specific websites are minimized to ensure that the book remains relevant, as the shelf life of most aspects of the Internet tends to be fairly limited, and many websites disappear or devolve due to "digital decay" (Dougherty, 2010, p. 445).

Structure of the Book

In terms of technology, it is important to consider the ramifications of technological change. The past twenty years of change have been so enormous and all-encompassing for information technology that things may have changed more in the past two decades than in the past five centuries. Even the most creative minds of science fiction in 1990 could not have imagined the world of interconnectedness, personalization, omnipresence, and miniaturization that technology now provides. Far too many people accept such changes unthinkingly, as if a rapid pace of technological change that threatens to leave many groups behind is a natural and acceptable byproduct of progress and a fair exchange for all of the applications in the newest Web-enabled mobile device.

Technological change has meaning to and ramifications for users and nonusers alike. Children who avoid television, the Internet, and video games still are affected by the decisions of the majority of their age group to focus on those same technologies as primary sources of entertainment. The rare teenager who is not constantly sending text messages is isolated from many peers by the decision to try to communicate face-to-face.

Accepting technological change without analyzing it allows technology to assert prominence over the users of the technology. "We shall never experience our relationship to the essence of technology so long as we merely conceive and usher forward the technological, put up with it, or evade it" (Heidegger, 1977, p. 287). While most people accept the Internet as a revolutionary good for society and for their own lives, it is essential to ponder those disenfranchised by the Internet and the impact of such disenfranchisement from the central technology of the early twenty-first century.

Building on the large-scale issues and contexts discussed in this chapter, Chapter 2 examines the historical and legal issues raised by the intersection of disability and information technology, exploring the relationships between technology development and civil rights laws for persons with disability. Chapter 3 focuses on issues raised by online interactions for persons with disabilities in a range of important professional, personal, and public contexts. Chapter 4 discusses the roles of accessibility evaluation and policy reform in promoting a more inclusive Internet. Issues of online identity, representation, and advocacy for persons with disabilities are explored in Chapter 5. Finally, Chapter 6 synthesizes the themes from the book and offers a discussion of the ways in which individuals with disabilities, disability rights organizations, policymakers, technology developers, educators, and researchers can contribute to improving the accessibility of the Internet to promote the social inclusion of persons with disabilities.

The remainder of this chapter lays the groundwork for the subsequent chapters of the book. First, it discusses the different conceptual approaches to disability and the perspective used in the book. It then explores the different perspectives related to disability in societal contexts, the language of disability, and issues of access for persons with disabilities, three areas that inform much of the discussion that follows. The chapter next introduces the theoretical frame employed in the book—the theory of information worlds. The chapter concludes with a reflection on the implications of disability and the Internet both in terms of societal context and from the vantage point of an individual with a disability.

Conceptual Approaches to Disability

The conceptual foundations of this book exist within the larger contexts of disability studies research that shape approaches to disability, society, language, and technology. Building upon the discipline and perspectives of information policy, this text frames its discussion of disability and the Internet in terms of the theory of information worlds. This approach also informs the language choices of the text related to disability, information, and technology. The goal of these discussions is to establish the parameters of and reasons for the conceptual, theoretical, and language choices in the text and discuss their relationships to other approaches to the study of disability.

Any academic discussion of disability in contemporary society is at least partially framed by the work of advocates and scholars of disability to move away from what is known as the "medical model" toward a "social model" of disability and beyond. In this context, the term *model* indicates the general frame that society employs in relation to disability. The primary difference between these models is the perception of disability as being located inside the person or socially imposed upon the person. Or, more finely, the medical model focuses on fixing individuals, and the social model focuses on fixing the environment (Hahn, 2001).

The medical model was long the approach taken to disability, and the definitions used derived from health and medicine and focused on "the causes, symptoms, and interventions that will help that individual or others who have a similar disability" (Stroman, 2003, p. 15). The medical model assumes that persons with disabilities have deficiencies that they must compensate for, that they must adapt to the social, educational, professional, and political conceptualizations that serve to marginalize them. The medical model is also strongly associated with the decisions affecting the lives of people with disabilities being made by others, particularly medical professionals, and with the forced reliance on external supports by persons with disabilities.

The medical model emphasizes disability as a purely functional issue, and persons with disabilities often associate it with oppression. Sadly, the medical model reflects the way that disability is still most commonly viewed among general populations of many nations (Prince, 2009). In contrast, the social model focuses on the ways in which social, educational, professional, and political conceptualizations marginalize people with disabilities and the ways in which these conceptualizations can be altered to become inclusive of people with disabilities (Stroman, 2003). Under the social model, "disability is a form of social oppression involving the social imposition of restrictions of activity on people with impairments and the socially engendered undermining of their psycho-emotional well-being" (Thomas, 1999, p. 3).

The argument that disability is socially produced has much historical evidence in its corner. For example, the approach of the social model is supported by the fact that in the eighteenth century, Martha's Vineyard was renowned for openness toward and inclusion of people who were deaf, with one in twenty-five residents actually being deaf. In this community, everyone knew how to sign, and there were no differences in employment or educational attainment between the deaf and the hearing residents (Shapiro, 1993).

As an advance over the medical model, the social model "has the great advantage for advocacy of diverting attention from what *happened* to disabled people as individuals (what caused their impairments) to what *happens* to them collectively as the result of unnecessary social and cultural restraints" (Couser, 2009, p. 27). The social model is clearly a major step forward as a societal frame for disability.

The social model has proven instrumental as a tool for advocacy in promoting the sizable gains in civil rights for persons with disabilities in many nations over the past several decades. Prior to the assertion of civil rights perspective inherent in the social model, the bigotry toward persons with disabilities was socially accepted as "self-evident truth" (Johnson, 2006, p. 54). Building on the social model, the terminology of the disability rights movement has emphasized concepts of independence and self-reliance, concepts that are resonant with the general populace in many places (Bagenstos, 2009). For all of its value as a tool for changing perceptions about disability, however, the social model is also problematic.

While the social model is now the most common approach among disability scholars and activists, neither the medical model nor the social model in isolation presents an accurate picture of disability, as it is simultaneously an issue of individual difference and of social construction (Corker and Shakespeare, 2002; Stroman, 2003). "Both the medical model and the social model seek to explain disability universally, and end up creating totalizing, meta-historical narratives that exclude important dimensions of disabled people's lives and their knowledge" (Corker and Shakespeare, 2002, p. 15). Or, from a more individualized perspective, "the social model of disability proposes an untenable separation between body and culture, impairment and disability" (Hughes and Paterson, 1997, p. 326).

The social model also suffers from the fact that, if disability is indeed a social creation and not about the individual, then it makes little sense to provide legal rights specifically to people with disabilities as a population (Bagenstos, 2009). It is very hard to define policies to address social constructions, especially if the characteristic that defines the population is not actually a characteristic of the members of the population.

To address these types of issues, a postmodern model of disability has been proposed. The postmodernist approach to disability argues that there are no social structures that shape the individual lives of people with disabilities; instead, life is a series of opportunities for individuals to reinvent themselves (Corker and Shakespeare, 2002; Shakespeare, 1994). However, the postmodern model fails to adequately address the realities of disability as a personal, lived experience. "In most postmodern cultural theorizing about the body, there is no recognition of—and, as far as I can see, no room for recognizing—the hard physical realities that are faced by people with disabilities" (Wendell, 1996, p. 45).

As a result, there are currently multiple different ways in which scholars of disability may conceive of disability. There are also geographic differences in the conception of and approach to disability. In the United States, a good deal of the focus—both under the law and among disability scholars and advocates—has been on viewing disability as a minority group, with its own knowledge and experiences that others do not share (Siebers, 2006). The language of disability rights laws in the United States is all premised on disability as a minority group in society. From this sociopolitical standpoint, disability is "not a physical or mental defect but a cultural and minority identity" (Siebers, 2008, p. 4). As such, people with disabilities "are disadvantaged by the way society is organized," and the solution is a policy that "addresses various attitudinal and environmental barriers that prevent disabled people from participating" (Turmusani, 2003, p. xiii).

The problem with this approach, however, is that disability is not a binary experience but a range of very diverse experiences (Sherry, 2008). People with disabilities are all members of other populations as well, so individual experiences of people with disabilities are also shaped by race, gender, ethnicity, age, education, socioeconomic status, and other factors (Sherry, 2008). There are also limits to what can be accomplished by providing civil rights to persons with disabilities as a minority group. "We need to recognize that social justice and cultural change can eliminate a great deal of disability while recognizing that there may be much suffering and limitation that they cannot fix" (Wendell, 1996, p. 45).

These differences in perspective are exacerbated by goals for differing social outcomes among persons with disabilities, ranging from the desire to cast off any social support as a form of oppression to the desire for a considerable expansion of the social supports and welfare provided to persons with disabilities (Bagenstos, 2009). Yet, for all of the differing approaches and disagreements about perspectives on disability that can be found in contemporary scholarship on disability, these perspectives are all united by the genuine desire to establish a perspective—or multiple perspectives—that help to realistically portray the societal standing of persons with disabilities and the ways in which that standing can be improved and made equal with other members of society.

From an applied standpoint, a useful way to reconcile these differences is to view disability as simultaneously a natural part of human diversity and an environmental outcome shaped by social attitudes toward such diversity (Enns and Neufeldt, 2003). A similar approach to understanding disability is to conceive of it as being the manifestation of two interrelated elements: (1) the ongoing presence of a physical or cognitive condition that society deems unusual; and (2) the social and institutionalized discrimination or exclusion resulting from this physical or cognitive condition that society deems unusual (Jaeger and Bowman, 2002, 2005). In the context of the discussions in this book, *physical* impairments include the range of sensory and mobility impairments that affect use of the Internet and related information and technologies, while *cognitive* impairments include the range of intellectual, developmental, and learning impairments that affect use of the Internet and related information and technologies.

In this book, the perspective toward disability in society is definitely on the applied side, driven by the disciplinary perspective of information policy that frames the text. Information policy is a discipline that encompasses elements of law, public policy, information studies, computer science, and communication to analyze issues of access to and use of information and related technologies (McClure and Jaeger, 2008; Relyea, 2008; Schmetzke, 2007a). A key part of this research is a focus on populations in society that face gaps in such access and use, which are often socially imposed differences created by technology design and implementation or articulation of law and policy (Jaeger et al., 2011; McClure and Jaeger, 2008). Information policy research is strongly oriented toward identifying such gaps, isolating their causes, and changing policy to mitigate them.

Such gaps have come to be collectively known as "the digital divide," though common understandings of the term do not capture the complexities of the issues. In fact, these gaps result in populations being variously disadvantaged, underrepresented, and underserved in terms of information and technology (Jaeger et al., 2011). This status derives from a combination of social attitudes, educational and employment opportunities, technology development and implementation, and legal and policy decisions that negatively impact or discount the needs of persons with disabilities in relation to information and related technologies. Persons with disabilities are not alone in facing such disadvantages, because socioeconomic status, educational attainment, gender, language, literacy, age, and geography, among others, can influence access to and use of information and related technologies (Baker, 2001; Jaeger et al., 2011; Kinney, 2010).

These gaps have been especially pronounced for persons with disabilities, however. Such a lack of access can be seen as a civil rights violation that requires rethinking of technology design and social policy (DePoy and Gilson, 2006, 2008). As I detail throughout the book, persons with disabilities historically have been strongly disadvantaged—and continue to be in contemporary society—in access to and use of information and technology, deriving from a range of interrelated social, educational, technological, and political biases.

A key part of the approach of information policy is the analysis of the established legal context. As such, for an analysis rooted in the laws of the United States, the approach is inherently tied to the sociopolitical approach of persons with disabilities as a minority population. But that does not mean that assumptions under the law are not deconstructed as part of this analysis. Several of the major causes of the information gaps faced by persons with disabilities are a direct result of the constructions within the law itself.

Disability rights laws in the United States have been built on an antisubordination approach, meaning that rights are only available if one is a member of the legally defined class of people protected; in contrast, all other types of civil rights laws in the United States are based on an antidifferentiation approach, meaning that anyone has protections under the law if they are being discriminated against (Colker, 2005). This difference means that disability rights laws are much harder to enforce, as people with disabilities must first prove that they have standing under the law, something no other population must do under civil rights laws. The law also has many exceptions, loopholes, and inherent contradictions in terms of information and technology that serve to increase and even encourage discrimination against persons with disabilities.

The approach I take here, however, does not mean that a post-modernist approach to the interrelations between disability and the Internet would not prove insightful and useful. In fact, any additional detailed engagement with the topic of disability and the Internet in disability studies would be extremely valuable. Despite the enormity of the Internet in the social, political, educational, and economic lives of every member of society, the Internet is fairly neglected in the field of disability studies. One could read a great many disability studies books and articles from the past fifteen years and find few references to Internet-related issues. Most existing research and discourse on the issue of disability and the Internet has been generated by the fields of information studies, education, computer science, law, communication, universal design, and media studies. This curious neglect of the nexus of disability and the Internet needs to change, as the Internet will continue to increase in importance in individual lives and society into the foreseeable future.

Disability in Society

Paralleling the complexities of the approaches to and perspectives on disability within the scholarly discourse, disability is a difficult issue within society, though the approaches in society rarely fit neatly into one category or model. Part of the difficulty is tied to the fact that disability is not static. Most people with disabilities have variations in their condition that means they have different levels of impairment on a day-to-day level. The variable nature of an individual's disability may make it harder for someone without a disability to understand; for example, one might be confused about why a person some days uses a cane and on other days uses a wheelchair. However, a larger variable of disability is the fact that the population of persons with disabilities is not static.

Disability is the only minority group that can be joined during the course of one's life. Most people with disabilities acquire them during the course of their life, typically without the intent to acquire them. So, not only is disability the only minority group that people can join, but it is also one that people do not want to join but lack a choice in the matter. People do join the group, nonetheless. "In nearly no other sphere of existence, however, do people risk waking up one morning having become the person whom they hated the day before" (Siebers, 2008, p. 26). Though disability can happen to anyone, some populations are more likely to experience disability as a result of unequal distribution of factors that cause disability, such as war, violence, disease, and famine (Sherry, 2008). In the United States, people with disabilities are actually the largest minority group, with more members than either Latinos or African Americans. Another indicator of the size of the population of people with disabilities is that, after English and Spanish, American Sign Language (ASL) is the third most widely used language in the United States.

There are many ways that societies view disability. As noted previously, the medical model approach of focusing on physical, sensory, or cognitive difference is still widely held across many cultures. In other circumstances, the focus follows the social model, emphasizing the issues of social, economic, religious, cultural, educational, and employment discrimination that result from societal reactions to differences. However, clear distinctions that specifically follow medical, social, or postmodern approaches rarely exist in daily life.

Consider the basic issue of difference. Not all differences carry the negative social connotations of disability. People with naturally occurring red hair carry a gene that results in an obvious physical difference that is very rare in the overall population. However, their ability to function in society is rarely questioned and they are not often looked down upon. It seems absurd to imagine children with red hair being put in special classes in school or their parents having support groups. While natural red hair may have no particular social or economic advantages for the individual, it likewise does not result in the individual experiencing discrimination.

Some differences even are celebrated. Students who perform very well on certain standardized tests are given their own advanced classes and labeled "gifted." Being tracked this way benefits the gifted students as they progress through elementary and secondary school and heightens their chances of attending a prestigious college that will ultimately improve their career opportunities. Certain physical differences are considered large advantages in life as well. Professional athletes are very well compensated and highly regarded for their physical differences, a group that some persons with disabilities call the "severely able-bodied."

Not all physical, sensory, or cognitive differences, therefore, are viewed as disabilities in society. However, disability is tied to specific individual differences that result in exclusion and social distancing. This situation clearly reinforces the notion that "to a large extent, disability is a social construct" (Schmetzke, 2002, p. 135). Society has made the decision that red hair is irrelevant, a high IQ is to be celebrated, basketball is a high-paying career option, and deafness is a deviation. Such social decisions are as old as human society. The concept of disability, in fact, has been part of human culture through known history (Scheer and Groce, 1998).

Disability clearly is "part of the natural physical, social, and cultural variability of the human species" (Scotch and Shriner, 1997, p. 154). A more humane approach to disability than is generally taken would be to acknowledge that disabilities are simply part of the spectrum of human variation, present in every culture and geographic outpost of human life (Higgins, 1992; Scheer and Groce, 1998; Zola, 1993). The predominant social reaction to disability has not been acceptance as natural variations, though, as most reactions through time have emphasized disability as otherness and deviation (Barnes and Mercer, 2003; Barnes, Mercer, and Shakespeare, 1999; Jaeger and Bowman, 2005). "From the moment a child is born, he/she emerges into a world where he/she receives messages that to be disabled is to be less than, a world where disability may be tolerated but in the final instance, is inherently negative" (Campbell, 2009, p. 17).

Though disabilities vary widely, people with disabilities share common social experiences through their treatment by others (Ziporyn, 1992). Throughout recorded history, the noted presence of disability is paralleled by judgments about the meaning of disability (Albrecht, 1992). As societies have articulated standards of normalcy, disability has been the juxtaposition of normalcy (Campbell, 2009; Davis, 1997, 2000). Through time, disability has been associated with prophecy of pending negative events, wrath of supernatural powers, demonic possession, burdens on society, fodder for public sport, and entertainment; but all of the associations have been linked by perceptions of little social value or outside of the conception of society (Baynton, 2001; Bessis, 1995; Braddock and Parish, 2001; Bragg, 1997; Bryan, 1996; French, 1932; Hibbert, 1975; Rosen, 1968; Stone, 1999; Warkany, 1959).

Disability, as a social factor, has been so powerful across time and societies that some scholars believe that it has functioned as a "master status" in society, the element that defines a person regardless of any other personal characteristics (Albrecht and Verbugge, 2000, p. 301). The presence of disability "floods all statuses and identities" of an individual in society, such that "a woman who uses a wheelchair because of multiple sclerosis becomes a disabled mother, handicapped driver, disabled worker, and wheelchair dancer"

(Charmaz, 2000, p. 284). According to this line of thinking, a Latina who owns a successful business, has two children, and happens to be visually impaired would be most prominently perceived as blind by society. Supporting this assertion is the fact that discrimination against women, people of color, and immigrants has historically been justified by representing these groups as having disabilities (Baynton, 2001). This apparent situation has led to conclusions by many people with disabilities that "my disability is how people respond to my disability" (Frank, 1998, p. 111).

The discriminatory reactions to disability are strange given the number of persons with disabilities. Disability is not uncommon and it will become more common in the near future. In the United States, 54.4 million people have a disability (18.7 percent of the overall population in 2005), and the number of persons with disabilities worldwide is approaching 1 billion in 2010 (Albrecht and Verbugge, 2000; Metts, 2000; US Census Bureau, 2008). Disability does increase with age—13 percent of people age 21 to 64 have a disability, but 53 percent of persons over 75 have a disability. The number of people in the United States age 55 or older is increasing rapidly as a percentage of the total population; as a result, the number of persons with disabilities will grow significantly in the next few years as the baby boom generation ages (Rehabilitation Research and Training Center on Disability Demographics and Statistics, 2007). In fact, only 15 percent of persons with disabilities are born with them.

Disability, then, becomes more common with age but is much less common among the population in schools and in the workforce, which emphasizes the perceptions of otherness. A further aspect of disability that contributes to this sense of otherness is the fact that it is not a unifying, static, or immutable state. Numerous variables shape the ways in which a disability affects a specific person. The same type of disability can vary by severity, visibility, stability, age of onset, type of onset, levels of accompanying pain, and extent of impacts (Vash and Crewe, 2004). Most people with disabilities acquire them during the course of their life, so disability is very different from a characteristic like gender, which is constant through the lives of the vast majority of people. Disability also does not have a unifying cause; it can result from genetics, age, accident, or other external circumstances.

Nor are people with disabilities unified by a defining common characteristic—they cannot be recognized by a factor like skin color or language. Disability really is "the all-inclusive minority" (Riley, 2005, p. xiv). It touches people of all different cultures, ages, backgrounds, religions, pigmentations, and sexual orientations. Some people with conditions that society classifies as a disability do not consider themselves to have a disability, such as the many people with hearing impairments who view the use of ASL simply as speaking another language (Branson and Miller, 2002). Perhaps most significantly, there is a wide range of physical and cognitive conditions that are considered disabilities, ranging from sensory impairments to learning disabilities to mobility impairments to limitations on cognitive development. The range of different disabilities leads to varying views of disability as, for example, a process, an interaction, a binary condition, or a continuum of abilities (Baldwin, 1997; Brandt and Pope, 1997; Cunningham and Coombs, 1997).

All of these differences make disability more unpredictable than other variations among humans. People can comfortably anticipate that their gender and skin color will remain fairly constant through their lives. The possibility of acquiring a disability, however, looms over the life of every person. The unpredictability of disability may make it harder for people without disabilities to accept people with disabilities, as people with disabilities may seem an unwelcome reminder of the randomness of life. In spite of the major gains in terms of civil rights and social inclusion for persons with disabilities over the past several decades, much of the overall population still does not regard persons with disabilities as an integral part of society, but instead views them with a mix of stereotyping, sentimentality, oppression, feigned concern, indifference, and even hostility (Barnes and Mercer, 2003; Barnes, Mercer, and Shakespeare, 1999; Campbell, 2009; Jaeger and Bowman, 2005; Siebers, 2008; Stiker, 1999; Switzer, 2003; Thomas, 1982).

The underlying social aspects of disability become clear by thinking about the basic design of buildings. Consider a society in which wheelchair users were the majority of the population and people who walked were the minority. Such a society would naturally be designed around the needs of the majority of the population—the wheelchair users. People who did not use wheelchairs would face the social stigma of disability and would find barriers at every turn. Stairs would be uncommon, doorways would be too short, places to sit would be very hard to find, and tables and other flat surfaces would be at very low levels. Navigation would be very difficult for the minority of walkers, and the users of wheelchairs would rarely think about these problems. Chairs and stairs, in fact, would be only grudgingly provided as accommodations in this society.

Even in the reality that we have, the example of wheelchairs points out the level of subjectivity of disability. Many wheelchair users ironically view chairs as an accommodation for the people who don't think ahead to bring their own place to sit. To the minority of wheelchair users, chairs are an accommodation for the majority. For the majority, ramps and curb cuts are the accommodations for wheelchair users.

Disability can be particularly hard to relate to if one neither has a disability nor is close to someone who does. Media presentations of disability tend to emphasize people with disabilities either as objects of pity, ridicule, charity, sickness, and menace or as paragons of heroism, innocence, nobility, and sweetness (Black, 2004; Condeluci, 1991; Mitchell, 2008; Norden, 1994; Riley, 2005; Thompson, 1997). Outside of entertainment portrayals, popular exposure of disability tends to be limited to telethons and other charitable functions (Charlton, 1998). The distancing of persons with disabilities from mainstream activities is reflected in the common occurrence of descriptions of disabilities being turned into slurs and social metaphors for negative things (LaCheen, 2000).

This social distancing of persons with disabilities directly translates into exclusion from many key parts of society. Persons with disabilities already face unemployment at more than three times higher levels than the rest of the population (54.4 percent versus 16.5 percent) and suffer similar gaps in educational attainment (US Census Bureau, 2008). For some types of disability, the gaps in employment are even higher—for people considered to have a severe disability by the Census Bureau, 69.3 percent are unemployed and 27.1 percent live in poverty, three times the national average (US Census Bureau, 2008). Yet, 75 percent of people with disabilities who are not employed want to work (Dispenza, 2002). Only 30 percent of high school graduates with disabilities enroll in college, compared with 40 percent of the general population; one year after graduation, only 10 percent of students with disabilities are still enrolled in two-year colleges, while only 5 percent are still enrolled in four-year colleges (Stodden, 2005; Wagner et al., 2005). These educational challenges are tied to the large number of postsecondary faculty who feel unprepared or disinterested in working with students with disabilities (Banard et al., 2008; Bourke, Strehorn, and Silver, 2000; Dona and Edmister, 2001; Hindes and Mather, 2007; Izzo, Murray, and Novak, 2008; Weimar, 1990; Zeff, 2007).

These exclusions also directly affect the usage of services and of technologies like computers and the Internet. When seeking health services, for example, 74 percent of persons with disabilities report facing difficulties in getting the health care they need (Shigaki, Hagglund, Clark, and Conforti, 2002). Among persons with disabilities, 30.2 percent use a computer at home, 33 percent live in a household with Internet access, 26.0 percent use the Internet at home, and 30.8 percent use the Internet at any location (Dobransky and Hargittai, 2006). All of these percentages are less than half of the percentages for the rest of the population (Dobransky and Hargittai, 2006). People with disabilities who live in nonmetropolitan areas have the lowest Internet usage of any population in the United States (Simpson, 2009). These exclusions are not unique to the United States; in Canada, persons with disabilities are three times more likely to live in poverty and are less than half as likely to have Internet access as the overall population (D'Aubin, 2007; Jongbloed, 2003).

The Language of Disability

As with the differences in the approaches to the study of disability and the complicated roles of disability in society, the language of disability is also an area of disagreement. "People with disabilities? Disabled people? There are ongoing and unresolved debates about ways to talk about disability" (Church et al., 2007, p. 1). In part, this derives from the desire to find terminology that does not carry any of the stigmatizing or bigoted connotations of previous terms that have been applied to people with disabilities throughout history. Many terms that have been created as medical terms have quickly morphed into derogatory terms for people with disabilities.

Additionally, in Western culture, disability historically has served as a dividing line between "worthy poor" and "undeserving poor," creating other linguistic connotations that raise concerns of economic subjugation (Oliver and Barnes, 1998). For centuries the language used to describe persons with disabilities promoted dehumanization, dependence, and exclusion. The term *handicapped* used for so long was derived from cap in hand, based on the fact that persons with disabilities in England were long permitted to support themselves exclusively through begging. Other venerable terms like *crippled, retarded,* and *feebleminded* have equally disturbing connotations for persons with disabilities. As attempts are made to advance the language beyond historical biases, terminology that has been accepted at one time is often cast off as being outdated or offensive not many years later. This trend is reflected in the abrupt change in the mid-1980s from the use of the term *handicap* to the use of the term *disability* in the legislative language of the United States (Stroman, 2003).

The biggest challenge with disability, however, may lie in the fact that persons with disabilities are primarily associated together by social exclusion. "Disability acts as a loose rubric and as an amalgam of dissimilar physical and cognitive traits that often have little in common other than the social stigma of limitation, deviance, and inability" (Mitchell and Snyder, 1997, pp. 7). Disabilities can be sensory, affecting sight, speech, or hearing. They can be mobility impairments, affecting control of the limbs due to injury, loss, palsy, paralysis, arthritis, and other conditions that restrict movement and muscle control. They can be impairments that impact the functioning of internal organs, such as difficulty breathing. Disabilities can also be cognitive, affecting the processing of information generally or in a specific area. Cognitive disabilities include impairments that range from severely limiting general cognitive functions to affecting specific cognitive functions. The array of cognitive disabilities includes more commonly known conditions such as autism, amnesia, aphasia, dementia, Down syndrome, and Asperger's syndrome, as well as much less common conditions such as Cri du Chat syndrome. Additionally, learning disabilities are cognitive impairments that impact the processing of specific types of information with extremely specific impacts, such as the ability to process numbers for computation.

Disabilities can also be described in terms of impact—the term *print disabilities* is sometimes used to describe any visual, learning, or mobility impairment that limits the ability to access physical or electronic print in standard means. Across these types of disabilities, there are often few linkages between persons with various physical, cognitive, and sensory disabilities beyond the social, economic, political, religious, cultural, educational, and employment discriminations that result from societal reactions to these differences. As a result, when it comes to disability, "there is virtually no vocabulary which has universal support" (Pollack, 2009, p. 5).

Currently, many scholars and advocates draw a distinction between disability and impairment. The social model asserts that *impairment* should be used to refer to the physical or cognitive condition, and *disability* should refer to the social construction of exclusion and oppression resulting from the impairment. However, this distinction is logically flawed due to the fact that *impairment* is also a social construction of what is considered a normal body and what is considered not normal (Hughes and Paterson, 1997; Lupton and Seymour, 2000).

As noted earlier, in North America the language and thinking of disability rights has been much more focused on disability as a minority group than in Europe (Barnes, Mercer, and Shakespeare, 1999). The minority group approach is reflected in the language used to define disability in legislation—a physical, sensory, or cognitive difference that results in impairment of a major life function, the diagnostic record of such impairment, or the social stigmatization associated with such impairment. The advantage of this legal language of disability used in the United States is that it encompasses "the social, historical, political, and mythological coordinates" of disability (Mitchell and Snyder, 1997, pp. 2–3).

In terms of disability, the language throughout this book employs what is known as person-first terminology, reflecting both the common language of the United States and its disability rights laws. This literally means that the person receives greater emphasis than the impairment: a "person with a disability" rather than a "disabled person." The former is the terminology generally employed in North America, while the latter is the terminology generally employed in Europe.

The goal of person-first language is to avoid terminology that equates the person to the disability and language that disempowers or devalues the person, such as the difference between describing a person as a "wheelchair user" rather than "wheelchair bound." The former emphasizes that the person uses the wheelchair as a tool, while the latter allows the wheelchair to define the identity of the person. The European perspective on language, in contrast, sees placing the *disabled* term first as emphasizing the socially imposed discrimination against the individuals. Cross-culturally, person-first terminology is the language more commonly used by people with disabilities themselves (Lupton and Seymour, 2000).

In truth, there is no definitive answer to these language issues, despite claims to the contrary that can readily be found on both sides of this linguistic divide. These linguistic differences, however, do serve as a reminder of the complicated nature of the larger social challenges faced by persons with disabilities. The terminological awkwardness of disability is a potent symbol of the distancing and exclusion of disability in society.

The Language and Goals of Access

Following the language of disability, the terminology of access for persons with disabilities has its own differences. Unlike the terminology of disability, however, these differences are often more tied to different terms across disciplines for similar goals than rooted in inherent differences in goals. As will be shown, *access* as a general term has multiple meanings, but *access for persons with disabilities* has been variously described in terms of accessibility, universal design, universal access, and universal usability.

The oldest of these terms—at least in its use to indicate access for persons with disabilities—is *universal design*. Universal design has its roots in making commercial products and architecture more inclusive, taking focus away from the traditional design approach of creating things for an imagined average user. Instead, universal design focuses on making "products and environments welcoming and useful to groups that are diverse in many dimensions, including gender, race and ethnicity, age, socio-economic status, ability, disability, and learning style" (Burgstahler, 2008a, p. 3). Universal design is one approach to making products that are more inclusive of persons with disabilities, without focusing specifically on accessibility (Ostroff, Limont, and Hunter, 2002; Burgstahler, 2008b).

Traditional standards in design enable and create order for those with standardized bodies but disable and exclude those who do not fit the standards; in this way, the lack of compliance with standardization can be seen as a key means by which people are disabled by society (Moser, 2006). Universal design originated with the realization in architecture that born-accessible structures were both more inclusive of people with disabilities and of people belonging to other populations. For example, curb cuts on sidewalks not only support wheelchair access but also help parents with baby strollers, people with shopping carts and rolling luggage, bicyclists, skateboarders, rollerbladers, and many others (Zeff, 2007).

Following on the principles of universal design, the concept of universal access—or universal service—has been articulated in telecommunication and computer science contexts as the goal of making technology equally available to all (Shneiderman, 2000). The language of universal access can be found in government policy documents, business plans of communication companies, and computer science researchers, among others. While a worthy goal, universal access overlooks the very significant issue of usage. After access is available to all, people still need to be able to use what they have achieved access to. Universal access does not overcome barriers to access such as language, literacy, technological literacy, and disability.

The concept of universal usability overcomes these problems if it achieves its goal of creating technologies that can be accessed and used by most, if not all, people. Established information technologies—postal services, telephones, television—successfully provide universal usability; that is, the vast majority of the population has access to, can use, and regularly does use the technology (Shneiderman, 2000). Thus, the belief is that information technologies should be designed to provide the same kind of widely usable products from the outset (Shneiderman, 2000). Universal design, universal access, and universal usability focus on a broad range of populations that the design is intended to reach, including age, gender, race, ethnicity, and other factors, as well as disability.

In this book, I use the language of universal usability to discuss broad goals of access across populations. However, the discussion focuses on information and technology for persons with disabilities in terms of accessibility. There are several reasons for this choice. First, *accessibility* is the term most commonly used within information policy to discuss access for persons with disabilities in particular. Second, it is a more finely grained term than *universal design, universal access*, and *universal usability*, as accessibility refers narrowly to the population of persons with disabilities, the topic of this book. Third, achieving accessibility in design is central to achieving universal usability—an accessible design will generally be more inclusive of many types of users disadvantaged by factors such as age, literacy, experience, and education. Finally, people with disabilities have a different kind of relationship to technology than other groups, as it plays specific supportive roles in the lives of many people with disabilities.

Because of these unique relationships, people with disabilities conceptualize technologies in two main ways: "as tools assisting bodily function and as contributing to the body/self as it is experienced and presented to others" (Lupton and Seymour, 2000, p. 1861). They associate technology with potentially facilitating communication, mobility, safety, autonomy, control, independence, competence, confidence, and participation in the workforce and social relationships. However, many people with disabilities are also uncomfortable with their reliance on technologies.

People with disabilities often want to be early adopters of new technologies, which may serve to increase independence and facilitate life outside the home, but people with disabilities often find the costs of new mainstream and specialized technologies prohibitive, and the design typically fails to account for the needs of people with disabilities (Harris, 2010). People with disabilities report a feeling of being continually left behind by new information technologies, due to the lack of accessible versions or training (Lupton and Seymour, 2000). Generally, people with disabilities find that information technologies can provide the means to more easily engage in social relationships, so long as the technologies have a "normalizing" rather than "stigmatizing" function (Lupton and Seymour, 2000). For example, people with visual impairments find that they are more accepted when using a guide dog rather than a cane, because the cane is a symbol of difference, but dogs, beloved as they generally are in society, are a symbol of commonality.

Given these unique relationships with technology in general and information technology in particular, to analyze the issues most effectively, it is necessary to isolate the needs of persons with disabilities in terms of accessibility. The focus on accessibility for persons with disabilities in particular also fits with the theoretical frame used in this book.

The Theoretical Approach of Information Worlds

Building on the information policy–based approach to disability and the Internet discussed in a previous section, the conceptual framework I use here is a theory constructed within the study of information policy. The theory of information worlds, which I codeveloped, is a conceptual framework for understanding the information behavior of specific populations within the broader social and policy context. This conceptual framework helps reveal the relationships between persons with disabilities and the Internet in two key ways. First, it illuminates the different levels of access to information and technology that are necessary for inclusion. Second, it demonstrates the ways in which access to the Internet—or lack thereof—shapes the information behavior of persons with disabilities at both the individual and broader social levels.

The theory of information worlds is designed to provide a framework through which the multiple interactions across information,

information behavior, and the many different social contexts within which it exists—from the individual to the social group to the society—can be understood and studied (Jaeger and Burnett, 2010). The theory posits that information behavior is shaped simultaneously by both immediate influences, such as friends, family, coworkers, and trusted information sources of the small worlds in which the individual lives, as well as larger social influences, including public sphere institutions, media, technology, and politics. These levels, though separate, do not function in isolation, and to ignore any level in examining information behavior results in an incomplete picture of the social contexts of the information. Explorations of information behavior need to account for the different levels if the social drivers of information behavior and the uses of information in society are to be fully understood. The theory of information worlds attempts to account for all of these social and structural elements at work in the shaping of information behavior within a society.

Levels of Access

A pillar of the theory of information worlds is that there are three levels of access to information and information technology: physical access, intellectual access, and social access (Burnett, Jaeger, and Thompson, 2008). Physical access is the most basic and familiar aspect in disability rights law—the ability to reach something, which in this case is information. Physical access to information is generally viewed as access to the document or other form embodying information, be it conveyed through print, electronic, verbal, or another means of communication—literally the process of getting to the information that is being sought (Svenonius, 2000). Most discourse on information access tends to focus on physical issues, such as the physical structures that contain information, the electronic structures that contain information, and the paths that are traveled to get to information (Jaeger and Bowman, 2005). While it is a necessary prerequisite, mere physical access is not sufficient for full access. "It is a common, but mistaken, assumption that access to technology equals access to information" (McCreadie and Rice, 1999, p. 51). The ability of a user to get to information and the ability of that user to employ information to accomplish particular goals are very different (Culnan, 1983, 1984, 1985).

    The next level of access is intellectual access—the ability to understand the information. Intellectual access can be understood as the accessing of the information itself after physical access has been obtained (Svenonius, 2000). Intellectual access to information "entails equal opportunity to understand intellectual content and pathways to that content" (Jaeger and Bowman, 2005, p. 68). Issues of intellectual access involve understanding how the information is presented to people seeking information, as well as the impact of such presentation on the process of information seeking; intellectual access to information includes the means through which the information is categorized, organized, displayed, and represented.

Social access is the most advanced level of access—the ability to communicate and use the information in social contexts (Burnett, Jaeger, and Thompson, 2008). Such social contexts can range from personal communication for entertainment purposes to educational and work settings to democratic participation. Gaining and understanding information without the ability to communicate that information prevents social engagement through the information. People also have a stronger sense of community and belonging in situations in which they can exchange information in social contexts (Johnson, 2010; Williamson and Roberts, 2010). Social access is now heavily dependent on information technologies for communication in many contexts. The social access depends both on an individual user's attitudes toward information technologies and on the ability of the user to employ information technologies to engage in social interactions.

Thus far, the focus on accessibility online in the United States and elsewhere has been almost exclusively on concerns of physical access. This focus on physical access carries through to both information and information technologies. As a result, even training materials to help developers create accessible information technologies reflect this strong bias toward physical access (Law, Jaeger, and McKay, 2010). For social equality to be achieved in access to information technologies, accessibility needs to place greater emphasis on achieving intellectual and social access to information and information technologies—Internet-enabled and beyond. This emphasis depends on a better understanding of information behavior in the online environment.

Information Behavior in Information Worlds

The theory of information worlds argues for the examination of information behavior in terms of the immediate social groups of everyday life, the mediating social institutions of the public sphere, and the context of an entire society (Burnett and Jaeger, 2008). Building on previous developments of information theory, the social groups are known as small worlds, and the entire society is known as the life-world. These social structures constantly interact with and reshape one another, forming the ways in which individuals and groups interact with information and information technology. In examining these interrelated parts, the theory of information worlds focuses on five social elements:

- *Social norms:* a world's shared sense of the appropriateness of social appearances and observable behaviors.
- *Social types:* the roles that define actors and how they are perceived within a world.
- *Information value:* a world's shared sense of a scale of the importance of information.
- *Information behavior:* the full range of behaviors and activities related to information available to members of a world.
- *Boundaries:* the places at which small worlds come into contact with each other and across which communication and information exchange can—but may or may not—take place.

As with the social structures within small worlds, the elements are interrelated and constantly interact with and influence one another (Jaeger and Burnett, 2010).

As localized worlds of information, each small world has its own social norms, social types, information behavior, and understanding of information value. The members of each small world have established ways in which information is accessed, understood, and exchanged within their world and the degree to which it is shared with others outside the small world. Few individuals, however, exist in only one small world; it may not even be possible except in extreme circumstances of social isolation. In contrast, there is no real limit to the number of small worlds to which an individual can belong. A typical person is a part of many small worlds—for example, friends, family, coworkers, fellow students, people with shared hobbies, and people with similar disabilities.

Any one of these small worlds may offer many places where its members are able to interact with members of other small worlds. Information moves through the boundaries between worlds via people who are members of two worlds or through interaction between members of two small worlds in a place where members of different small worlds are exposed to other perspectives. Further, the contact between small worlds and other inputs from the lifeworld can lead to the creation of new worlds as information passing over the boundaries between worlds either blurs those boundaries or otherwise transforms or changes information behaviors and perceptions of information value. Encountering other small worlds can occur through public sphere institutions, such as in a public library, or through new technological avenues of communication and exchange, such as social networks on the Internet. As information moves through boundaries between small worlds, the information is treated, understood, and used differently in each small world in line with the social norms of that world. As a result, the same information may have a different role within each small world.

Together, these small worlds constitute the lifeworld of information. The way that the small worlds as a group in the lifeworld treat information will shape how the information is treated within the lifeworld as a whole. As the information moves between small worlds, more and more small worlds will decide how to treat this information, generating an overall perception of the information across the lifeworld. The more small worlds that are exposed to information, the more exchange between small worlds there will be, and the better chances there will be for a democratic perception of and approach to the information.

However, beyond the small worlds, there are also influences at play in the lifeworld that shape the way that small worlds perceive information. Some of these influences increase contact between small worlds and promote democratic engagement in the lifeworld. Libraries, schools, and other public sphere organizations exist specifically to ensure that information continues to move between the small worlds and that members of each small world are exposed to other small worlds. In sharp contrast, other influences serve to constrain the movement of information between small worlds or constrict the socially acceptable perceptions of information. The most influential small worlds of information—such as those that possess political power or those that control the media—can use their power to push back against the collective small worlds to enforce a minority perception on the majority, asserting control over the information in the lifeworld.

Some influences on small worlds and the lifeworld are inherently neutral but can be used for the objectives of either increasing or decreasing information access. Information technologies act as a way for small worlds to connect in new ways and to reach other small worlds that would not otherwise touch their boundaries. The Internet and online social networks represent particularly powerful examples of this phenomenon. But information technologies—like the Internet and more traditional media—can also work to homogenize perspectives or enforce hegemonic perspectives of small but powerful small worlds on the lifeworld. In total, the small worlds are shaped by all of these larger influences but also have the power collectively to define the parameters of the external influences.

For persons with disabilities, there are a multitude of small worlds at multiple levels of social organization. People with different types of disabilities, and different levels of severity of each disability, will likely have different information access needs, different information behavior, and different accessibility challenges. Each of these different groups, then, would be a small world, unified by the information and access issues. As such, people with no vision would be one small world, and a somewhat larger small world would be people with visual impairments. However, persons with disabilities as a whole are also an even larger small world, joined by broader information and access goals and challenges, heavily influenced by social perceptions of disability within the lifeworld of information.

In the subsequent examinations of online accessibility and the social impacts of the Internet on persons with disabilities, the information worlds framework will be of use in several ways. The three levels of access will help assess the emphases given to accessibility in the contexts of law, education, employment, commerce, communication, entertainment, and government on the Internet, as well as assess the ways in which accessibility could be improved. The framework for information behavior in information worlds will shape the discussion of the online social activities—education, employment, government, communication, entertainment, and commerce—of persons with disabilities and help to place them within the greater context of online activities. The levels of access will also inform analyses of policy related to the Internet and persons with disabilities. The framework for information behavior will additionally play a role in the considerations of identity, advocacy, and policy. The issues raised by the theory of information worlds will ultimately be considered in the discussions of accessibility policy and the future of accessibility.

Considering Disability and the Internet

Since the development of movable type, the evolution of the means by which information can be made available and accessed has moved with increasing rapidity from books to newspapers to telegraph to telephone to radio to movies to television to the Internet. Yet, the dizzying technological changes of the twentieth century seem quaint in a new century that has already produced wireless computing, mobile Web-enabled devices, GPS-based navigation devices, social media and networking, e-book readers, and websites with hundreds of millions of users. By 2008, billions of people with Web access could visit tens of billions of Web pages, over 100 million of which were blogs (Golbeck, 2008). Google has made most of the Web searchable, while retail giants like Amazon sell virtually everything purchasable. Recent innovations in social media services such as Facebook, YouTube, and Twitter have created new levels of social interaction online. In 2010, Facebook had over 500 million users and Twitter had 200 million users posting 650 million messages a day, truly astounding numbers in a world of 6 billion people.

The promise of the Internet and its related technologies has been predicted in every corner of life, and many of these promises have already come to fruition to some extent. In an age where a message can crisscross the globe in a matter of seconds and all news is instant, it almost defies belief that the ability of the telegraph to share news across continents over a period of days was an undisputed wonder of its time (Hanson, 2008).

As with any new technology, the strongest proponents of the Internet have oversold its impact. It is unlikely that the Internet will ever lead to the elimination of poverty, 100 percent voter turnout, or a public fluent in the intricacies of all of the pressing issues of the day. But even the staunchest resisters of the influence of the Internet cannot escape the fact that education, employment, government, entertainment, communication, and socialization rely more and more on the Internet. Even many people who do not own home computers can still use the Internet constantly through their mobile devices.

Like most information technologies in human history, however, the Internet and its opportunities are not equally available to everyone. Factors of geography, socioeconomic status, literacy, and language can all affect how available the Internet really is. All of these factors are external to the Internet and its technologies. If the network is built, free access is universally provided, technology training is available, and content is produced in local languages, these barriers to access to the Internet can be made to disappear.

The barriers to Internet access related to disability, however, run much deeper. Inaccessible technologies and content—and accompanying incompatibility with assistive technologies—are built directly into the Internet, creating enormous barriers to the Internet for many people with disabilities. Making the Internet accessible to persons with disabilities requires many significant adjustments to design, development, and implementation of Internet-related technologies and content. These barriers replicate the long-running barriers to all other aspects of society that people with disabilities have struggled against through time. "Perhaps the word that best describes the historical treatment of persons with disabilities is separation" (Switzer, 2003, p. 31). This description unfortunately remains true in the age of the Internet.

Equal access to the Internet—with its central role in communication, socialization, education, employment, government, and entertainment—is vital for equal participation in society. Advocates, researchers, and policymakers can try to promote equality of access through changes in civil rights laws that encourage or mandate the development of accessible technologies and content and that foster changes in social attitudes about people with disabilities. However, equal access to the primary technological means of disseminating, accessing, using, and exchanging information rises to the scale of a human rights issue when one group of people is at the center of the greatest exclusions.

Such exclusions are all the more pointed in light of the fact that the Internet has the potential to be the greatest mechanism for inclusion of people with disabilities ever invented. The ability to communicate and participate in activities in real time anywhere in the world without leaving home opens up enormous new avenues of participation for people with the entire range of physical, sensory, and cognitive disabilities. Physical barriers, transportation challenges, communication difficulties, and other major barriers to participation can be overcome through an accessible Internet and create wide new vistas for civic engagement, education, employment, and social interaction. These revolutions in the lives of people with disabilities, however, rely entirely on an accessible Internet. An inaccessible Internet is as threatening to persons with disabilities as an accessible Internet is exhilarating.

Throughout history, people with disabilities have usually had to wait for the accessible versions of technology to become available to catch up to the information access and other opportunities available to the rest of the population. Since the advent of the World Wide Web in the mid-1990s, this race to establish equal access to information and communication technologies has grown increasingly untenable for persons with disabilities, as the introduction and evolution of technologies has accelerated to the point that most new technologies introduced are obsolete before they become accessible. If the Internet is to fulfill its promise of providing new levels of inclusion for people with disabilities, the barriers to equal access need to be eradicated. Otherwise, the opportunities for social inclusion that people with disabilities have fought so hard to win over the past half century will recede as participation in education, employment, government, and society as a whole become less possible due to technological barriers. The failure to address issues of accessibility for persons with physical, sensory, and cognitive disabilities ultimately threatens to segregate people with disabilities as the permanent second-class citizens of the information age.

An Individual Perspective

This book is of great personal importance to me not only as someone who has been a scholar of disability and information for a decade, but as an individual with a disability. My own personal experiences with the Internet are woven into the fabric of this text, given that I have had a significant visual impairment my entire life and my lifespan has neatly paralleled both the development of personal computers and the implementation of civil rights laws for persons with disabilities. I was born in the 1970s, the decade that saw the passage of the first substantial disability rights laws in the United States. Had I been born a decade earlier, I might not have been allowed to attend public school, as it was then common for schools to refuse to admit students with disabilities.

When I began school in the early 1980s, schools were still struggling with the implementation of the notion of equal—or at least vaguely equivalent—education for students with disabilities under the Individuals with Disabilities Education Act (IDEA). My experiences at different schools varied from being the only student with a disability in a class to being sent off on my own to learn at my own pace. My time in elementary school coincided with the period when personal computers began to widely appear in schools as educational tools. The first one I ever encountered was unusable for people like me, so it was hard to understand what everyone was so excited about. It was a while before these computers were accessible to most students with disabilities.

By the time I got to college, the Americans with Disabilities Act (ADA) was only several years old, so institutions of higher education were still fumbling toward the inclusion of students with disabilities. I found myself part of the struggle by students with disabilities to have these new civil rights enforced in terms of access to classrooms, course materials, activities, and dorms, as well as technology. Computers, at least, had become much more accessible, and the Internet—at that point, a text-based medium using simple and easy-to-memorize keyboard commands that could be made relatively accessible using optical character recognition (OCR) software and some other basic programs—was quite usable for me. Though, for people with other types of impairments, the early Internet was not as accessible; many people with mobility impairments, for example, were significantly disadvantaged due to the reliance on keyboard commands. The turning of the tide came soon after, with the explosion of the World Wide Web as the graphics-based environment that would soon utterly dominate the Internet. As the Internet became far more widely accessible, most people found it inviting and easy to use. Each new development, however, challenged my ability to use it. For years, I have wondered at the ways in which the Internet makes my life as a researcher and educator more powerful, but simultaneously have despised always feeling like a second-class citizen online.

These experiences spurred me to learn as much about disability and technology in different contexts and disciplines as I could, and I wound up with graduate degrees in law, information, education, and library science. Over the past ten years, I have written literally scores of books, articles, and book chapters about disability and technology. I now oversee a master's degree program devoted to making information and technology available to all. Yet, I still approach new versions of programs and software updates with trepidation, because that tiny, new update to some minor software program may negatively affect the functioning of the various accessibility programs and features on which I rely. And an update of a program or service means that the screen reader program I use may once again be trying to play catch-up to the changes. As a result, I feel pretty much shut out of new Web-enabled technologies when they are launched. Even the Web-enabled phone system on the campus where I work—which was installed while I was writing this book—is utterly inaccessible, being a touch screen product with a gray-scale screen the size of a credit card and completely lacking accessibility features.

I mention this personal perspective not only so that the reader knows where I am coming from as author, as such context is important, but also to emphasize the extent to which accessibility of the Internet is really a human issue. It involves technology, but it truly is a matter of civil rights, social inclusion, equality, and human dignity. Jonathan Young, chairman of the National Council on Disability, recently stated that people with disabilities "should participate fully in all aspects of our communities and have opportunities to take risks, to succeed, and—yes—to fail" (Young, 2010, p. 6). However, when it comes to new technologies, people with disabilities are usually relegated to fail as a result of inaccessible design. To build a system that potentially could benefit everyone but that constantly ignores the basic needs of persons with disabilities has tremendous ramifications for each person with a disability. As you read this book and consider the issues discussed herein, always keep in mind that these issues have very large and very real impacts on many, many people who could one day include some of your friends, members of your family, or even yourself. These issues are not just the concern of people who design and study technology. Issues of disability and the Internet matter to everyone.

2

The Digital Divide: Historical and Legal Issues

Focusing on the historical and legal issues raised by the intersection of disability and information technology, I trace in this chapter the relationships between technology development and civil rights laws for persons with disabilities. While the pace of technological change now significantly affects accessibility for persons with disabilities, the struggles for inclusion in older information technologies has usually been a long process. However, many information technologies that became commonly used during the twentieth century were initially conceived as technologies to help a certain population of persons with disabilities. Technology also serves to create a standard of normalcy within society, the impacts of which are examined in terms of persons with disabilities. In this discussion, I place current issues of online access within the larger historical context of access to information technologies and the legal framework for accessibility. I also examine the tensions of technological change for persons with disabilities. New technologies and new versions of existing technologies may serve to increase access for persons with disabilities or they may be inherently inaccessible or incompatible with assistive technologies, may necessitate modifications to the ways in which an individual uses a technology, and may render a previously accessible technology unusable.

While persons with disabilities are strongly affected by limitations on equal access to the Internet, other populations also remain on the wrong side of the digital divide due to factors such as socioeconomic status, literacy, geography, and education. In this chapter I examine disability as part of broader gaps in access to the Internet. The commonalities and differences in the access issues for these different groups are used to show the unique challenges encountered by persons with disabilities, as well as the important unique benefits that the Internet can provide to persons with disabilities.

I conclude the chapter by analyzing the attempts to legislate for equal access to the Internet for persons with disabilities and the success levels of these laws in the United States and other nations, as well as the governmental structures established to try to enforce equality of access. Other nations have taken different approaches and established different types of requirements. I analyze the reasons for the success and failures of these laws and the roles of courts in interpreting them.

Technological Change and Information

Until roughly 150 years ago, the rate of technological change related to information would not be called rapid. Writing appeared thousands of years ago, while the printing press and movable type began the process of democratizing literacy about 500 years ago. For thousands upon thousands of years, the means of communicating information were very limited. People could speak face-to-face and written materials could be conveyed by foot, horseback, or, eventually, boat. Direct long-distance communication was limited to smoke signals and flags, neither of which could cover a very long distance.

Within the scope of human history, the modern period of the development of information technologies is breathtaking in its speed. A technology that now seems quaint or commonplace was utterly revolutionary not that many decades ago. Consider two developments that were groundbreaking in the mid-1800s. Mechanization of the printing, cutting, and folding of papers led to dramatic increases in distribution and readership of printed materials—particularly newspapers—and in levels of literacy (Hanson, 2008). Soon after, the telegraph increased the power of the press by allowing the reporting of events soon after they occurred and the spreading of these reports around the world. "The telegraph was the first technology to inform the public as well as leaders about events as they were still occurring. There was less time to make decisions. The press gained influence. Public opinion could be more easily aroused" (Hanson, 2008, p. 20). The increased speed of the spread of news forced governments to react to events at a much faster pace, and the telegraph in turn gave empires the technology to more tightly control their colonies. Mechanized printing is completely taken for granted now, and the telegraph has been consigned to the dustbin of history; newspapers may soon be as well. Yet these technologies were enormous advances a very short time ago in the overall course of human history.

Since then, the advent of the telephone, the radio, the television, the computer, the Internet, the mobile phone, and wireless communication have all resulted in similar shocks in society and personal interactions that have been absorbed and now seem perfectly normal and unremarkable. Many information technologies and features of information technologies actually began as devices meant for persons with disabilities. Telephones, typewriters, scanners, modems, voice activation, closed captioning, keyboard shortcuts for computer commands, synthesized readers, and computerized speech, among others, were all originally developed for persons with disabilities and then embraced by society at large (LaCheen, 2000; Winzer, 1993, 1997). Alexander Graham Bell, in fact, originally began work on the telephone as a device for people with hearing impairments and even later invented a device that would transmit handwriting from one stylus to another over phone lines for people with complete hearing loss (Winzer, 1993). Sadly for all of us, the latter device never became widely used.

Prior to the age of the Internet, when the speed of information technology change was much slower, equality of access for persons with disabilities moved by comparison at a glacial pace. For people with visual impairments, the gap between printed books and standardized reading and writing systems, such as Braille, was literally hundreds of years. Today, however, people with visual impairments can interact with text not only through Braille, but also through enlarged print, talking books, electronic texts, screen readers, screen magnification, reading machines, and video enlargers. With more recent information technologies, the gap between invention and equal access has, generally, still been slow in coming. Given that the origin of the telephone is rooted in helping people with disabilities, the struggle for equal access to telephones and televisions for persons with hearing impairments serves as a pointed example.

There was a gap of decades between the widespread use of telephones and the widespread availability of TTD/TTY services, and another gap of decades between the omnipresence of television and the requirements for closed captioning. During the campaign for the implementation of closed captioning, the term *media justice* was employed to convey the importance of equal access to the content of television programs for all (Downey, 2008, 2010). Multiple pieces of legislation were ultimately required to force those two information technologies to be made accessible for persons with hearing impairments—the Telecommunications for the Disabled Act of 1982, the Hearing Aid Compatibility Act of 1988, the Telecommunications Accessibility Enhancement Act of 1988, the Television Circuitry Decoder Act of 1990, and the Americans with Disabilities Act of 1990 (Hinton, 2003; Jaeger, 2006b; Lang, 2000). Ironically, the new smartphones and other mobile devices—with their visual interfaces—are much more useful to and usable by many persons with hearing impairments than by persons with visual, mobility, or cognitive impairments (Higgins, 2009; Portner, 2010). Nevertheless, people with hearing impairments still often face technical issues with mobile devices, such as speech-to-text conversion, interoperability, and hearing aid compatability (Baker and Moon, 2008). Furthermore, regardless of levels of acessiblity, people with many different disabilities may find the costs related to mobile devices and data plans prohibitive (Baker and Moon, 2008).

With the Internet, the concerns about equal access are considerably broader than they were with previous information technologies, because the Internet facilitates far more than information activities. The Internet is central to communication, social interaction, employment, education, and participation in government. Being excluded from the Internet makes an individual tremendously disadvantaged in society in terms of not only social communication and interaction, but also employment, education, and interaction with government (Jaeger and Burnett, 2010). Unfortunately, the average time between the introduction of a new information technology and the availability of a version that is accessible to persons with disabilities is three years (Kanayama, 2003b). These resulting unequal levels of access for persons with disabilities threaten to turn a physical or cognitive impairment into a social disability (Goggin and Newell, 2000, 2003; Moser, 2006).

Once it became a commonly used technology, scholars and policymakers proclaimed the Internet to be an equalizing force for persons with disabilities (Dobransky and Hargittai, 2006). These assertions parallel many other pronouncements about the ways in which a new technology will change everyone's life. However, the uptake and usage of information technologies make little statistical difference in the quality of life for users, particularly in terms of direct impacts on everyday activities (B. Anderson, 2007). "Despite the large number of policy references to the positive effects of information and communication technologies on people's lives, few of these claims are supported by empirical research" (Heres and Thomas, 2007, p. 176).

For persons with disabilities, the disjunction is even more pronounced, as the Internet remains primarily a place of limited access and multitudinous barriers. Many people with disabilities find the early and continuing claims of the equalizing nature of the Internet quite hollow: "The Internet would eradicate the loneliness of being disabled because everybody would be connected, and nobody could see or hear your disability online, eliminating stigma and discrimination. Virtual reality would turn everybody into the gymnast, ballet dancer, or sex god he or she longed to be" (Riley, 2005, p. 199). Not only has this situation patently not happened, equal access to the Internet and its content remains an ongoing challenge for most persons with disabilities.

The Quest for Accessibility

Technologies that are inherently designed to be inclusive of all users regardless of ability are known as accessible technologies or universally usable technologies. For a technology to be accessible, it needs to be usable in an equal or equitable manner by all users without relying on specific senses or abilities, and it needs to be compatible with the assistive technologies that users may rely on, such as narrators, scanners, enlargement, voice-activated technologies, alternate input devices, refreshable Braille, and many other devices that persons with disabilities may employ (Jaeger, 2009; Lazar, 2006; Lazar and Greenidge, 2006; Lazar and Jaeger, 2011). The utility of different assistive technologies will vary widely between individuals, depending not only on type and scope of impairment, but also on a range of factors related to personality, environment, support, and the nature of the technology itself (Draffon, 2009). The utility of assistive technologies will also be impacted by the other programs being used. For example, screen readers work much better with Microsoft browsers than Mozilla browsers due primarily to the attention Microsoft gives to support of assistive technologies (Yesilada et al., 2007).

On the Internet, this means that technologies used to access the Internet and the content found on the Internet should be designed to be accessible to persons with disabilities and compatible with the assistive technologies they may use. However, even when assistive technology is available and works, it is an extra cost persons with disabilities face that other users do not (Stienstra, Watzke, and Birch, 2007). For many people with disabilities, "while accessibility of content is a serious issue, the larger problem is getting Internet service at home" as a result of economic circumstances or the cost of acquiring assistive technologies to use the Internet (Rothman, 2011, n.p.). "When a piece of adaptive equipment to make the Web accessible costs up to several thousand dollars and you're living on a fixed income as many people with disabilities are, the Internet becomes less of a priority" (Moe, 2011, n.p.).

Accessibility is, admittedly, an objective in the design and production of a technology that requires thought and planning. For a website to be inclusive of persons with visual impairments, it will need to be designed so that all of the text, buttons, and links can be read by a screen reading program like JAWS, Kurtzweil, or Window-Eyes; that all graphics have "alt" tags—text describing the image; that it has sufficient contrast between text and background; that it works with screen magnifiers, screen enlargement software, and Braille readers; that it can be navigated by keyboard or other alternate input device rather than a mouse; and that text size and color contrast can be adjusted. For users with hearing impairments, all audio content on the website will need to have closed captioning or a textual equivalent. For users with seizure disorders, flashing items need to be avoided on the website. For users with cognitive disabilities, the navigation of the site and instructions should be clear, while the layout needs to be uncluttered. For users with mobility impairments, the lack of clutter, the ability to navigate without a mouse through voice and other alternate input devices, and compatibility with a range of other assistive technologies are also extremely important.

In the case of meeting the needs of users with these different types of disabilities, the website needs to be designed to be inherently accessible and to work with the assistive technologies that many users with disabilities employ. Most websites and Web-related technologies are specifically designed to work with a keyboard and a mouse or similar pointing device, creating barriers for those who rely on other input devices (Carter et al, 2006; Loiacono, 2003; Wang and Mankoff, 2003). However, assistive technologies allow users to change the relationship between the user and the technology (Litvak and Enders, 2001).

Assistive technologies, which include a wide range of hardware or software devices that provide enhanced accessibility, are literally technologies that make another technology accessible. In the preceding paragraphs, screen readers, screen magnifiers, screen enlargement software, and Braille readers are all examples of assistive technologies that could be used to access the Internet. Other types of assistive technologies that might be used to access the Internet include voice recognition software, joysticks, trackballs, wands and sticks, modified keyboards, sip-and-puff systems, touch screens, and electronic pointing devices, most of which are primarily used by people with mobility impairments. Specific brands of assistive technologies for people with sensory impairments include JAWS, a prominent screen reader; and Dragon, a prominent voice recognition program. For people with mobility impairments, brands of assistive technologies include Tracker Pro, a camera system that allows the user to direct the cursor by moving a reflective dot worn on clothing, and Integra Mouse, a joystick that is controlled by the lips and mouth. Additional assistive technologies are always being designed to try to find new ways to help people with disabilities better use the Internet (Curran, Crawford, and O'Hara, 2004; Yang et al., 2009).

In addition, different website users will have different levels of impairment and different approaches to navigating the impairment. People with different types of disabilities will approach technologies, use assistive technologies, and seek accommodations in different ways, depending on the specific type of disability they have and when they acquired it (Jaeger, 2009). However, with many technologies, little attempt is made to account for accessibility.

Accessibility also is not an absolute concept. An information technology can be accessible, partly accessible, or completely inaccessible. One information technology may be fully accessible for persons with mobility impairments and yet utterly inaccessible to persons with visual impairments. The key to website accessibility is making sure that the content of the site is equally available to all users. It is not a one-time process, though, since modifications to an information technology over time can lead to increased problems with accessibility (Hackett, Parmento, and Zeng, 2004; Lazar and Greenidge, 2006). The tremendous benefits of accessibility outweigh any concerns, however, as accessible design typically makes interacting with the technology easier for all users. Even if a particular user receives no benefit from an accessible technology, there is no downside for that user; accessible design will be clear to users with disabilities but not noticeable to other users.

Information technologies could be accessible from the outset if they were designed to include all users and if the accessibility solutions were designed to carry through subsequent generations of an information technology (Kennard and Lyle, 2001; Stephanidis and Emailiani, 1999; Vanderheiden, 2003). However, for most information technologies, accessibility is not part of the design process, and accessibility testing infrequently occurs in the development and implementation of many information technologies (Jaeger, 2006b; Kanayama, 2003b; Keates and Clarkson, 2003; Theofanos and Redish, 2003; Tusler, 2005). The most commonly cited reason by industries and governments for this neglect of accessibility in the design process is the extra cost of making information technologies inclusive (Bowe, 1993; Kanayama, 2003b; Lang, 2000). Using cost as an excuse to not design inclusive technologies dates back to the development of the first telephone networks, when accounting for the needs of people with hearing impairments was deemed too costly (Lang, 2000).

The cost of accessibility, when accounted for from the outset of design, is practically nothing (Slatin, 2001). However, significant challenges and expenses often arise in the process of retrofitting an existing technology to be made accessible. For example, redesigning a basic tic-tac-toe program into an accessible game increases the lines of code from 192 to 1,412, a difficulty that could have been avoided if the program had been originally designed to be accessible (Ossmann, Miesenberger, and Archambault, 2008). Products that have been designed to be inherently accessible have also been shown to have increased value to the designer—as much as a 100-fold return on investment (Bias and Mayhew, 1994).

Throughout history, though, because few technologies have been introduced to be accessible, assistive technologies have had to be created. The easiest assistive technologies to conceptualize are the most familiar ones; wheelchairs, braces, prostheses, and canes, for example, are assistive technologies that make navigation in less-than-accessible physical environments possible for people with mobility impairments. These are also the oldest types of assistive technologies that we know of; wooden prostheses are mentioned in writings as early as 500 BCE, and a tomb from approximately 300 BCE was discovered to contain a skeleton with a bronze prosthetic leg (Braddock and Parish, 2001).

The screen reader software programs mentioned are an example of assistive technologies that are important on the Internet. Such programs are designed to verbalize all content on the screen, making the Internet usable to people with very low vision or no vision. A skilled user of a screen reader can listen to the Web much faster that other people can visually read the same content. Screen readers, however, are of little use when a website is designed so that it is not compatible with screen reading technology. Sadly, many websites still are incompatible with screen readers and many other assistive technologies that persons with disabilities rely on to access the Internet. In fact, one of the biggest barriers for persons with disabilities online is incompatibility with assistive technologies (Russell, 2003).

Concerns regarding accessibility have accompanied every change in information technologies. However, the relationship between individuals and information technologies has changed significantly in the past century or so, shifting the importance of information technologies in everyday life. In a world of small communities and primarily face-to-face personal, educational, and employment interactions, the lack of equal access to television or radio may have been unjust, but it would not undermine the ability to engage in socialization, work, or school. In sharp contrast, personal, educational, and employment interactions now depend heavily on information technologies, with interactions often occurring only through those technologies.

Given the importance of the Internet to employment and education, the lack of accessibility to websites can be disastrous. Of the more than 13 million people with disabilities who are employed, 90 percent rely on accessible technologies to accomplish their jobs (Dispenza, 2002; Johnson, 2004; Schartz, Schartz, and Blanck, 2002). For many people with disabilities, the Internet has provided "an opportunity to join the workforce for the first time (Rich, Erb, and Rich, 2002, p. 51). Without accessible Internet content, many of these jobs would be difficult or impossible.

Similarly, with the move toward online education—in terms of both totally online courses and online course materials for face-to-face courses—the accessibility of course websites has become a tremendously important issue for students with disabilities in elementary, secondary, and higher education. Many academic websites are inaccessible, and many educational institutions lack effective accessibility policies (Bradbard, Peters, and Caneva, 2010; Carlson, 2004; Wattenberg, 2004). Since its introduction a decade ago, students and faculty with disabilities at colleges and universities have struggled with the accessibility challenges posed by the most widely used online course system (Abram, 2003; Riley, 2005). As with employment situations, inaccessible online academic materials threaten the ability of students and faculty with disabilities to fulfill their educational goals.

Because of the rapid changes in information technologies, staying engaged in society is moving from information technologies being necessary just for information access, to information technologies being central to information access, communication, and interaction (Jaeger and Xie, 2009). In considering the ways in which the law could move to promote sustained equality of access to information technologies and whatever follows next, it is necessary to acknowledge that access is a multifaceted concept. Even an update to an existing information technology may change the accessibility of the technology or the ways in which the user interacts through assistive technologies. Equality of access depends on equality of all elements of access. To try to ensure such vital accessibility, governments and nonprofits have created laws and standards for equal access online.

Accessibility Laws and Standards

The United States has the world's largest and most comprehensive set of disability rights laws related to information technologies, including Section 508 of the Rehabilitation Act, the Americans with Disabilities Act, the E-Government Act, and the Telecommunications Act of 1996 (Jaeger, 2004a). These disability laws focus either on providing specialized services or on protecting and advancing civil rights (DePoy and Gilson, 2009). This suite of laws is intended to guarantee equal rights online for persons with disabilities. Like many other conceptions about the Internet, under the law, each issue with the Internet "is understood primarily as a *technical* one" (Boyle, 1996, p. ix).

However, like in all other nations with disability rights laws related to information technologies, the US laws are based on static assumptions about information technologies, making them unable to comfortably adjust to technology development and change (Crawford, 2003; R. Frieden, 2003). The legal approaches in the United States and elsewhere also rely on purely technical approaches to promoting accessibility, rather than conceiving of accessibility as a social goal that is accomplished through technology. These static notions of technology and disability limit the success of laws online (Ellcessor, 2010; Jaeger and Xie, 2009).

A further key limitation on the development of laws and standards mandating accessibility is that the voices of industry are more powerful and more present in the discussions than the perspectives of persons with disabilities (Adam and Kreps, 2009; Jaeger, 2006b; Simpson, 2009). As a result, the laws do not account sufficiently for the actual needs of users with disabilities and tend to create distinctions between people with disabilities and all other users of the technology. This binary approach—average user or user with disabilities—tends to obscure discrepancies in the system and validate different levels of access for different users (Carling-Jenkins, 2010).

At the federal government level in the United States, there are six major laws that establish the foundation of mandates for equal online access for persons with disabilities; the first three are more general, while the later three more specifically target the Internet (Jaeger, 2004a). The first disability rights law related to technology, Section 504 of the 1973 Rehabilitation Act, established broad standards of equal access to government information and rights to accessible information technologies related to government activities. Passed shortly thereafter in 1974, IDEA established requirements of equal access for educational materials, including technology-based educational materials. In 1990, the ADA created broad prohibitions on exclusion of persons with disabilities from public services or the denial of benefits related to public services. All three of these laws were written before widespread use of the Internet, yet they firmly establish the core principles of inclusion, and the rights they establish have been generally brought into the online environment.

Since use of the Internet became commonplace, the federal government has passed three further major laws that affirm and extend guarantees of accessibility online. The Telecommunications Act of 1996 promotes the development and implementation of accessible technologies in telecommunications systems, including the Internet. The E-Government Act of 2002 compels all federal government agencies to provide their online materials in accessible format. The key law of online access, though, is Section 508 of the Rehabilitation Act, which mandates accessible online materials and the use of accessible technologies by government agencies and any entities receiving government funding.

Section 508 focuses directly on equality in "the access to and use of the information and data" (29 U.S.C. § 794d(a)(1)(A)(ii)).

Section 508 establishes accessibility requirements for Web-based information and applications, telecommunications products, software applications, operating systems, video and multimedia products, self-contained or closed products, and computers. The key requirements of Section 508 for the discussion at hand are those related to websites, which focus wholly on making information accessible.

The requirements of Section 508 for websites value content over presentation to ensure that all users can get to the information and service content on a website (Mueller, 2003). The primary guidelines for website design and implementation that are required to comply with Section 508, known as the Internet and Intranet Accessibility Standards (www.section508.gov), can be summarized as:

- Ensuring that the elements of the site work with assistive technologies.
- Providing alternate formats for all nontext content.
- Providing alternate formats for all multimedia content, synchronized with the presentation.
- Not relying on color to convey content.
- Using redundant links.
- Making documents readable without associated style sheets.
- Identifying row and column headers on tables and markup for multiple row and column headers.
- Providing identifications to facilitate navigation and location.
- Titling frames with text.
- Using scripting language that provides functional text that can be read by screen readers.
- Using client-side image maps.
- Avoiding flicker rates that can cause seizures.
- Providing direct links to any required plug-ins.
- Making online forms compatible with assistive technologies.
- Providing methods to skip repetitive navigation links.
- Having a text-only equivalent page available for every page that cannot otherwise be made completely compliant with all other requirements.
- Providing accessible versions of all software and forms on the site.
- Not timing users out of applications (Electronic and Information Technology Accessibility Standards, 36 C.F.R. § 1194.22).

The actual guidelines are more specific and technical in the explanations and offer examples of when each applies.

In fact, the guidelines are very technology centric. Nevertheless, the guidelines are seen as being very successful, if applied correctly, in terms of guaranteeing equal access to websites (Slatin and Rush, 2003). For example, "more than 90 percent of sensory accessibility issues can be resolved through steps outlined in Section 508" (Fulton, 2011, p. 38). The standards address many of the online needs of persons with visual, auditory, mobility, and cognitive impairments, as well as the needs of persons with very specific conditions, such as seizure disorders.

Nongovernmental agencies have also worked to create standards for online access that will be used by private entities. The most prominent of these efforts is the Web Accessibility Initiative (WAI). Tim Berners-Lee, one of the creators of the World Wide Web, has been a supporter of the WAI since its founding in 1997. Nearly concurrently to the United States federal government beginning to develop the guidelines for Section 508, the nongovernmental World Wide Web Consortium (W3C) began to establish its WAI. Founded in 1994, the W3C is made up of over 500 organizations originally spearheaded by the Massachusetts Institute of Technology (MIT) and the European Laboratory for Particle Physics (CERN). The goal of the W3C is to produce consensus-based, internationally recognized guidelines, software, and tools to advance the utility and effectiveness of the Web. Because it has no governmental status or enforcement mechanism, the W3C standards are adopted only voluntarily.

The WAI offers a set of recommended guidelines and checkpoints for creating accessible websites, known as the Web Content Accessibility Guidelines (WCAG), as well as tools for promoting Web content accessibility for persons with disabilities (http://www .w3.org/WAI). The WAI originated in 1997, the first recommendations were offered in 1999, and they have been updated since. The WCAG offered the first Web accessibility guidelines that "represented a broad, international consensus among industry representatives, academic researchers, and members of the disability community" (Slatin and Rush, 2003, pp. 4–5). The WCAG breaks guidelines into three levels: Priority 1 guidelines are necessary for accessibility, Priority 2 guidelines are suggested to improve basic accessibility, and Priority 3 guidelines are not necessary for accessibility but would be helpful to users with disabilities. Each guideline at each level of priority includes checkpoints by which to measure progress. The key principles of the WCAG are:

- Use of alt tags for images and animations.
- Use of client-side image maps.
- Provision of captioning for and transcripts for audio and descriptions of video.
- Use of hyperlink text that makes sense.
- Maintenance of consistent page orientation.
- Provision of summaries of tables, graphs, and charts.
- Creation of alternate content for features that rely on inaccessible external software.
- Use of meaningful titles for frames.
- Validation of work with tools guidelines, and checklists provided by W3C.

The WCAG has recently been updated and organized around four unifying principles, under the acronym of POUR:

- *Perceivable* accessibility features, including alternate forms of content and captions, compatibility with assistive technologies, and sufficient contrast to make content easy to see and hear.
- *Operable* features, including keyboard accessible functions, time to read and use content, navigation and search assistance, and avoidance of seizure-causing features.
- *Understandable* content, including readable text, predictable content and layout, and easy-to-find help features.
- *Robust* compatibility with current and future technologies.

The WCAG and Section 508 guidelines are the two most thorough and most commonly used sets of rules for creating accessible websites worldwide (Lazar et al., 2003; Slatin and Rush, 2003). Both of these sets of accessibility guidelines aim to create websites that provide equal access to all users. They do have somewhat different approaches, though, because the Section 508 guidelines place emphasis on technology and the WCAG focus mainly on design.

For the most part, the WCAG principles and the Section 508 principles are similar. The Priority 1 guidelines of the WCAG, those that are necessary for accessibility, are all covered in the Section 508 guidelines. However, the Section 508 guidelines include a number of other accessibility requirements that are accompanied by detailed specifications. The most significant difference is that the Section 508 standards give greater considerations to the needs of persons with cognitive and learning disabilities, though this greater specificity is still not sufficient attention to the issues.

There are significant similarities between the two sets of guidelines but also some very important differences. Whereas the Section 508 requirements were designed to be a detailed set of enforceable standards, the WCAG serve as suggestions of best practices, as emphasized by the conceptual approach of the four unifying principles. Strict adherence to the WCAG, however, does not necessarily provide full accessibility for all users (Lazar et al., 2003; Witt and McDermott, 2004). In contrast, Section 508 standards include overarching accessibility principles and detailed requirements by which these principles are to be achieved. The Section 508 requirements generally are more specific than the WCAG checkpoints. However, with its checkpoints and self-assessment tools, the WCAG may be much more user-friendly for those trying to implement accessible websites and likely offers better guidance to those trying to follow the standards (Slatin, 2001; Slatin and Rush, 2003). This broader, more guided focus of the WCAG gives it the potential to maximize universal usability of technologies if implemented fully, but the specificity of Section 508 gives more clear targets for accessibility.

Guidelines are often considered to aid accessibility, although the guidelines, even if followed to exacting standards, would not create an Internet that was equally accessible by all persons with disabilities. Most significantly, both Section 508 and the WCAG focus heavily on sensory and mobility impairments but give too little consideration to cognitive impairments (Lazar, 2007). People with sensory impairments and mobility impairments generally want to achieve the same information goals as people without impairments; they just need to utilize different software and hardware to accomplish the similar information goals. Cognitive issues, however, are more complicated in terms of information goals. The lack of focus on cognitive impairments derives from the fact that most of the research about information access and Internet access for people with disabilities has been on issues related to the needs of people with sensory and mobility impairments. The small amount of research conducted regarding accessibility for persons with cognitive impairments has demonstrated important elements of accessible design for these users—large size text, descriptive text, clear alignment of content items, visual guidance and orientation, and color change on mouse over—but this research still receives less attention than acessibility related to sensory and mobility impairments (Sears, Hanson, and Myers, 2007; Sevilla et al., 2007). Even the process of revising the Section 508 requirements did not result in a consensus on guidelines for accessibility for cognitive impairments, noting that any such guidelines would not be specific or measurable (Access Board, 2010b).

As a result, while there is generally a very good understanding of how people with sensory and mobility impairments utilize computers, there is not yet an equivalent understanding of the ways in which people with cognitive impairments use computers (Jaeger and Bowman, 2005; Lazar, 2007; McGrenere, Sullivan, and Baecker, 2006). The guidelines, then, reflect this lack of research on the various cognitive impairments, which can be extremely different from one another in impacts. Amnesia, aphasia, dementia, autism, and Down syndrome will each result in widely different goals in relation to information and technology—goals that are also potentially different from those of people with other disabilities (Lazar, 2007; Mankoff, Hayes, and Kasnitz, 2010; McGrenere, Sullivan, and Baecker, 2006). For example, many people with Down syndrome, which often makes the verbalization of thoughts difficult, are now extensively using the means of instant communication via text— through microblogging tools like Twitter and through mobile Web-enabled technologies—to communicate much more effectively than they previously could. This situation is similar to that of persons with speech and hearing impairments. However, a person with dementia would not likely be able to engage in the same kinds of information and communication activities. Even learning disabilities—such as dyslexia, dyspraxia, and dyscalculia—have varying issues with technology access; for example, dyslexia has implications for user interfaces, software, hardware, and language (Pollack, 2009; Smythe, 2010).

Mobile devices can also help people with cognitive disabilities in other ways, and these need greater consideration in accessibility guidelines. People with amnesia can use mobile devices to orient themselves when feeling lost or disorientated and to help store and retrieve new information that might otherwise be lost, while users with autism and aphasia can use mobile devices to communicate by typing or using graphics and to keep them aware of their appointments and other important information (Moffat et al., 2004; Wu,

Baecker, and Richards, 2005). Similar orienting benefits have been found for users with Down syndrome (Carmein, 2004). Due to the facilitation of communication and focus, mobile devices have become particularly important in the education of students on the autism spectrum.

Early enthusiasm for the potential impacts of the guidelines, particularly Section 508, was extremely high. When the Section 508 guidelines for Web accessibility were announced, the National Council on Disability (NCD), the government agency responsible for advocating for the needs of persons with disabilities, labeled these guidelines "the most far-reaching source of legal authority for accessible electronic and information technologies" (National Council on Disability, 2001, p. 56). The regulations, which the NCD called "landmark" and "revolutionary," were considered a "powerful influence" on government and industry that would avoid the limitations of many other disability rights laws (National Council on Disability, 2001, p. 57). The NCD was also enthusiastic in its assessment of the means of implementing and enforcing compliance with the Section 508 regulations, noting that Section 508 represented "the most sophisticated model to date of a civil rights law that closely integrates accessible design and enforcement strategies" (National Council on Disability, 2001, p. 58).

The NCD's assessment of the law and accompanying regulations was far from isolated. When the law was to be implemented in 2001, the chairman of the Federal Communications Commission (FCC) lauded Section 508 as a means to make government and private industry more responsive to and responsible for the needs of persons with disabilities who are interacting with information and communication technologies (Kennard and Lyle, 2001). Longtime disability rights advocates saw Section 508 and its regulations in a similar manner. One advocate for accessible technology stated that the Section 508 regulations "have the potential for being as important for assuring access to the information age as the Architectural Barriers Act was for assuring access to the constructed environment for people with disabilities" (Wakefield, 1998, n.p.). Legal scholars even wrote law review articles praising the law and its intent (McLawhorn, 2001; Nadler and Furman, 2001). Support for the law and its regulations also extended to President George W. Bush, who stated that Section 508 will allow "more opportunities for people of all abilities to access government information" (quoted in Access Board, 2002, p. 1).

These projections, unfortunately, parallel the enthusiasms that the Internet would completely change life for persons with disabilities. The actual impacts of these laws and guidelines have been mixed. A wide range of studies have shown low levels of compliance with the law (Ellison, 2004; Jaeger, 2006a, 2008; Lazar and Greenidge, 2006; Rubaii-Barrett and Wise, 2008). Both the FCC's *National Broadband Plan* and the National Council on Disability's *National Disability Policy: A Progress Report* noted in 2009 the continuing widespread failure of the federal government to comply with Section 508 requirements, with the latter report equating noncompliance with Section 508 with the common inaccessibility of commercial websites (Federal Communications Commission, 2010; National Council on Disability, 2009).

Just as significantly, the technology-specific nature of the laws and guidelines have become problematic as the Internet has rapidly matured (Jaeger and Xie, 2009). While government and industry accessibility standards have been developed to make information-oriented websites more inclusive to persons with disabilities, the existing guidelines are not as useful in the communication-oriented Internet environment that has developed in recent years. As much Web activity has moved beyond the one-way transfer of information to multidirectional information flows through social media—popularly known as Web 2.0—the laws and guidelines have not evolved to keep up with these new means of interaction online.

Because of the rapid changes in information technologies, staying engaged in society is moving from Web-enabled information technologies being necessary just for information access to Web-enabled information technologies being necessary for information access, communication, and interaction (Jaeger and Xie, 2009). In considering the ways in which the law could move to promote sustained equality of access to Web-enabled information technologies and whatever follows next, it is necessary to consider that access is a multitiered concept. Even an update to an existing information technology may change the accessibility of the technology or the ways in which the user interacts through assistive technologies. Equality of access depends on equality of all levels of access.

The challenges that persons with disabilities face online are significant and unique. People with disabilities, however, are not the only population that faces barriers to online access and participation. A number of other populations grapple with limited Internet access, and the online barriers to persons with disabilities fit within a larger spectrum of gaps in access and societal implications of these access gaps.

Gaps in Internet Access

From the beginning of the explosion of popular usage of the Internet, there have been many proclamations that the Internet would quickly become an all-inclusive, completely egalitarian medium that would eliminate many societal differences and provide opportunities for everyone. Such wildly optimistic projections have never approached accuracy, with many populations being left behind, for many reasons. Often, "the problems of Internet access are common to the problems of access to other communication and information technologies" (Norris, 2001, p. 66). Currently, nearly 40 percent of US homes lack Internet access, and the percentage of households without Internet access jumps to 62 percent in rural communities; among homes with Internet access, 45 percent lack broadband access, and 10 percent continue to rely on dial-up Internet service (Horrigan, 2008, 2009).

In 1995, the National Telecommunications and Information Administration (NTIA) began a series of reports, called *Falling Through the Net,* that documented the gaps in access to the Internet in the United States, in the process popularizing the term *digital divide* (US Department of Commerce, 1995, 1998, 1999, 2000). Under the George W. Bush administration, two more reports in the series were issued under the much more optimistic name of *A Nation Online* (US Department of Commerce, 2002, 2004). The more optimistic title, however, poorly hid the fact that the numbers had not changed all that much from 2000 to 2002 (Bertot, 2003; Jaeger and Thompson, 2003, 2004; Fairlie, 2005).

Over the course of the reports, the groups that were on the wrong side of the digital divide did change, due in part to the reports figuring out the appropriate areas to focus on (Kinney, 2010). The 1995 report identified urban and rural poor, urban and rural minorities, older adults, young adults, and those of lower education levels as the groups being left behind. Three years later, the 1998 report identified the groups on the wrong side of the divide as rural poor, rural and urban racial minorities, young households, and female-headed households. The 1999 report found that the disadvantaged groups were determined by education level, income level, race and ethnicity, and residence (rural or urban). The final *Falling Through the Net* report in

2000 highlighted growing Internet access among most populations, though the report also noted the clear divides based on education, income, age, and disability. The 2000 and 2002 *A Nation Online* reports avoided the use of the term *digital divide,* instead focusing on levels of adoption online. The reports emphasized the growing adoption of the Internet among the groups already using it, sidestepping the groups not being included in the growth of Internet access and usage.

By not considering the larger social contexts and the reasons for gaps in access, the reports painted a fairly limited picture of those gaps and the ways to address them (Bertot, 2003; Stevenson, 2009; Warschauer, 2003a, 2003b). However, across the reports, they did demonstrate a clear trend that groups that suffer other disadvantages in society—such as lower socioeconomic status, lower educational achievement, disability, and rural residency—were also the most likely to have difficulties in accessing and using the Internet. Other studies have demonstrated that the gender, racial, and ethnic disparities that the reports identified were actually far more tied to economic differences (Hoffman and Novak, 1998; Lenhart et al., 2000; Spooner, Meredith, and Rainie, 2003; Organisation for Economic Co-operation and Development, 2000). Additionally, nations with the largest economic disparities tend to have those disparities reflected in socioeconomic gaps in Internet usage (Booz Allen Hamilton, 2002).

There are also key reasons for divides that are not addressed in the reports. Lower levels of availability of non-English materials related to the United States have hindered many Americans who do not speak English from using the Internet. For example, 32 percent of Latinos in the United States who do not speak English use the Internet, but 78 percent of Latinos who speak English use the Internet (Fox and Livingston, 2007; Livingston, 2010). Similar language-related differences can be found in other groups (Fairlie, 2005; Spooner, Rainie, and Meredith, 2001). Additionally, lower levels of formal education are typically linked to lower levels of technological literacy—understanding how to use technologies like computers and the Internet (Jaeger and Thompson, 2003, 2004; Powell, Byrne, and Dailey, 2010).

The availability of access is not the only issue. On an Internet dominated by social media, streaming audio and video, and other bandwidth-intensive applications, the level of access is as important as the presence of access. Nonbroadband connections are "minimally useful" and becoming "increasingly strained" as the content on the

Internet becomes richer (Boyd and Berejka, 2009, p. 7). Levels of access now present some very significant access gaps. In April 2008, only 55 percent of American adults had home broadband access (Horrigan, 2008). Rural Americans are least likely to have home broadband access (38 percent), as compared to suburban (60 percent) and urban (57 percent) Americans. Higher educational attainment and higher income levels correlate to higher home broadband penetration. For example, whereas 85 percent of Americans earning over $100,000 per year have home broadband access, only 25 percent of Americans earning less than $25,000 per year have it. Many current users of lower-speed connections would not be able to switch because of the cost (Horrigan, 2009).

These gaps in access speed are now being paralleled in some ways to gaps in access to mobile Internet-enabled technologies, as more and more development of Internet content is likely to focus on such mobile technologies, which some populations have more ability to access and afford than others (Baker and Moon, 2008; Horrigan, 2009; Rainie and Anderson, 2008). Given their potential importance as an emergency communication tool, access to mobile devices is a particularly important issue for persons with disabilities (Baker and Moon, 2008).

Another issue that is generally ignored in discussions about the gaps in Internet access is the literal availability of access. In a nation in which phone service is still not available in some rural areas, the availability of the Internet cannot be taken for granted. In fact, a wide range of factors—including physical geography, levels of urbanization, condition of infrastructure, corporate priorities, local politics, and success in applying for government funding—affect the levels of access, availability, and affordability of the Internet in any location (Gabel, 2007; Grubesic, 2008; Jaeger et al., 2007; Jaeger, McClure, and Bertot, 2005; Mack and Grubesic, 2009; Mandel et al., 2010; Sgroi, 2008; P. K. Yu, 2002). In some communities, Internet access is limited to low-speed access or is not available at all because the areas are so rural, while in other locations the same access scenario occurs because the area is high poverty and telecommunications companies do not feel it economically worth their time to provide service (Gabel, 2007; Grubesic, 2008; Mack and Grubesic, 2009; Sgroi, 2008).

In other cases, the combination of geography and federal funding has created regional differences in quality of access. The monies to support Internet access by the federal Universal Service Fund have not been evenly distributed based on population size or need. Instead, the application process and thereby the distribution of funds have favored certain states and regions of the country (Jaeger, McClure, and Bertot, 2005). Ironically, some of the most successful states in receiving these funds have been among the wealthiest, while some of poorest and least connected states have received limited benefits, resulting in areas such as the Gulf Coast states having much lower levels of access than the national average (Jaeger et al., 2007; Jaeger, McClure, and Bertot, 2005).

The great recession that began in 2008 has led many people to drop their home Internet access, considering it to be a luxury that can be cut to save money in harsh economic times (Horrigan, 2008). This recession has exacerbated the situation of those of lower socioeconomic status who were already the least likely to use the Internet, have Internet access, or use advanced online tools (Horrigan, 2008). A great many people who no longer can afford home Internet access have turned to the free Internet access made available in public libraries (Carlton, 2009; CNN, 2009; Nicholas et al., 2010; Van Sant, 2009). In most communities in the United States, the public library is the only source of free Internet access (Bertot, McClure, and Jaeger, 2008). To meet these needs, public library branches in 2009 averaged 14.2 workstations for public use, and 82.2 percent of public libraries offered free wireless access for patrons, both increases over previous years (American Library Association, 2010). At the beginning of the recession in 2008, applications for library cards were already 10 percent higher than 2006 levels (American Library Association, 2009). Among those using libraries for Internet access, 52.4 percent do not own a computer, 42.4 percent lack access both at home and at work, 40 percent are there because access is free, and 38.1 percent rely on the assistance of librarians (Gibson, Bertot, and McClure, 2009).

In the economic downturn, use of public libraries and library computers for applying for unemployment benefits and social services, seeking employment, and other e-government activities has increased substantially (Bertot, 2009; Bertot, Jaeger et al, 2009; Jaeger and Bertot, 2010a, 2011; Powell, Byrne, and Dailey, 2010). However, "this is not the same as having automatic access via high-speed connections at home and at the office" (Norris, 2001, p. 92). In spite of these levels of Internet access available, 73.5 percent of libraries still have insufficient workstations some or all of the time (American Library Association, 2010). In 2009, 75.7 percent of libraries reported increased usage of workstations over the previous year, while 71.1 percent reported an increase in wireless usage (American Library Association, 2010). Additionally, 45.6 percent of libraries reported increases in usage of electronic resources, and 26.3 percent had increases in requests for training services; to manage the scope of access demands, 92.3 percent of public libraries have established time limits for access to workstations (American Library Association, 2010).

Disability Among Access Gaps

Clearly, people with disabilities are not the only population that faces disadvantages in accessing the Internet. It has been accurately stated that equal access to the Internet is an issue where the disadvantaged are those "who have fought for civil rights in other areas of our society" (First and Hart, 2002, p. 385). While people with disabilities are not alone when it comes to gaps in Internet access and usage, the barriers faced by persons with disabilities are unique.

As noted in Chapter 1, 30.2 percent of people with disabilities use a computer at home, 33.0 percent live in a household with Internet access, 26.0 percent use the Internet at home, and 30.8 percent use the Internet at any location. Each of these percentages is approximately half of the equivalent percentages for the rest of the population (Dobransky and Hargittai, 2006). Persons with disabilities can be limited in their access to and use of the Internet by a wide range of factors—from the ability to afford the hardware to accessibility problems with Internet Service Providers (ISPs), to Web browsers that are not compatible with vital assistive technologies (Fox, 2004; Fox and Madden, 2005; Jaeger and Bowman, 2005; University of California Los Angeles, 2003). If the statistics existed for the use of mobile Internet-enabled devices, the discrepancies would likely be even higher between people with disabilities and the rest of the population. Persons with disabilities are very much on the wrong side of the digital divide, and the growing use of mobile technologies threatens to widen this gap.

This gap for persons with disabilities may also become wider as the number of older adults, and thereby the number of people with disabilities, increases as the baby boom generation ages. Older adults are the group most likely to not use the Internet entirely by choice (Horrigan, 2008, 2009). This rise in the number of older adults has paralleled the time in which the Internet has become an important—

even essential—new platform for information and communication in contemporary societies (Fox, 2006; Fox and Madden, 2005). Like persons with disabilities, older adults are much less likely to regularly use the Internet—and are more likely to limit Internet usage—than many other populations as a result of these barriers to initial access (Loges and Jung, 2001; Jaeger and Bowman, 2005; Xie, 2003).

The barriers that persons with disabilities face are not necessarily as fixable by intermediaries as the barriers other groups face. The free access and training in public libraries can overcome the gaps faced by people who cannot afford access and who lack the education to use the Internet without assistance. In fact, 99 percent of public libraries in the United States provide free Internet access, 90 percent of public libraries have Internet training courses for patrons, and more than that offer informal assistance with the Internet whenever patrons need it (American Library Association, 2010). With more than 16,500 public libraries covering the United States, free Internet access and training are available to those who need it in most cities and towns in the nation. While library access may not be as convenient as home access, public libraries ensure that Internet access is available to most of the nation's population.

For people with access that is limited due to lack of sufficient infrastructure, the Obama administration is working to overcome these infrastructure challenges. Obama's charge to the FCC to create a national broadband plan is an opportunity to close the digital divide due to infrastructure; a National Broadband Plan has been developed, and billions of dollars in grants have been distributed to expand the broadband infrastructure in rural and urban areas (Federal Communications Commission, 2010; Turner, 2009).

For all of those groups, the challenge is one of access to the Internet, be it overcoming cost, education, or availability issues. The more complex access barriers are the ones that are built into the Internet itself. For persons with disabilities, many of the challenges tie to economic and educational reasons, as many people with disabilities are disadvantaged in terms of employment and education compared with national averages. However, even if every person with a disability had sufficient money, time, and technological literacy to master the Internet, that does not mean equality of access would be achieved.

For persons with disabilities, the greatest access barrier is in the infrastructure and content of the Internet. Like the people whose Internet usage is limited because they do not find relevant much of the content that is available in the language they speak, people with disabilities are disadvantaged in the limited amount of content that is in a form they can use. In addition, many of the technological channels by which to reach that content are not usable either.

So many websites are not designed to be accessible to individuals with various disabilities that large portions of the Internet are of limited access or totally inaccessible to people with sensory, mobility, and cognitive impairments. As so much of the Internet content and so many of the technologies used to access the Internet are developed without consideration of accessibility for persons with disabilities, the entire Internet environment is riddled with barriers from a nearly infinite number of sources.

No group faces barriers to Internet access that are as multifaceted, numerous, and hard to address as persons with disabilities. Until producers of content and technologies realize the need to better account for the needs of persons with disabilities—or are forced to by legal mechanisms—this situation will not likely change.

As fewer users are excluded from a technology, the costs to those excluded rise exponentially (Tongia and Wilson, 2007). Unfortunately for persons with disabilities, the social, economic, educational, and other deficits created by lack of participation in the Internet are clear and becoming ever more significant as the Internet becomes central to more aspects of life. If people with disabilities are the only group significantly left out of the Internet of the future, the results will be disastrous. Determining ways to rectify these gaps while they can still be overcome technologically is of utmost importance to persons with disabilities.

The Law in the United States and Access Gaps

As mentioned earlier, the United States has long been the world's leader in establishing legal protections of rights for persons with disabilities. The Architectural Barriers Act, the Rehabilitation Act, IDEA, and the ADA have all provided major advances in promoting the rights of people with disabilities in the United States and also inspiring many other nations to pass similar legislation. In terms of the Internet, the United States has pursued a robust legal program to promote equal online access through Section 508 of the Rehabilitation Act, the E-Government Act, the Telecommunications Act of 1996, and other laws.

Equal access to the Internet for persons with disabilities has been an enormous challenge since the advent of the World Wide Web but was not necessarily a major issue needing extensive legal protections before the Web. Before the Web, some individuals with disabilities actively used many e-mail programs, bulletin boards, Internet support groups, and other forms of computer-mediated communication for advocacy, peer support, and information gathering (Fullmer and Walls, 1994; Ritchie and Blanck, 2003). While the pre-Web Internet, as a simple text-based medium, was relatively accessible for most persons with disabilities who had access to basic assistive software, the graphics-based World Wide Web poses tremendous access difficulties for persons with a wide range of disabilities, including visual, mobility, cognitive, auditory, and learning (Jacko and Hanson, 2002; Stephanidis and Savidis, 2001). In 1998, just a few years after the advent of the Web, 40 percent of the US population was using the Internet, but only 10 percent of persons with disabilities were (Ritchie and Blanck, 2003).

Over time, the law in the United States has shifted from treating disability as a medical issue to focusing on it as a civil rights issue; but it has not made this transition completely smoothly (Switzer, 2003). Originally, the US law, like laws elsewhere, treated disability purely as a medical problem within the individual, ignoring the roles of social influences and discrimination. The medical model emphasized that it was the responsibility of the individual to overcome the disability in order to be part of society. In this medical model, the premise was for the law to ensure support and services, not guarantee an equal place in society. The Architectural Barriers Act began a philosophical shift in the law, focusing on the rights of persons with disabilities—in this case to have equal access to public spaces—rather than on the medical needs of persons with disabilities. The Rehabilitation Act focused on rights to participate in government places and services, while IDEA brought the right to a public education. The ADA then extended these notions to many other contexts of public accommodation—hotels, restaurants, transportation, and entertainment, for example—as well as to state and local government.

US laws now emphatically focus on the civil rights aspects of disability, which emphasize the ways in which society can better allow individuals with disabilities to function. However, protective policies carry several potentially negative aspects: they assume that persons with disabilities need specialized legislation when general legislation protects the rights of all others; they can be unclear about who is to be covered by the protections; and they can include exemptions that allow discrimination to persist (DePoy and Gilson, 2004, 2008, 2009).

Not all of these laws are coordinated, and the rights are not overseen by a government agency with enforcement powers. In the federal government, the Access Board—formally the Architectural and Transportation Barriers Compliance Board—is the closest thing to a disability rights watchdog. It establishes design criteria and guidelines for the federal government in relation to buildings, transportation, information technology, and other areas. It also issues reports about compliance with disability laws. However, it does not have the power to enforce compliance with the laws. Instead, many government agencies and industries are left to self-regulate their actions.

In 1987, it was asserted that "America has no disability policy. It maintains a set of disparate programs, many of them emanating from policies designed for other groups, that work at cross purposes" (Berkowitz, 1987, pp. 193–194). In many ways, this statement still holds true. The United States has the widest array of laws to protect the rights of persons with disabilities anywhere, but it does not necessarily have the means to maximize the impact or success of these laws. For the Internet, the United States has not only the major laws cited, but also many smaller related pieces of legislation that support these primary laws (see Simpson, 2009, for a cataloging of these acts). Simply creating the legal rights is not sufficient, however.

The US federal government has created numerous laws related to accessibility of information technology, but these laws focus primarily on government agencies and entities receiving direct government funding (Jaeger, 2004a). For websites, the most prominent law is Section 508 of the Rehabilitation Act, which mandates specific design requirements that reduce barriers to access for different types of disabilities and promotes compatibility with assistive technologies that users may be employing. As detailed earlier, Section 508 has an explicit set of technological and accessibility requirements as well as guidance for implementation (www.section508.gov). Many government websites are still inaccessible, despite the fact that, by law, the websites were required to be accessible from 2001 (Cullen and Hernon, 2006; Jaeger, 2006a, 2006b, 2008; Jaeger and Matteson, 2009; Olalere and Lazar, forthcoming). While statistics for website accessibility vary depending on the assessment method used—as discussed in greater detail in a subsequent chapter—the levels of accessibility of websites are extremely limited regardless of the methodology employed, with the percentages of accessibility ranging from the low single digits to less than one-third in different studies.

Until late 2010, there was no statement or legal mandate from the US federal government specifically directing accessibility for nongovernmental websites. As a result, levels of accessibility on commercial websites tend to be even lower than those on governmental sites. As a result of both a lack of education about ways to achieve online accessibility and social biases against persons with disabilities, many studies have demonstrated significant gaps in access and an accompanying lack of interest on the part of many companies to provide equal online access to persons with disabilities (e.g., Baker and Moon, 2008; Lazar et al., 2007; Lazar et al., 2003; Lazar, Dudley-Sponaugle, and Greenidge, 2004; Lazar and Greenidge, 2006). Perhaps not surprisingly, legal efforts to create equality of access in the commercial realm have been largely unsuccessful and confused. Courts typically are reluctant to view websites as being "places of public accommodation" that are covered by social inclusion legislation like the ADA (Jaeger and Bowman, 2005).

A primary feature of US laws related to the Internet is the notion of "undue burden," which appears in the major laws as a reason that can be used to avoid compliance, allowing for inaccessibility when the company or government agency claims that making a technology accessible would be too expensive or time-consuming. Both government and corporate developers and creators of information technologies have relied heavily on the undue burden exemptions written in many of the laws to avoid making accessible versions. Many corporations have employed this exemption liberally as a defense against making any accessible versions of information technologies, including both the means to access the Internet and the websites on the Internet (Jaeger, 2006b; Kanayama, 2003b; Lazar and Jaeger, 2011). Yet, reliance on industry standards is insufficient to promote accessibility (Stienstra, 2006), and disability rights laws cannot be revised fast enough to match technological change at this point. As a result, the passage of Section 508 did not lead to major changes: "Due to the indirect method of enforcement (through government procurement policies and agents) and due to compliance being 'voluntary' on the part of vendors to comply, little improvement in the overall availability of accessible [information technology] has been reported" (Maskery, 2007, p. 189).

In most cases, the main recourse for persons with disabilities is to file a discrimination claim in the court system. For discrimination claims against private entities, the cases enter the civil court system, while discrimination claims against government agencies enter the administrative law courts. This approach places a curious burden on people with disabilities to be able to afford legal counsel and have the time to file a case to assert their rights. Sadly, courts have also not been particularly receptive to disability discrimination cases. For example, persons with disabilities lose up to 96 percent of the cases they file under the ADA (Davis, 2002; Lee, 2003). Perhaps more significant, the Supreme Court has spent the past two decades limiting the disability rights laws passed by Congress, and many state courts and state legislatures have followed the lead of the Supreme Court (Jaeger and Bowman, 2005; Switzer, 2003). Many states have changed state disability rights laws to mirror the limitations imposed by the Supreme Court on federal laws, while other states have strengthened state laws to counter the rulings of the Supreme Court (Switzer, 2003). Most distressing, the majority opinion in a 2001 Supreme Court decision on disability dismisses the history of discrimination against persons with disabilities as exaggerated and inconsequential (*Board of Trustees of the University of Alabama v. Garrett*, 2001). Nor have court decisions necessarily resulted in the resolution of issues. As a result of the limitations of disability laws and the overall lack of clear direction on website accessibility by courts, states now have widely varying accessibility laws, with few providing specific legal guarantees for website accessibility (Fulton, 2011).

The difficulties in enforcing website accessibility for persons with disabilities through the courts is amply demonstrated by a federal district court opinion that found that the Target website, as it was closely integrated with physical stores, could be seen as being legally required to be accessible only because of this nexus (*National Federation of the Blind v. Target*, 2006). However, the same opinion explicitly limited the holding to companies with an online presence that is closely integrated to a physical presence.

So, while these issues will likely continue to be debated in the courts, the current case law says that Target should have an accessible website, but online-only retailers like Amazon.com, Priceline.com, and Overstock.com may not need to worry about accessibility. It also implies that a company can have both physical and online presences—with the online presence being inaccessible—so long as the website is not too integrated with the physical presence. Legal scholars have generally found this holding—with its clear lack of understanding of technology and its social implications—to make matters more difficult for persons with disabilities seeking equal access to commercial entities in the online environment (Abrar and Dingle, 2009; Bashaw, 2008; Else, 2008; Kessling, 2008). Some have even suggested that the *Target* holding will make it harder to seek equal access to other forms of online content, such as educational websites (Ogden and Menter, 2009).

Disability Law and Internet Access Around the World

For all of the flaws in the US approach, legal assertions of the civil rights of persons with disabilities are rare, and guarantees of legal rights in relation to information technologies are extremely rare. Internationally, "responses to the needs of persons with disabilities have oscillated between charity on the one hand and welfarism on the other" (Devlin and Potheir, 2006, p. 1). Most nations do not have—and have never had—protections of the civil rights of persons with disabilities. While some of these nations have legal guarantees of support for persons with disabilities in some fashion, many others do not. Those nations with laws related to disability most frequently focus on public services or education (D. L. Baker, 2006).

In many societies, there are no legal protections. People with disabilities are often "the poorest and most powerless people" in societies around the globe (Charlton, 1998, p. 25). In many less developed nations, it is estimated that up to 90 percent of children with physical impairments may die before the age of twenty, while a similar percentage of children with cognitive impairments may die before the age of five (Barnes and Mercer, 2003). Currently, in many less developed nations, persons with disabilities are frequently abandoned, left to die, killed in infancy, deprived of education, trained as beggars, sterilized, banned from marriage, forcibly locked in state institutions, or denied rights of citizenship (Charlton, 1998; Ghai, 2001; Ingstad, 2001; Preistley, 2001). In many of these less developed nations, worrying about Internet access may seem a moot point, as Internet access is terribly limited. However, persons with disabilities are marginalized in their access to the Internet relative to the rest of the population even in societies where overall access is limited (Mehra, Merkel, and Bishop, 2004; Selwyn, 2004).

The passage of the ADA did inspire quite a few other nations to pass their first civil rights legislation for persons with disabilities. Australia, Austria, Brazil, Canada, Denmark, Finland, France, Germany, Malawi, South Africa, Sweden, Uganda, the United Kingdom, Venezuela, and Zimbabwe all enacted legislation modeled directly on the ADA (Barnes, Mercer, and Shakespeare, 1999; Blanck et al., 2003; Metts, 2000). The scope of these laws ranges from establishing who has a disability to actively reducing social barriers for persons with disabilities.

Some international organizations also followed the lead of the ADA, with the European Union (1996) adopting guidelines—encouragements, not requirements—for member nations regarding the rights of persons with disabilities, and the United Nations (1994) creating standards that all nations were encouraged to adopt to promote equal opportunities for persons with disabilities. Since the 1990s, the Council of Europe, with mixed success, has been encouraging member nations to pass stronger disability rights laws and to increase access to social rights. These Council publications and statements have addressed employment, access to buildings, antidiscrimination, and technology access, among other topics (Doyle, 2003). The Council of Europe (2003a, 2003b) also has accessibility and participation guidelines based on the WCAG.

In 2007, eighty-two nations signed the United Nations Convention on the Rights of Persons with Disabilities, including most nations with existing disability rights laws. This convention includes provisions in which signatories agree to promote the creation of accessible information technologies and equal access to existing technologies, including specific mention of the Internet (United Nations, 2007). However, although the International Organization for Standardization (ISO) has existed for many years, it only recently has shown interest in user issues rather than purely technical ones, and it has as yet to focus on accessibility (Stienstra, Watzke, and Birch, 2007).

There are typically several key differences between US laws and the laws of other nations: the United States views social problems as human rights and civil rights issues in light of the Constitution; the United States has fewer statutory services than other developed nations and no universal health care; and the United States has a smaller organized volunteer sector than many other developed nations (Barnes, Mercer, and Shakespeare, 1999; Oliver, 1990). Additionally, disability rights groups in the United States have relied on lobbying and mass political action, whereas other nations typically rely on changes in social policy (Barnes and Mercer, 2003). As a result, a civil rights focus is more natural in the United States than in other nations, where a service-oriented focus better fits the larger societal and legal structures. The latter approach, however, does not provide the same levels of legal rights or protections.

Germany was one of the few nations to draw heavily from the approach of the ADA and focus their legislation on the civil rights of people with disabilities. "Inspired by the passage of the 1990 Americans with Disabilities Act, German activists adopted a disability rights model and successfully worked toward passage of a constitutional equality amendment in 1994 and antidiscrimination legislation in 2002" (Heyer, 2002, p. 723). Intriguingly, the primary opponents to disability rights laws in Germany were the business community, paralleling the battle over the ADA in the United States (Poore, 2007). The language of disability rights used in the debate over and the text of the ADA transformed the discourse about disability in Germany and changed the course of the government's approach to disability; the concepts of disability rights were tailored to meet the needs of German social structures (Heyer, 2002).

Such changes were badly needed in Germany. Since reunification, surges in right-wing political activity in Germany have been accompanied by attacks against not only foreigners, but also against people with visible disabilities (Poore, 2007). In 2003, 93 percent of children with disabilities were segregated in special schools in Germany, and only 24 percent of men with disabilities and 18 percent of women with disabilities were in the workforce, though changes in these numbers are hoped to follow the passage of stronger antidiscrimination laws in recent years (Poore, 2007).

In the United Kingdom, however, the Disability Discrimination Act of 1995 focused on a medical view of disability as being exclusively in an individual. As a result, it gives limited protections and wide exemptions for cost and burden, basically ignores social discrimination, and lacks an enforcement mechanism (Barnes, Mercer, and Shakespeare, 1999). To compensate for the failings of the act, such as not applying to 90 percent of employers, the government has since created a committee to produce standards and codes of practice to encourage inclusion of persons with disabilities (Barnes and Mercer, 2003). Note the notion of encouraging inclusion rather than guaranteeing it. The notion of encouragement of inclusion follows other disability laws passed through time in the United Kingdom, where laws have provided for community-based social supports to persons with disabilities since 1948, but these services were historically discretionary and often not provided at all (Oliver and Barnes, 1998).

Canada takes an entirely different approach. In Canada, issues of inclusion of persons with disabilities are generally handled through the Canadian Standards Association—which develops voluntary industry standards through involvement of stakeholders—rather than through the law (Jongbloed, 2003; Stienstra, 2006). However, because industry is much better organized and financed than disability rights groups, this type of system "privileges the voices of industry while creating a discourse of public accountability and corporate social responsibility" (Stienstra, 2006, p. 336). Relying on industry to volunteer to make things accessible based on market perceptions is not likely to be very successful. Some Canadian provinces have been more active in the creation of legal protections for persons with disabilities, and the national government has added disability to the list of groups entitled to human rights under the Canadian Charter of Rights and Freedoms.

One in six Canadians is identified as having a disability (Puttee, 2002). However, disability policies have been shaped by tensions between a predominant perspective that regards people with disabilities as "worthy poor" and the people with disabilities who argue that disability is an aspect of human rights (Rioux and Prince, 2002). Canadian public policy continues to focus on individual limitations, in line with the worthy poor perspective (Prince, 2009). Perhaps not surprisingly, given the standards approach, Canadians hold highly ambivalent attitudes toward the social inclusion of persons with disabilities (Prince, 2009). The Canadian parliament has had some success bringing online its discussions of proposed regulations related to disability, though it is not clear how many persons with disabilities are represented among the people using these electronic participation options (Prince, 2009).

In Ireland, antidiscrimination legislation passed in the late 1990s outlawed discrimination against people with disabilities; in 2002, the government mandated compliance with the WCAG by government agencies, yet the national census did not collect information on disability until that same year (Doyle, 2003). Rates of completion of secondary education and employment for people with disabilities in

Ireland are less than half that of the rest of the population (Quin and Redmond, 2003).

Following many other nations, New Zealand added disability discrimination to its Human Rights Act in 1993. However, in New Zealand, unlike in other nations, the development of rights for people with disabilities has been primarily through the development of community partnerships among individuals with disabilities, family members, community groups, and corporations (Sullivan, 2001). The unique experience in New Zealand has also been shaped by the fact that the native Maori population does not classify physical, cognitive, or sensory impairments as disabling conditions in their culture, instead associating the concept of disability with poverty, homelessness, and loss of connection to their culture (Kingi and Bray, 2000).

The approach of the Italian government has been to pass disability rights laws and then primarily not comply with them. For example, a law mandating online accessibility was passed in 2004 with the stated goal of compliance with WCAG standards in 2005. Yet, in 2008, only 3 percent of government sites met these requirements (Burzagli et al., 2008). One can wonder if the passage of the law was meant for show, though the government of Italy has had many unique problems in implementing e-government (Jaeger, 2003).

In Sweden, the government has taken an approach that encourages accessibility not through legal mandate, but through programs emphasizing the regular evaluation and testing of government and corporate websites (Gulliksen et al., 2010). These efforts have at least led to widespread awareness of inclusive design with 90 percent of government agencies being familiar with the WCAG, though not necessarily implementing them; for real impact the nation needs "a more coherent accessibility policy" (Gulliksen et al., 2010, p. 29).

Without laws specifying a legal right to Internet access, many nations like Sweden now rely on standards or guidelines encouraging use of some version of the WCAG. In addition, regulation of access to information technology is accomplished through economic regulations in many nations (Stienstra, Watzke, and Birch, 2007). As a result, many countries emphasize industry self-regulation—which has become widely used in many contexts in the past two decades—as the primary means by which to promote access to the Internet for persons with disabilities (Goggin and Newell, 2007). Even the provision of legal rights under the law does not necessarily reach into the area of information technology. When Australia originally passed its Disability Discrimination Act in 1992, the law initially exempted telecommunications from accessibility standards for persons with disabilities and continued to do so for five years.

In nations without legal guarantees along the lines of an ADA, access to technology for persons with disabilities varies as widely as other forms of access in society. For example:

• In China, people with disabilities have moved from being social outcasts in the 1980s to having limited opportunities to participate in society now as a result in changes in government policies (Kohrman, 2005). However, disability is still generally seen as a stigma on individuals and their families, negatively impacting social status and marriage opportunities, and the government still has sterilization programs for some people with disabilities (Bulmer, 2003).

• In Indian culture, "disability represents horror and tragedy" and infanticide of a child with a disability would not even be considered a crime in many cases (Ghai, 2002, p. 89). Less than 1 percent of children with disabilities are educated in India.

• In Japan, the marginalization of disability is closely tied to language—common abbreviations and official bureaucratic terminology are both intentionally marginalizing and abusive of people with disabilities (Valentine, 2002). This situation is not that unusual, however, as the word for disability carries explicitly negative connotations in many modern languages (Charlton, 1998; Stone, 1999).

• In Jordan, people generally hold negative views of people with disabilities, and, like in China, disability is seen as negatively impacting social status and marriage opportunities (Turmusani, 2003). These attitudes are reflected in commonly used cultural proverbs.

• In Malta, all social progress for people with disabilities has come from a small group of interested government officials rather than from a grassroots movement, due in large part to the tiny size and small population of Malta and the fear of social impacts of admission of disability in such a small society (Camilleri and Callus, 2001).

As this international overview shows, rights to technology access and to broader social access are far from guaranteed to individuals with disabilities in most parts of the world. The belief that the inclusion of persons with disabilities is a human rights issue may ultimately be the approach that many countries settle on, but thus far it is a concept that has proven difficult for countries to implement (Quinn and Bruce, 2003).

Industry, Internet, and the Law

Leaving accessibility up to industry and allowing industry the option to opt out of making technologies accessible—if they consider the burden too high in terms of cost or effort—is not the most productive path to creating accessible technologies. Generally, the information and information technology industries have reacted to accessibility requirements with "outright opposition, passive ignorance, acts of omission, or unwillingness to embrace required change" (Goggin and Newell, 2007, p. 160). In many cases, corporations view people with disabilities as a niche market that they are not interested in or not worth the effort to design for (Kanayama, 2003b; Jaeger, 2006b; Tusler, 2005). Sadly, few businesses view people with disabilities as an important market or see positive public relations benefits to meeting the needs of persons with disabilities (Neufeldt et al., 2007).

The most frequently cited reasons by industry for not providing accessible technologies are that incorporating accessibility into the technology will:

- Increase costs of the technology.
- Lengthen time of development.
- Serve only a small market.
- Necessitate special design requirements.
- Result in low-tech and uncool products.
- Sacrifice aesthetics.
- Create difficulties in supporting accessible products.
- Never meet the needs of each different disability.
- Make the product worse for all other users (Maskery, 2007).

All of these are unfounded assertions, yet they are constantly repeated by companies. Additionally, many claims have been made by companies that they lack sufficient guidance on accessibility, which is a curious assertion in light of WCAG and Section 508 guidelines. These corporate objections to accessibility are ironic in light of the fact that more than three-quarters of people who do not have a disability believe that the benefits of including people with disabilities outweigh the costs associated with accessibility for businesses (United States Department of Education, 2004a).

As a result of negative attitudes toward accessibility, many organizations simply have not educated their managers and staff about accessibility. Though accessibility can be viewed as an issue of professional ethics for developers, most Web developers lack accessibility experience (Mankoff, Fait, and Tran, 2005; Peters and Bradbard, 2003). A 2009 survey of Web developers found that 86 percent of developers do not have adequate training in accessibility, 64 percent felt management was unaware of the importance of accessibility, and 48 percent believe that development life cycles are too short to incorporate any forms of accessibility (Loiacono, Romano, and McCoy, 2009).

Were accessibility "incorporated in the technology—rather than having to be an expensive and not particularly compatible add-on and afterthought," it would not only be more usable by persons with disabilities, but "the technology would be accessible, easier to use, and more attractive for many people without disabilities" (Goggin and Newell, 2007, p. 160). A key advantage is that accessible technologies also benefit people with different levels of technological literacy and education. The design concept of universal usability prioritizes access to all users regardless of age, disability, skill level, technological literacy, and other factors (Shneiderman, 2000). The most efficient and effective way to promote universal usability would be to create inherently accessible technologies.

From the beginning of the widespread use of the Internet, even large corporations have resisted making accessible products. "Some of the worst offenders in implementing basic Internet accessibility have been large corporations, entities that surely enjoy sufficient resources to ensure that their website administrators and developers understand and put in place accessibility measures" (Goggin and Newell, 2003, p. 120). Microsoft and America Online (AOL)—perhaps the two biggest titans of the Internet in the 1990s—spent much of that decade making inaccessible products. For a period of time in the 1990s, the leading software company and the leading Internet service provider (ISP) both had significant accessibility problems that went unfixed until considerable pressure from disability rights groups was exerted.

Even the entity organizing the Sydney Olympic Games website intentionally built a site that was inaccessible to users with visual impairments, claiming that to do otherwise would compromise the experience for all other users. The organizing committee then fought against making it accessible, ultimately being forced to make it accessible by an Australian government wishing to mitigate the politically embarrassing situation. Since the 1990s, discussions and considerations of accessibility have become more commonplace and more widely acceptable, but accessibility has not yet become a standard element of new technologies. In fact, most new information technologies—such as the current wave of Web-enabled mobile devices—are introduced with little or no thought to accessibility.

Even long-standing products can avoid accessibility. PDF files are widely used in employment, education, government, and many other contexts, despite the fact that they are "notoriously inaccessible" to people using screen readers (Vandenbark, 2010, p. 27). Fortunately, some products do mature into accessibility. Since its days struggling with accessibility, Microsoft has embraced accessibility in their products, with some analysts believing that their operating system offers a greater range of built-in assistive technologies, more powerful built-in assistive technologies, and better compatibility with external assistive technologies than other operating systems (Vandenbark, 2010).

The overall disinterest in creating accessible technologies strongly influences website developers and webmasters, as well. A number of studies of the perceptions of website developers and webmasters—in both the public and private sectors—about accessibility have found commonly held beliefs that accessibility only benefits a small number of people, that accessibility features will ruin the site, and that people with disabilities do not matter as a population; studies have also revealed widespread lack of knowledge of accessible design and requirements (Jaeger, 2006a; Lazar et al., 2003; Lazar, Dudley-Sponaugle, and Greenidge, 2004; Lazar and Greenidge, 2006).

Some organizations try to avoid creating inherently accessible products by creating reduced or parallel versions that have fewer features than the standard version, but which may be better able to work with assistive technologies (Lazar and Wentz, 2011; Wentz and Lazar, 2011). Yahoo recommends that users of assistive technologies use the "Yahoo Mail Classic" version of its e-mail interface rather than the current version of the interface, even though the older interface has fewer features. A similar situation exists for Microsoft Outlook Web Access 2007. Due to accessibility problems with its standard Web-based interface for accessing corporate e-mail, Microsoft recommends that users of assistive technologies use a different interface called Outlook Web Access Light with significantly reduced features and capacities. Google also recommends its "basic HTML" version of Gmail as the best version that has compatibility for assistive technologies, yet it is missing extremely basic features, including spell check and contact management (Annam, Reid, and Kaki, 2009).

This practice of parallel sites has primarily replaced an older tactic of maintaining a separate, text-only version of a site. Section 508 and the first version of the WCAG permit this practice, though the revised WCAG does not and Section 508 notes that separate, text-only sites are the alternative of last resort for online accessibility and must be updated consistently with the primary site. Of the organizations that continue to take this approach of a parallel, text-only site, many rely on products like Usablenet Assistive from the company Usablenet, which attempts to dynamically convert current website content into a text-only format.

It should not be surprising, then, that "people with disabilities have little faith that market forces will eventually yield accessible [technologies]" (D'Aubin, 2007, p. 199). It has clearly been demonstrated that legal solutions to improving accessibility can take a long time to result in social change, and court cases can delay the potential impacts. However, decades of experiences with industry show that it is not an effective route to accessible technologies. Even advocates for market forces creating accessible technologies admit that economic incentives will only create change slowly (Karasik, 2005). In an environment of rapid technological change, a slow evolution in attitudes is never going to keep pace with the new technologies.

Information Access and the Law

Because of the rapid changes in information technologies, staying engaged in society is moving from Web-enabled information technologies being necessary just for information access, to Web-enabled information technologies being necessary for information access, communication, and interaction (Jaeger and Xie, 2009). In considering the ways in which the law could move to promote sustained equality of access to the Internet and related Web-enabled information technologies, it is necessary for the law to acknowledge that access is a multitiered concept. Even an update to an existing information technology may change the accessibility of the technology or the ways in which the user interacts through assistive technologies. Equality of access depends on equality of all levels of access.

As was discussed in Chapter 1, there are three types of access to information and information technologies—physical access, intellectual access, and social access (Burnett, Jaeger, and Thompson, 2008). Thus far, disability rights laws in the United States and elsewhere have focused almost exclusively on concerns of physical access. This focus on physical access carries through to laws related to information and information technologies. In fact, the original text of the ADA focused primarily on visual and hearing impairments (Bowe, 1993). A narrower example of this trend can be found in closed captioning. The current law mandates that closed captioning be available, without considering the types of content or levels of content that would be available in that format. As a result, a large amount of closed captioning text is rewritten to reflect a much lower reading level than the spoken words, demonstrating a lack of consideration of intellectual access; and the types of programming available with closed captioning have varied widely in usefulness and educational value, evidencing a lack of consideration of social access (Downey, 2008, 2010).

On the Internet, a similar focus on physical access can be seen in Section 508 of the Rehabilitation Act, which is intended to ensure equal access to government information technologies and online content. The Section 508 guidelines focus on physical access for persons with disabilities, emphasizing visual, hearing, and mobility impairments, but mostly leaving out cognitive impairments (Jaeger and Bowman, 2005; Lazar, 2007). This focus of the law on physical access results in limited consideration of intellectual and social dimensions of access. Compliance with Section 508 means that a website, software application, or operating system can technically be accessed by someone using an assistive technology input or output device. Technical accessibility, however, does not necessarily equate to an interface that is usable, understandable, or functional for communication (Theofanos and Redish, 2003). Without these latter components, an information technology can be technically accessible under the law and virtually preclude intellectual and social access for some or all persons with disabilities.

To achieve true equality of access to information technologies under the law, the legal guarantees of access need to be reconceptualized to simultaneously focus on ensuring physical, intellectual, and social access to information and information technologies in addition to the creation of technical accessibility standards. For social equality to be achieved in access to information technologies, disability rights laws will need to place greater emphasis on achieving intellectual and social access to information technologies—Web-enabled and beyond. In the next chapter, we explore the ways in which accessibility on the Internet has been implemented in different contexts—education, employment, communication, commerce, entertainment, and government. The extent to which accessibility has or has not been implemented in these contexts is considered in light of the various legal requirements and concepts of access.

3

Barriers to Online Access: Personal, Public, and Professional Spheres

This chapter examines the issues raised by online interactions for persons with disabilities in professional, personal, and public contexts. All of these contexts are vital to participation online and in society as a whole. Because persons with disabilities disproportionately face lower levels of educational attainment and higher levels of unemployment than any other population, the Internet offers many potential opportunities for success in these areas and for increased access to institutions that support education, such as libraries. However, without equal online access, the Internet can serve to become yet another hindrance to success in education and employment beginning at the initial application stage.

Beyond employment and education, the Internet also has become a hub for personal communication, commerce, and entertainment, ranging from keeping up with friends through social media, to shopping, to seeking out video clips and games. From its inception, the Web has been viewed by many as a way that persons with disabilities could become more widely engaged in these types of social activities. However, accessibility has received very different levels of emphasis in the contexts of communication, commerce, and entertainment.

At the societal level, the most significant issues of online access are perhaps those of access to government online. At national, state/provincial, and local levels around the globe, governments have embraced using the Internet as a platform for government information, communication, and services. In the United States, many government functions are now primarily or exclusively online. Unfortunately, many government technologies are no more accessible than commercial technologies. The area of accessibility and e-government is particularly important for persons with disabilities to avoid being excluded from both accomplishing personal tasks—like filing income taxes—and participating in democratic governance. As e-government is quickly becoming a key part of access to social services, to fulfillment of obligations of citizenship, and to civic engagement, equal access to e-government for persons with disabilities is one of the most significant issues related to disability and the Internet.

The Internet at Work and School

While the Internet has revolutionized many aspects of society, its impacts in education and employment have been particularly profound. Proficiency with computers and the Internet is a central part of education, beginning in elementary school. Even in the earliest years of education, assignments now require the use of the Internet, and many course materials are posted on the school's website. At the college and university level, many courses and entire degree programs exist exclusively online, while assignments for all other courses require the use of the Internet to read course materials and conduct research. Public, school, and academic libraries—central repositories of educational materials—now provide many of their materials and services online. Many libraries have phased out much of their print collections in favor of electronic resources.

The Internet is equally central to most jobs. Communication, research, design, record keeping, accounting, time sheets, and innumerable other functions of most employers are now online. Most employers now depend on e-mail and PowerPoint to function. Except for the noisiest and hottest forms of manual labor, it is becoming increasingly hard to find employment that does not involve computers and the Internet. In fact, even the most basic jobs demand that an applicant submit an online application to be considered for the job.

With these technological changes, all students and members of the workforce have had to adapt to these changing expectations. For digital natives who have grown up accustomed to such changes, this period has not seemed like one of transition; but, for the rest of the population, the Web-enabled classroom and workplace have resulted in a seemingly constant cycle of new technologies appearing, changing the ways in which things are done, and then being replaced by something different.

In exchange for dealing with the bewildering parade of new information technologies, these same technologies open up new opportunities for education and employment. The resources available for use in the classroom are much richer and more varied. Thanks to the Internet, Web cameras, and the right software, a person no longer has to be in the same place as his or her school to be part of real-time interactions. Online research conducted by students and faculty members is an infinitely faster and easier process than digging through print materials at the library with little sense of where the needed information might be. Libraries now can provide access to much more content than they could previously afford. Employees can regularly work from home or other places and still meet all of their job requirements. The information of any company can be used to improve performance of the entire organization. Business meetings do not require travel. It truly is a whole new world for education and employment. Since people with disabilities "work less, earn less, and have lower levels of economic well-being than those without disabilities" (Burkhauser and Daly, 1996, p. 164), any changes to education and employment have to be welcomed.

Many of these new opportunities with work and school seem especially conducive to helping people with disabilities. Telecommuting, online education, and electronic library catalogs are tremendous opportunities for people with impairments that affect mobility and traveling. For people with impairments that fluctuate in severity, the option of working via distance can be enormously helpful when it is needed. For students with a range of different disabilities, accessible educational materials can mitigate many of the problems students with disabilities have traditionally faced in accessing and using course materials. In each of these circumstances, however, the barriers of the Internet shape the experiences of people with disabilities, often diminishing the potential benefits.

To return to some differences mentioned earlier, people with disabilities face very different employment and education opportunities than the rest of the population. A person with a disability is more than three times more likely to be unemployed than the rest of the population, even though approximately three-quarters of unemployed persons with disabilities want to work (Dispenza, 2002; US Census Bureau, 2008). In 2005, 81 percent of individuals without disabilities were employed full- or part-time, but only 32 percent of persons with disabilities were; 66 percent of these unemployed persons with disabilities wanted to work (Colker, 2005). A 2008 study found that the employment rate of working-age people with disabilities was 39.5 percent and the full-time employment rate was 25.4 percent (Cornell University, 2010).

For people considered to have a severe disability by the Census Bureau, the gaps in employment are even higher: 69.3 percent are unemployed and 27.1 percent live in poverty, three times the national average (US Census Bureau, 2008). Even among working-age people, 25.3 percent of persons with disabilities live in poverty (Cornell University, 2010). People with physical disabilities have long been more likely to have a job than people with cognitive disabilities (Drehmer and Borieri, 1985; Hayes and Macan, 1997; Stone and Sawatzki, 1980). Because policies rarely focus on economic self-sufficiency for people with disabilities, many are cyclically trapped in poverty (Stapleton et al., 2006).

Even an economic boom does not improve the overall economic state for people with disabilities, the majority of whom "did not share in the economic prosperity of the late 1990s" (Stapleton et al., 2006, p. 701). In 2005, 29 percent of people with disabilities were living below the poverty line, compared with 10 percent of the rest of the population (Colker, 2005). Six years later, 46 percent of adults with disabilities were living in a household with $30,000 or less in annual income, compared with only 26 percent of the rest of the population (Fox, 2011a, 2011b).

In terms of education, 95 percent of six- to twenty-one-year-old students with disabilities are now in regular schools, an enormous change from three decades ago (US Department of Education, 2010). However, the rates of failure to complete high school are nearly three times higher among persons with disabilities than the rest of the population. As a result, 78 percent of people with disabilities complete high school, compared with 91 percent of the rest of the population (Colker, 2005). A 2011 study found that 61 percent of adults with a disability had a high school education or less, compared with only 40 percent of other adults (Fox, 2011a, 2011b).

Only 30 percent of high school graduates with disabilities enroll in college, compared with 40 percent of the general population; one year after graduation, only 10 percent of students with disabilities remain enrolled in two-year colleges, and only 5 percent remain enrolled in four-year colleges (Stodden, 2005; Wagner et al., 2005). As a result, only 12 percent of people with disabilities ultimately graduate from college, compared with 23 percent of the rest of the population (Colker, 2005). In 2008, the percentage of working-age people with disabilities who had attained a bachelor's or higher degree was 12.3 (Cornell University, 2010). For most people with disabilities, higher education "is still just a dream" (Mates, 2010, n.p.). If used to their full potential for inclusion, however, the Internet and related technologies have the potential to level many of these disparities.

Disability, the Internet, and Employment

Online materials are now a central aspect of employment from the beginning of the job-seeking process. The federal government is the largest employer in the United States, for example, and applicants of all of their jobs must apply through the www.usajobs.gov site. A 2005 study found that only 3 percent of companies did not use the Internet and online services as part of their hiring and human resources processes, such as requiring applicants to apply online and have an e-mail account (Bruyère, Erickson, and Van Looy, 2005). It seems reasonable to imagine that that number has decreased since then. Unfortunately, the same study found that only 13 percent of responding companies were familiar with the guidelines for accessible website design, and only 10 percent of companies could confirm that their online hiring and human resources materials had been evaluated for accessibility (Bruyère, Erickson, and Van Looy, 2005). The progress to online applications has been swift. Of the top 100 US retailers (including Walmart, Home Depot, and Kroger) in 2006, 70 percent accepted online applications for hourly positions, up from 41 percent in 2004, while 16 percent accepted *only* online applications (Taleo Research, 2006). Herein lies the first conundrum of employment in the age of the Internet—inaccessible online hiring processes are not likely to benefit people with disabilities in the job market.

More positively, for many people with disabilities, the Internet has provided "an opportunity to join the workforce for the first time" (Rich, Erb, and Rich, 2002, p. 51). The ADA actually inspired most companies to attempt to become more accessible in their practices. Despite initial fears about the financial cost of accommodating employees with disabilities, 95 percent of private companies had made accommodations to support the hiring and success of employees with disabilities less than a decade after the passage of the ADA (Kruse and Hale, 2003; Lee and Newman, 1995). However, such efforts have had varying levels of success in increasing the number of employees with disabilities (Batavia and Schriner, 2001; Bound and Waidmann, 2002; Kruse and Schur, 2003; Schur, 2003a, 2003b). In 2007, the Department of Labor even began a tax credit program— known as a Targeted Jobs Tax Credit Incentive—to encourage small businesses to employ persons with disabilities. Yet, "no study has been able to establish that the ADA has had any positive impact on the employability or poverty rate of individuals with disabilities" (Colker, 2005, p. 69).

A key reason for the lack of progress in employment for people with disabilities is that prohibitions against hiring discrimination do not end discrimination, because negative hiring decisions "can be disguised as having been based on other criteria, such as job qualifications" (Premeaux, 2001, p. 293). Employment barriers to persons with disabilities include more than overt and subtle forms of discrimination, however. Additionally, social isolation limiting awareness of job opportunities, lack of transportation, lack of adequate education and training, family responsibilities, and fear of loss of social benefits all factor into employment rates for persons with disabilities (Loprest and Maag, 2001). For example, people with disabilities much more commonly face barriers to employment due to challenges with health care (28 percent versus 12 percent) and transportation (30 percent versus 10 percent) than the rest of the population (Colker, 2005). A lack of support from courts for people suing in cases of disability discrimination exacerbates the employment inequalities in the United States. The only group of litigants less successful in court than people claiming disability discrimination is prisoner plaintiffs, who rarely have access to or representation by counsel (Bagenstos, 2009).

Worldwide, people with disabilities are particularly vulnerable to unequal opportunities in economic life (Doyle, 1995). "Capitalism has favored the non-disabled not only by granting them almost exclusive entry into the workforce but also by manufacturing products for the largest share of the market, which generally excludes consumers with disabilities" (Hahn, 2001, p. 70). Sadly, such intentional economic discrimination against persons with disabilities is often logical from an employer's perspective—especially when there are no legal protections—in light of social biases, customer preferences, coworker prejudices, and fears of safety risks related to employees with disabilities (Bagenstos, 2009).

In the United States, the combination of the Rehabilitation Act and the ADA not only prohibit public and private employers from discriminating against persons with disabilities in the hiring and promotion processes, but also mandate that employers provide reasonable accommodations to employees with disabilities. Many of these reasonable accommodations now center on assistive technologies necessary to use computers and the Internet.

Many processes in a job that might have made a position difficult or impossible for a person with a disability now can be negotiated with the help of computers, the Internet, and assistive technologies. For the employee with a visual impairment, all materials that would have been in print—and thereby unreadable—can now be in an electronic form that a computer can read aloud. An employee with a mobility impairment can telecommute and still participate in all the activities of the job. A hearing or speech impairment no longer needs to be an obstacle to communication with coworkers and customers in an office if the employer makes available instant messaging, e-mail, and the speech and translation capacities of Web-enabled mobile devices. Employees with disabilities are now also better able to organize, using the Internet for advocacy, peer support, and living skills (Ritchie and Blanck, 2003). The Internet has made all of this possible.

Not surprisingly, assistive technologies play an essential role in the work lives of the majority of people with disabilities. Among persons with disabilities who are employed, 90 percent use assistive technologies to accomplish their jobs (Dispenza, 2002; Johnson, 2004; Schartz, Schartz, and Blanck, 2002). The combination of Internet-enabled occupations and the availability of assistive technologies has led many to believe that increased equality of employment opportunities will be the inevitable result. However, employment statistics show that the first few years of the Web actually paralleled declines in employment of persons with disabilities (Bound and Waidmann, 2002). For those who are employed, the use of accommodations in the workplace may present problems, with several studies indicating that fellow employees tend to view accommodations as an unfair advantage for persons with disabilities (Colella, 2001; Colella, Paetzold, and Belliveau, 2004; Paetzold et al., 2008).

Curiously, much of the employment literature that discusses information technology and disability uses language that suggests that information technologies will rehabilitate the people with disabilities, along the lines of the medical model of disability. Much of the discourse uses verbs such as *rescue, neutralize, offset, overcome, restore, compensate,* and *augment* (Roulstone, 1998). This type of language implies that technology is seen as making people with disabilities whole rather than providing equal opportunities for people with different types of abilities (Roulstone, 1998). The mentality evidenced by this language is not as fine a point as it may seem at first. The assumption that the presence of the technology will alleviate all disparities in the workplace leads to the false belief that other barriers will no longer be of concern. Even in workplaces with all of the needed accessible technologies, persons with disabilities will still likely face challenges in organizational culture, physical environment, coworker attitudes, and continuing changes in technology (Roulstone, 1998).

Telecommuting has been suggested as a means to overcome these other sorts of barriers in traditional workplaces for persons with disabilities. Even before the advent of the Web, suggestions were being made that "telework can open up new employment opportunities for people whose disability has excluded them from the workplace" (Murray and Kenney, 1990, p. 206). For people with many kinds of disabilities, the online environment does provide increased opportunities to search for and apply for employment; it also helps persons with disabilities remain employed, because they have more personal control over their circumstances (Anderson, Bricout, and West, 2001; Hesse, 1995b). Employees with disabilities who telecommute can better manage their symptoms and treatments, maintain their stamina, and spread out their work in line with their condition, resulting in healthier and more productive employees (Hesse, 1995a). It has been suggested that harnessing the capabilities of unemployed persons with disabilities through telecommuting could save US employers billions of dollars every year (Anderson, Bricout, and West, 2001).

Telecommuting presents several challenges for persons with disabilities, though. First, it works only if the employee has the necessary technology to engage in the telework or if the employer is willing to provide such technology. Second, courts have not been willing to accept that people with disabilities have the legal right to telecommute as a reasonable accommodation, rendering any agreement of telecommuting severable by the employer (Ludgate, 1997; Tennant, 2009). Third, there is a danger that persons with disabilities who telecommute will be limited in their career options and career advancement opportunities (Baker, Moon, and Ward, 2006; Bricout, 2004; Light, 2001). In spite of these potential pitfalls, however, the Internet and related technologies really do provide many new opportunities for persons with a range of different disabilities. Of course, eligibility for most of these information economy jobs hinges on educational attainment, which offers its own range of opportunities and challenges for students with disabilities in the age of the Internet.

Disability, the Internet, and Education

A main priority in disability rights legislation focuses heavily on access to and success in education (L. Frieden, 2003; Levy, 2001; Wattenberg, 2004). More than 6 million elementary and secondary school students in the United States have a disability, with nearly half of those students having a specific learning disability. Educators—at least some of them—have a long history of trying to meet the needs of students with disabilities. In the 1700s, educational reformers in Europe established the first methods of systematized education and residential schools for individuals with hearing and visual impairments (Daniels, 1997; Morton, 1897; Winzer, 1997). In 1812, the first school for students with visual impairments opened in the United States, with the first school for students with hearing impairments following five years later (Shapiro, 1993). In the 1840s, Dorothea Dix began a successful public crusade for better treatment of persons with cognitive disabilities (Brown, 1988). The first special education courses for teachers were available in 1905 (D. D. Smith, 2001), but these efforts were often marginalized by educators' generally negative perceptions of students with disabilities. The same year that IDEA was passed, guaranteeing the right to public education for students with disabilities, education researchers were still debating whether children with sensory disabilities were capable of the same levels of cognition as other children (Suppes, 1974).

For elementary and secondary students with disabilities, IDEA mandates an education that is as inclusive as possible. For postsecondary students with disabilities, the ADA mandates an inclusive education. Under both of these laws, equal access to information technologies is a part of an appropriate education. The focus on inclusion in information technology has primarily centered on technologies being used in the classroom, though courts have supported the idea that education websites need to be accessible under these laws (Ogden and Menter, 2009). During the few decades that students with disabilities have had legal rights, much of the focus has been on creating plans and materials that meet the needs of individual students.

Online educational materials, however, create a situation where entire courses and programs may present accessibility challenges.

With the move toward online education—both in terms of totally online courses and of online course materials for face-to-face courses—accessibility has become a tremendously important issue for students with disabilities in elementary, secondary, and higher education. As for employees with disabilities, the Internet also provides many new potential opportunities for students with disabilities to have greater access to materials in the formats that best meet their needs and to engage in educational activities on their own schedules without transportation hassles. Entirely online courses and degree programs offer the same benefits to students with disabilities that telecommuting does for employees with disabilities. Also, like employees with disabilities, students with disabilities are able to use the Internet to share and collaborate in advocacy, peer support, academic strategies, and living skills (Ritchie and Blanck, 2003).

The Internet also can be used to create new educational programs and opportunities that would never previously have been conceivable. For example, using Internet video conferencing and speaking in sign language, education students and educators who are hearing impaired can interact with and tutor students over the Internet (Kiernan, 2006). Schools of education use the same technology to work with teachers who are hearing impaired. Another software program now allows students with visual impairments to write down musical compositions, a process that was previously impracticable (Kelderman, 2010). Programs have even been designed to provide signed content online through avatars that take the place of reading textual transcripts of audio content (Kennaway, Glauret, and Zwitserlood, 2007). Many schools now use interactive online spaces—such as Second Life—to hold class meetings, a potential boon to students with mobility issues.

The Internet has also facilitated the creation of educational software and materials for students with different disabilities that are designed to their specific educational needs, such as the materials from companies like AbleNet. For example, a number of different programs have been created for elementary and secondary students at different levels of the autism spectrum that are based on interactive electronic content. These Web-enabled educational programs open new educational opportunities by providing content through means that the students best understand, emphasizing visual and pictoral content with clear context, and enabling communication about the content through means such as touch screens and typing. Widely used programs can have significant impacts on students with disabilities, as well. PowerPoint slides, for example, are used by many students on the autism spectrum as a means to help organize and communicate thoughts, particularly on mobile devices.

However, accessibility issues with online course systems and materials can also raise significant concerns for educational equality on the Internet, especially when they are not designed with the needs of students with disabilities in mind. Online education options create many new learning opportunities if they are designed to be inclusive; otherwise, they create new barriers for students and teachers with disabilities (Burgstahler, 2002; Burgstahler, Corrigan, and McCarter, 2004). As educational institutions began to rely on the Internet more, a number of sources offered guidance in creating and implementing accessible educational websites, but these were not widely followed (Hawke and Jannarone, 2002; Wall and Sarver, 2002). Such inattention to accessibility occurred in spite of the common interpretation of Sections 504 and 508 of the Rehabilitation Act requiring public and private institutions of higher learning to have accessible websites (Providenti and Zai, 2007a).

Inaccessible online academic materials threaten the ability of students and faculty with disabilities to participate in their own courses, and many institutions of higher education apparently are comfortable ignoring these barriers to education. A 2008 survey found that only 20 percent of institutions of higher education had a policy requiring that websites be accessible (Connell, 2008). "Colleges that wouldn't dare put up a new building without wheelchair access now routinely roll out digital services that, for blind people, are the Internet equivalent of impassable stairs" (Parry, 2010, n.p.). For example, the new Facebook-based virtual student union at Arizona State University that was made to increase a sense of community among students is inaccessible for students using screen readers. Inaccessibility can even make applying to higher education difficult, as evidenced by the National Federation for the Blind's 2009 lawsuit against the Law School Admissions Council (LSAC) and a bevy of law schools for having inaccessible application materials and online tests for aspiring law school students (Qualters, 2009).

The accessibility of school websites has steadily decreased as videos, animations, and social media have become more prevalent in the content (Carlson, 2004; Harper and DeWaters, 2008). College websites are widely inaccessible, and most colleges lack a policy or process to ensure compliance with accessibility requirements online

(Parry, 2010). Further, the use of social media and interactive online spaces for education purposes are heavily limited by overall low levels of accessibility in social media and networking services, including such major services as Facebook and Twitter (Howard, 2011; Lazar and Wentz, 2011; Wentz and Lazar, 2011). One Department of Education official estimates that only about 10 percent of online materials for higher education are accessible (Parry, 2010). As a result, some colleges try to get around accessibility needs of students with disabilities by simply waiving courses other students have to take (Kelderman, 2010).

During the 2007–2008 school year, 69.8 percent of school districts were offering online courses of some type, and many face-to-face elementary and secondary courses utilized online materials; at the same time, increases in enrollment in online courses in higher education were far outpacing increases in enrollment in face-to-face courses (Ogden and Menter, 2009). However, many academic websites are inaccessible, with an overview of studies of higher education accessibility showing more than 75 percent of the sites examined to be inaccessible (Bradbard, Peters, and Caneva, 2010). Online standardized testing of elementary and secondary students is an area of particular concern. In online standardized testing, students with disabilities typically fare far worse than other students, with nearly half of students with disabilities failing some of these tests (Lanterman, 2007). Additionally, many educational institutions at all levels lack strong accessibility policies, with the majority of policies lacking specific standards, responsibilities, time frames, enforcement, and other vital components (Bradbard, Peters, and Caneva, 2010; Carlson, 2004; Riley, 2005; Wattenberg, 2004).

Often, the adoption of new Internet technologies at educational institutions does not sufficiently consider accessibility issues. Around the turn of the millennium, educational institutions at all levels were enthusiastically adopting the Blackboard online course software, which was primarily inaccessible when it launched (Abram, 2003; Riley, 2005). Blackboard now thoroughly dominates the market for online courseware, but it only became disability-friendly in 2010. In late 2010, following a complaint filed by the National Federation of the Blind (NFB), a court found that Pennsylvania State University engaged in "pervasive and ongoing discrimination" against students and faculty with disabilities due to inaccessible departmental and library websites, Internet-enabled podiums in the classrooms, student banking, and course management software (Parry, 2010). These problems at Penn State are likely to be found at many other colleges and universities. Perhaps it should not be a surprise that the Department of Justice began to focus greater attention on the inaccessibility of post-secondary education websites following this ruling (Manister, 2010).

Teachers are usually ill prepared to handle the technical problems students with disabilities face in accessing their online course materials (Carlson, 2004; Harper and DeWaters, 2008). This lack of technical knowledge adds to a general problem of most educators not successfully responding to the needs of students with disabilities (Molloy and Nario-Richmond, 2007; Wolanin and Steele, 2004). Such problems are not necessarily related to the Internet. A survey of university faculty conducted during the debate over the ADA found only 57 percent supporting admission of students with disabilities into higher education and the majority questioning the ability of students with disabilities to earn a degree (Leyser, 1989).

Part of this problem is the paucity of educators with disabilities. For example, only 3.6 percent of higher education faculty members have a disability (US Department of Education, 2004b). Those faculty members with disabilities tend to exist in professional environments less than welcoming of disability (R. C. Anderson, 2007; Bowman and Jaeger, 2007; Crowder, 2006). For example, many objections have been raised in academia about the study of disability not being worthy of research or not being intellectually rigorous enough (Siebers, 2008). The unwelcoming environment toward students and faculty with disabilities extends into both electronic and more traditional print resources. Textbook publishers have been reluctant to create accessible print or electronic versions of textbooks, primarily because most professors do not insist on accessible texts (Keller, 2010; Parry, 2010).

Paralleling the employment arena, many in higher education resent accommodating students with disabilities by providing them with, for example, accessible versions of technology. Students with disabilities who receive accommodations are perceived as being less intelligent and are more likely to be socially stigmatized by their peers, and students with disabilities who are academically successful are particularly stigmatized (Egan and Giuliano, 2009). This stigma leads many students with disabilities to not seek the accommodations that they need (Baldridge and Veiga, 2006; Clair, Beatty, and Maclean, 2005).

Fortunately, because elementary and secondary schools have stronger and more established traditions of educating students with disabilities, they should be better equipped to create course materials, online tests, and websites that meet the needs of these students. Hopefully, this will lead to changes at the postsecondary level. For all levels of education, accessible online materials could be viewed not as a burden, but as an opportunity to expand the school's reputation. Schools with accessible online courses and materials can use the accessibility as a marketing tool to attract students (Ogden and Menter, 2009). Some schools have taken that exact approach.

California State University (CSU)—with an enrollment of almost 450,000 students—has used its size to try to force Google, Apple, and Blackboard to make their products more accessible, resulting in some important victories, including changes to make iTunes and Blackboard far more accessible in recent versions (Keller, 2010). Under this Accessible Technology Initiative, CSU refused to adopt software or hardware products systemwide until companies made their products accessible for students with disabilities. Unfortunately, the status of the California Accessible Technology Initiative is unclear now due to state budget cuts (Keller, 2010). Overall, however, the struggles with online accessibility in elementary, secondary, and postsecondary education also could learn from libraries—one societal institution of education that has a long history of embracing accessibility for patrons.

Disability, the Internet, and Libraries

Libraries made the commitment to provide equal access for persons with disabilities many decades before other social and government institutions did, and this commitment is evidenced in terms of Internet access. The first library services specifically for persons with disabilities were tactile print book libraries for people with visual impairments in the mid-1800s (Lovejoy, 1983). By the beginning of the 1900s, many larger public libraries had their own collections of materials in alternate formats (Brown, 1971; Dziedzic, 1983; Lovejoy, 1983). Libraries began providing talking books and talking-book machines to patrons with visual impairments in the 1920s, with the books being available first as records, then as tapes, and now as CDs and digital files (Majeska, 1988; Nieland and Thuronyi, 1994). Libraries also have traditionally incorporated new information-related assistive technologies as they have become available for acquisition—Braille, large print, talking books, reading machines, video enlargement, electronic texts, screen readers, and screen magnifiers, among others (McNulty, 2004). In their role as the primary social access and training center for the Internet, public libraries have had to focus on accessibility as a core part of meeting the needs of their patrons (Lazar, Jaeger, and Bertot, 2010).

Along with individual libraries, the American Library Association (ALA)—the largest organization of library professionals—has a history of outreach to persons with disabilities. The ALA created its first set of standards for patrons with disabilities in 1961. However, many libraries initially lagged behind in adopting these standards (Gibson, 1977). The ALA now has a statement, Access to Electronic Information, Services, and Networks (2000), and a policy, Library Services for People with Disabilities Policy (2001). The preamble of the latter includes the firm assertion that the ALA "is dedicated to eradicating inequalities and improving attitudes toward and services and opportunities for people with disabilities" (American Library Association, 2001, p. 1). Also, the vast majority of degree programs for librarians include service to patrons with disabilities and knowledge of their legal rights as a part of the required curriculum (Walling, 2004). Nevertheless, some feel that the ALA has not made online accessibility a significant enough priority (Blansett, 2008; Schmetzke, 2007a, 2007b).

The Rehabilitation Act and the ADA—and, in the case of school libraries, IDEA—all create legal obligations for public, academic, and school libraries to provide inclusive services to patrons with disabilities. As a result, libraries consider the accessibility not only of buildings and tangible resources, but of computers, software, digital libraries, and other electronic resources. The majority of libraries now have mission statements explicitly asserting that the library provides equal access and services to all patrons, including persons with disabilities, in both physical and electronic contexts (Jaeger, 2002).

As many library services are now being offered online, one of the greatest challenges is ensuring that these electronic information services are accessible for people with disabilities. Online library resources that need to be accessible include the computers and Internet access provided within the library; the library website and other original online content; the registration processes for a library account; and the subscription databases to which the library provides access (Bell and Peters, 2005; Bertot, Snead et al., 2006; Vandenbark, 2010; Will, 2005). The subscription databases and other services, since they are typically provided by commercial firms, are sometimes the hardest to manage in terms of accessibility (Byerley and Chambers, 2002; Stewart, Narendra, and Schmetzke, 2005). A purchased resource can decrease in accessibility, because natural modifications over time can lead to increased problems with accessibility (Hackett, Parmanto, and Zeng, 2004; Lazar and Greenidge, 2006).

Given their long-term professional stance toward inclusion, libraries generally tend to take Internet accessibility seriously. The challenges of inclusive access have received attention in the professional literature of librarians in terms of library websites (e.g., Ballas, 2005; Jaeger, 2002; H. Yu, 2002), online resources (e.g., Schmetzke, 2005; Stewart, Narendra, and Schmetzke, 2005), digital libraries (e.g., Bell and Peters, 2005), assistive technologies (e.g., Vaccarella, 2001), and the accessibility of electronic resources as part of more general discussions of inclusion of patrons with disabilities in library practice (e.g., Auld and Hilyard, 2005; Hawthorne, Denge, and Coombs, 1997; Holt and Holt, 2003; Mendle, 1995; Oliver, 1997; Will, 2005). Libraries began to develop online services specifically for persons with disabilities, with numerous resources being available in the early 2000s (Bell and Peters, 2005). Some of these early resources include the Audible E-Books project and the Unabridged digital audiobook delivery service, whereas the InfoEyes virtual reference and information service continues to be used by libraries around the country.

Libraries have made significant progress in making their websites accessible over time. In 2000, only 18.9 percent (14 out of 74) of the top 100 public library home pages were fully accessible, though at that time 26 of the 100 largest libraries did not even have a website (Lilly and Van Fleet, 2000). In a 2002 study, 42 percent of university library websites (79 out of 188) were found to be accessible (Spindler, 2002). A 2007 study found that 41 percent of the home pages of library schools in the United States and 55 percent of the home pages for campus libraries at US universities were accessible (Comeaux and Schmetzke, 2007). Between 2002 and 2006, both library school websites and campus library websites showed an improvement with regard to accessibility (Comeaux and Schmetzke, 2007; Schmetzke, 2003). In other studies of nonlibrary websites, accessibility has been shown to decrease over time (Hackett, Parmanto, and Zeng, 2004; Lazar and Greenidge, 2006), so this is certainly a good sign for the libraries and library schools. Another study of research libraries in 2008 found that 16.5 percent (20 out of 121) of libraries studied offer a separate text-only version of the home page, though establishing separate sites is not considered to be good accessibility practice, because having a separate text-only site often leads to an accessible home page that is out of date and does not provide current content (Hazard, 2008). It's important to note that most of these studies examined only the home page of a website. Some recent research indicates that, often, lower-level pages of a website may actually be more accessible than the home page, so that analysis of pages below the home page may be useful (Hackett and Parmanto, 2009).

In the contexts of employment and education, access for persons with disabilities is heavily dependent on the decisions of others. However, in other contexts online, persons with disabilities sometimes also have a greater role in shaping the level of access that is available to them. These issues are particularly evident in the contexts of communication, commerce, and entertainment.

Disability and Online Social Activities

The Internet can be seen optimistically as "a great equalizer" that will "eliminate disabling spaces by creating a barrier-free virtual commons" (Childers and Kaufman-Scarborough, 2009, p. 572). It also promises to "alleviate the physical, geographical, and attitudinal barriers to social interaction" faced by persons with disabilities (Guo, Bricout, and Huang, 2005, p. 51). The actual state of the Internet is more complicated, offering many new opportunities for social interactions, but also introducing new types of barriers to these interactions for persons with disabilities.

For Internet users in general, most social activities online are based not on the gathering of information, but on multidirectional communication and interaction. Through social media, instant messaging, e-mail, blogging, microblogging, chat, Usenet groups, and online communities, users engage in communication that is primarily multiple-direction interaction and information exchange. We live "in a world in which technology begs all of us to create and spread creative work differently from how it was created and spread before" (Lessig, 2008, p. xviii). The unique attributes of online social interaction and networking that occur through social media attract many users to the online environment (Preece, 2000; Maloney-Krichmar and Preece, 2005). The benefits of online social interaction can be present at the community, interpersonal, and individual levels (Xie, 2006). Additionally, research indicates that active participation in online communities is associated with an increased sense of individual well-being (Chen and Persson, 2002; Furlong, 1989a; 1989b; Gross, Juvonen, and Gable, 2002; Kanayama, 2003a; Shaw and Grant, 2002; Wright, 2000; Xie, 2007). Social networking tools are now used by a majority of Internet users; 86 percent of 18–29 year olds use social media every day (Madden, 2010). Similarly, 72 percent of adults and 87 percent of teens use text messages every day (Lenhart, 2010).

Online social interaction can be especially appealing to people with disabilities, for a number of important reasons:

• First, online social interaction can help persons with disabilities form new relationships in new communities—relationships that would otherwise be physically impossible for many because of physical limitations. While many persons with disabilities may not be able to physically travel to get together, they can interact in online communities (Guo, Bricout, and Huang, 2005).

• Second, persons with unique disabilities may not know others with the same disability in their physical location. Online social interaction, however, provides the ability to build socialization and support networks with other people with the same condition, whether they are next door or thousands of miles away. Thus, online social interactions help overcome not only physical but also geographical barriers.

• Third, asynchronous communication features enabled by online social interaction allow users to interact and communicate at their own pace, which eases the burden on physical and cognitive abilities (Kanayama, 2003a).

• Fourth, for persons with disabilities, physical and cognitive limitations are not just physical and cognitive issues but social issues as well. Support for dealing with these social issues can be found through the asynchronous and anonymous features enabled by online social interaction (Bowker and Tuffin, 2002; Seymour and Lupton, 2004).

In short, online social interaction can help overcome physical, cognitive, and geographical barriers that often inhibit the civic and social participation of persons with disabilities (Jaeger and Xie, 2009). All the benefits that online social interaction can provide for persons with disabilities demonstrate the importance of ensuring the accessibility of online social interactions.

Being involved in online social interactions has shown benefits for a number of different groups of persons with disabilities. For people with disabilities that limit their ability to leave their homes and for older adults with disabilities, online social interactions decrease a sense of isolation and increase feelings of friendship and camaraderie with people they interact with online and in the physical world (Bradley and Poppen, 2003). For middle-aged and older adults with disabilities, online social interactions increase a sense of well-being and also reduce the discomfort and anxiety that can accompany computer usage (Mann et al., 2005). Among youth and adolescents with disabilities, even though they use the Internet less than their peers without disabilities, online social interactions increase a sense of inclusion and acceptance with their peer group (DeBell and Chapman, 2003; Lathouwers, Moor, and Didden, 2009). Persons with disabilities whose conditions necessitate personal assistance benefit from online social interactions that are framed by the knowledge and experience of a very unique living situation (P. Anderson, 2007). These individuals find a sense of well-being in both interactions with peers and opportunities to engage in activities that are completely under their own control.

Online Social Interactions of People with Disabilities

For people with disabilities as a group, one of the largest benefits of online social interactions is that the greater levels of interaction and involvement lead to an increased sense of community, engagement, and social capital to facilitate general trust, reciprocal support, friendships, social participation, and the creation of social networks (Huang and Guo, 2005). Among the positive social benefits persons with disabilities derive from online social interactions are:

- Developing new friendships.
- Maintaining existing friendships.
- Connecting with people that distance or barriers would otherwise make impossible.
- Initiating and facilitating intimate relationships.
- Using disability-specific sites to talk to people with shared experiences.
- Engaging in communication where the physical body is not a factor.

- Building an online image.
- Making physically arduous tasks easily achievable online.
- Remaining anonymous in terms of disability if they choose.
- Feeling in control of their actions (Anderson and Jonsson, 2005; Bowker and Tuffin, 2002; Seymour and Lupton, 2004).

A common theme of many of these benefits is a sense of empowerment that results from a greater feeling of control over one's life.

In terms of a greater sense of independence online, people with disabilities feel enabled by being independent of the physical environment and physical limitations, avoiding being controlled by or having their decisions made by others, avoiding friction that may be present in relationships that involve a level of dependence in the physical world, avoiding human filters, and interacting at their own pace (Anderson and Jonsson, 2005; Bowker and Tuffin, 2002; Seymour and Lupton, 2004). Online social interactions may be the only place in which an individual with a disability can function "single-handedly, in full control, on equal terms" (Anderson and Jonsson, 2005, p. 730). Second Life, for example, includes a range of virtual clubs, groups, and islands for people with disabilities, with even an online nightclub named Wheelies being a hotspot in Second Life (Whittle, 2007).

People with disabilities also report significant feelings of empowerment in areas of interpersonal communication and information in "a more neutral context" than the physical world (Seymour and Lupton, 2004, p. 301). In communication activities, people with disabilities particularly embrace the chance to meet others as equals, where the presence of and extent of disability is revealed only as much as the individual wishes. This type of interaction allows the person with a disability to get to know people before disability enters into the relationship, defusing its potential impact (Anderson and Jonsson, 2005). People with disabilities also greatly appreciate the chance to be part of social networks comprised of others with disabilities, creating a safe environment in which to share lived experiences, seek advice, exchange information, and be supported by people who understand (Anderson and Jonsson, 2005; Seymour and Lupton, 2004).

In terms of information, people with disabilities benefit from being able to access a wide range of information when they want it and in the depth they need it without having to go anywhere. Among people with disabilities who are online, 65.6 percent regularly search for news, weather, and sports information (Dobransky and Hargittai, 2006). Benefits for people with disabilities are also reported in the presentation of information. For many people with disabilities, creating an online profile that accurately presents their life as a person with a disability in an affirming way provides a great sense of contribution and empowerment (Anderson and Jonsson, 2005). People with disabilities can use the online social interactions to contradict narratives of pity and tragedy imposed by others (Seymour and Lupton, 2004). The sense of using electronic information to create new electronic products also provides a sense of accomplishment that might not otherwise be possible for a person with a disability.

In online social interactions, people with disabilities often see the physical anonymity of the Internet as a "leveling ground" (Bowker and Tuffin, 2002, p. 327). They typically find the ability to control an online image and determine whether or not to disclose disability as enormously important—a means to choose whether or not to be seen as having a disability (Bowker and Tuffin, 2002; Seymour and Lupton, 2004). As a result of these benefits, a number of social networks related to disability now exist online.

These social networks specifically for people with disabilities include Disaboom (www.disaboom.com), Disability Social Network (www.disabilitysocialnetwork.com), and Disability Community (www.community.disabled-world.com). These broad communities provide social networking, dating, games, and even employment content. Others emphasize providing useful information to community members, such as Coping with Disability (www.copingwithdisability.com) and Disability Happens (www.disabilityhappens.com). More focused social networks also exist. Some focus on specific areas of networking, such as Disability Resource Exchange (www.drecrewe.org.uk), which is aimed at sharing ideas and resources among people with disabilities, and Xable (www.xable.com), which is focused on interactive media. Other communities focus on specific types of disabilities: Invisible Disabilities (www.invisibledisabilitiescommunity.org) is a community for people with chronic pain and illness, while CKfriends (www.ckfriends.org) is a community for people with learning disabilities.

The benefits of online social interactions do not come without potential downsides, however. There are clear barriers to online access for many people with disabilities. The cost and maintenance of the technology necessary to use the Internet—computer, Internet access, and any necessary assistive technologies—is a major barrier to the participation of many people with disabilities. Inexperience with and the complexities of the technology can also serve as a barrier to engaging in online social interactions for persons with disabilities (Mann et al., 2005; Seymour and Lupton, 2004). Additionally, using a computer over long periods of time can actually be quite painful to people with various disabilities (Loader, 1998; Riley, 2005; Seymour and Lupton, 2004). These painful physical reminders can reduce the sense of distance and escape that the Internet can truly provide (Loader, 1998).

Also, most social networking sites rely heavily on user-generated content, most of which is created by people with no knowledge of creating accessible materials (Whittle, 2007). As a result, social networks include major barriers for people with various disabilities. Users with visual impairments frequently encounter inaccessible logins, heavy reliance on tables, indecipherable color schemes, images that are links, images without alt tags, and background music that interferes with screen readers. The complexity of functions like friend invitations and privacy settings create problems for users with cognitive impairments. Users with mobility impairments face many features that rely on a great deal of mouse movement, that involve tiny buttons and icons, and that do not work with voice recognition software and other alternate input devices.

The gaps in technology access and physical ability to use the Internet leave many people with disabilities cut off from online social interactions. These divisions do not simply replicate the overall digital divide. They also split persons with disabilities into separate communities rather than creating a large community of persons with disabilities; they distance people with disabilities from one another and undermine the possibilities of broader actions for disability rights (Seymour and Lupton, 2004).

People with disabilities also risk reproducing problems of marginalization and isolation from the physical world in their online social interactions. People with disabilities most frequently interact with other people with disabilities online. Much of this communication is "problem-centered" and continues to focus on issues of disability, replicating interactions involving disability in the physical world (Seymour and Lupton, 2004, p. 301).

The empowerment that many people with disabilities experience by making their disability invisible online is also not without implications. Anonymity online can make disability disappear from the online conversations, interactions, and lives of people with disabilities. Visibility of disability is very important, however, because it can force others to question their stereotypes and misconceptions about disability (Marks, 1999). An online environment with less presence of disability will ultimately not serve to empower people with disabilities as a whole. Also, less presence of disability online may reduce the incentive and ability of persons with disabilities to organize online for civil rights and political action in the physical world (Cromby and Standon, 1999).

At a purely individual level, online social interactions pose another challenge to persons with disabilities. There exists the risk that "what is experienced as choice becomes restraint" (Anderson and Jonsson, 2005, p. 731). Because going online will likely avoid all the planning and logistics involved in physically going somewhere, people with disabilities may artificially limit their physical world interactions in favor of their online existence. This situation also has larger social ramifications, because a reduced presence in the physical world and an increased presence online, where disability is not necessarily known, will make people with disabilities less visible in society than they previously were. Reduced levels of visibility may ironically lead to a reduced focus on the need for accommodations in the physical world.

Online Shopping and Other Forms of Entertainment

Another area of social interaction in which the Internet has the potential to revolutionize the lives of people with disabilities is the realm of online shopping and entertainment. Without the hassles associated with traveling to and shopping in physical stores, the Internet offers the potential of a great savings of time and effort for people with disabilities. In terms of entertainment, the games available on the Internet also offer new opportunities for people with disabilities.

As with all other aspects of the Internet, these benefits will be available only if the online services are accessible. Much like other websites, e-commerce sites need to be developed with the intent to be inclusive of people with disabilities. If an online retailer expects and plans for patrons with disabilities, then shoppers with disabilities will have the opportunity to enjoy a successful shopping experience. However, if there is no planning for shoppers with disabilities—for example, the images all lack alt tags that describe the images, or the site is only navigable by mouse—then the shopping experience will not be successful for persons with disabilities (S. M. Baker, 2006). For example, the vast majority of shopping websites do not take into account the ways in which shoppers using screen readers will have to navigate the site, making these users spend much more time than other users navigating the sites (Tagaki et al., 2007).

There are fairly significant financial incentives for businesses to plan for the online shopping experiences of persons with disabilities. People with disabilities control discretionary funds that are more than twice the discretionary funds of teens and more than seventeen times greater than tweens, the two demographic groups currently most coveted by businesses (Loiacono, Romano, and McCoy, 2009). An accessible site will not only draw more shoppers with disabilities, but it will also likely increase traffic from members of other populations less experienced or typically disadvantaged in terms of access because an accessible site is usually easier for everyone to use. And an accessible site will not negatively impact the traffic of other users, because accessibility features, if designed correctly, are noticeable only by those users who rely on them.

Online shopping, however, has not been an area where accessibility seems to have been a key priority for many retailers. Early estimates of the inaccessibility of commercial websites ranged from 80 percent to 95 percent (Sullivan and Matson, 2000). One 1999 study found no shopping websites in the study population to be accessible (Jackson, 1999). One study of 1,080 commercial websites in 2002 found only 19 (1.76 percent) to be completely accessible (Milliman, 2002). Another 2002 study found 40 percent of retail sites and 15 percent of the most popular websites online to be accessible (Jackson-Sanborn, Odess-Harnish, and Warren, 2002). A 2004 study of 375 e-commerce sites determined that only 25 percent of sites were accessible, with accessibility receiving the least attention of twenty-five characteristics evaluated (Temkin and Belanger, 2004). Another 2004 study found that 9 percent of e-commerce websites met Section 508 accessibility criteria (Loiacono and McCoy, 2004b).

In studies of the top 100 companies and the top 100 nonprofit groups in the United States, only 6 percent of the corporations and only 10 percent of the nonprofit organizations were found to have accessible homepages (Loiacono and McCoy, 2004a, 2006). In 2009, fewer than 10 percent of leading corporate and e-commerce sites were found to be free of accessibility barriers (Loiacono, Romano, and McCoy, 2009). Travel sites, such as those that allow the purchase of tickets, have also been found to have high levels of inaccessibility, with the most positive study finding 12 percent of sites evaluated to be inaccessible (Gutierrez, Loucopoulos, and Reinsch, 2005; Lazar et al., 2010; Shi, 2006).

Although numbers vary by study, the overall picture is of limited accessibility to e-commerce and limited progress in overall levels of the accessibility of e-commerce over time. It is not surprising, then, that a 2007 survey of corporations found that a vast majority do not conduct accessibility tests of their products with users with disabilities, while those with accessible products rarely promote such accessibility in marketing efforts (Byerley, Chambers, and Thohira, 2007). Collectively, the findings from all of these studies demonstrate that most corporations have not "sufficiently recognized the importance of customers with disabilities to their business goals" (Loiacono, 2004, p. 82). Ironically, most businesses have made sure to include text and images that convey a sense of corporate responsibility as long as they have had websites (Esrock and Leichty, 1998).

The struggle to improve the accessibility of online commerce has led to legal battles between people with disabilities and leading companies like Barnes and Noble, Southwest Airlines, Target, Bank of America, and Wells Fargo over the inaccessibility of their Web presences. These cases have hinged on whether an online business is required to be accessible in the same way that a physical business is required to be. While the ADA lists many types of covered entities, the list was not meant to limit the entities covered, with the law asserting that it was meant to be interpreted broadly. However, because the law was written before the popularity of the Internet, it did not include any online entities in the list of types of covered entities. As a result, many businesses have claimed that their Web presence was not covered by the ADA and thus did not need to be accessible.

Courts have tangled with the issue without coming to a meaningful consensus. A late 1990s lawsuit by users with visual impairments against AOL raised some awareness of accessibility issues. A 2002 case involving Southwest Airlines over the accessibility of their site was dismissed, but another 2002 case held that the ADA required the Metropolitan Atlanta Rapid Transit Authority to have an accessible site (*Access Now, Inc. v. Southwest Airlines Co.*; Southeast ADA Center, 2002; Pierce, 1999). In 2004, Priceline.com and Ramada.com settled claims brought by the State of New York, agreeing to improve the accessibility of their sites (Fkiaras, 2005).

As was noted earlier, the holding in *National Federation of the Blind v. Target* (2006) resulted in case law establishing a nexus test for ADA compliance for e-commerce. If the website is closely inte-grated with the physical store, then the website is required to be accessible. If the website is not closely integrated with the physical store, or if there is no physical store, then there is no nexus and there-fore no need for ADA compliance under this holding. As Target chose to settle with disability rights groups rather than appeal the ruling, this nexus is the clearest picture of the way in which the courts will apply the ADA to e-commerce. The general consensus among legal scholars is that this holding is unrealistic and untenable due to a lack of understanding of technology and its social implications (Abrar and Dingle, 2009; Bashaw, 2008; Else, 2008; Kessling, 2008; Ogden and Menter, 2009). As a result, it is likely that this holding will be chal-lenged by future cases of online accessibility of e-commerce.

With these online barriers to inclusive e-commerce, it is not sur-prising that people with disabilities are less likely than other users to shop online. Among Internet users with disabilities, 53 percent engage in e-commerce activities, but 68 percent of other Internet users shop online (Childers and Kaufman-Scarborough, 2009). Of the people with disabilities who do shop online, they engage less fre-quently in e-commerce activities and purchase fewer products than other online shoppers (Childers and Kaufman-Scarborough, 2009).

The potential difficulties in accessing e-commerce aren't limited to website inaccessibility, however. Because there are lower levels of Internet access and lower levels of broadband connectivity among people with disabilities, fewer people with disabilities have the tech-nological capacity to use e-commerce. Again, the costs of a computer, Internet access, and necessary assistive technologies can be a prohibi-tive barrier to the large number of persons with disabilities who live in or near poverty. Even when e-commerce sites are accessible, the design of the site and the use of assistive technologies can make the process of shopping online slower for users with disabilities than for other online shoppers. Also, many of the features added to e-commerce sites to draw consumers—games, streaming video, and animation—detract from the experiences of shoppers with disabilities if they interfere with the accessibility of the site.

The possibility that games on sites could negatively impact acces-sibility is somewhat ironic, because beyond information seeking and social interactions, games are a key form of online entertainment for persons with disabilities. There are only a small number of areas of online activity that people with disabilities are more likely to engage in than other users. One of these areas is playing games—37.8 percent of Internet users with disabilities play games online, while 33.6 percent of other users do so (Dobransky and Hargittai, 2006).

There are several reasons that people with disabilities would be drawn to playing games online beyond the basic levels of games as a pastime, as a mental challenge, or as a way of making friends. Depending on the type of disability that an individual has, the online environment may offer a virtual representation that would allow a user to engage in activities that would be impossible in the physical world. Games that provide a comprehensive world to explore—such as Second Life and World of Warcraft—offer opportunities to engage in an extensive range of virtual activities. Such large-scale worlds offer users a stronger sense of the illusion of reality—that the game is not fiction and not a representation (Pasquinelli, 2010).

Games also offer a chance for people with disabilities to feel that they can compare their own abilities with those of other people in ways that are not possible in the physical world. Playing games online offers a chance to excel in competition against other players (Anderson and Jonsson, 2005). For many people with disabilities, playing games online provides a chance to compete with others on equal terms. Online gaming by persons with disabilities is an area in which further research could better illuminate the impacts of the Internet on the social lives of persons with disabilities, though conducting ethical research in large-scale worlds can be very difficult (Grimes, Fleischmann, and Jaeger, 2010).

Beyond the employment, education, commerce, communication, and entertainment contexts online, there are other online interactions that are extremely important—those between persons with disabilities and governments. These interactions are unique in terms of the role of disability, as disability is an unavoidable aspect of the interaction. In such interactions, people with disabilities do not have any incentives to choose not to reveal the presence of disability, while governments should be working to ensure that all citizens have equal access to government online. However, as with other contexts on the Internet, significant barriers affect the ability of people with disabilities to participate equally.

Government Online

The concept of government using the Internet to provide access to government information and social services, as well as to communicate and interact with citizens, dates from roughly the same time period as the explosion of Internet usage among members of the public. As members of the public were becoming more active online, governments envisioned the Internet as a means to make governance more efficient and effective and to encourage engagement among citizens. Government online soon became known as e-government. For the average citizen, e-government access—rather than access to printed government information—now stands as the primary means of getting government information and interacting with government (Bertot et al., 2009; Jaeger, Bertot, and Shuler, 2010; Shuler, Jaeger, and Bertot, 2010). Like other portions of the Internet, however, people with disabilities are often caught on the wrong side of equal access to e-government.

E-government is a dynamic sociotechnical system encompassing issues of governance, societal trends, technological change, information management, interaction, and human factors (Dawes, 2009). A key focus of e-government development has been on interactions between the government and members of the public, with many government agencies viewing e-government as their primary method for interacting with members of the public (Bertot and Jaeger, 2006, 2008; Ebbers, Pieterson, and Noordman, 2008; Streib and Navarro, 2006). Though the promise of e-government is often presented as being either to engage citizenry in government in a user-centered manner or to develop quality government services and delivery systems that are efficient and effective, the focus of government agencies has typically been on making the interactions easier for the agency, not the citizen (Bertot and Jaeger, 2008; Jaeger and Bertot, 2010a). A clear example of this situation was demonstrated by the Medicare Part D enrollment program in 2006, which required older adults—a group with large gaps in usage of the Internet—to examine the different plans and sign up for one online (Jaeger, 2008).

Governments at all levels are now showing a strong preference for delivering services via the Internet, primarily as a means of boosting cost-efficiency and reducing time spent on direct interactions with citizens (Ebbers, Pieterson, and Noordman, 2008). However, citizens still show an equally strong preference for in-person or phone-based interactions with government representatives when they have questions or are seeking services, though individuals with higher levels of education are typically more open to using online interactions with government (Ebbers, Pieterson, and Noordman, 2008; Streib and Navarro, 2006). In fact, many in public administration argue that the logic of cost savings and efficiency should be sufficient for citizens to embrace e-government (Teerling and Pieterson, 2010; Tung and Rieck, 2005).

Public satisfaction with the e-government services available, however, is limited. As commercial sites are evolving faster and providing more innovative services than e-government sites, public satisfaction with government websites is declining (Barr, 2007). Public confidence in government websites has also declined, because much of the post-9/11 public policy related to e-government since September 11, has involved the reduction of access to information through e-government (Feinberg, 2004; Halchin, 2004; Relyea and Halchin, 2003). The types of information that have been affected include many forms of socially useful information—from scientific information to public safety information to information about government activities (Jaeger, 2007). For these and other reasons, many citizens—even those with a high-speed Internet connection at home—seeking government information and services prefer to speak to a person directly in their contacts with the government (Horrigan, 2004).

Nevertheless, many citizens look to e-government as a valuable source of information and consider e-government sites to be "objective authoritative sources" (Office of Government Services, 2002, p. 1). Currently, the primary reason that people use e-government is to gather information (Reddick, 2005). In the United States, 58 percent of Internet users believe e-government to be the best source for government information, and 65 percent of Americans expect that information they are seeking will be on a government site, with 26 million Americans seeking political information online every day (Horrigan, 2006; Horrigan and Rainie, 2002).

Countless services are now available through e-government. Between local, state/provincial, and national governments, typical e-government services can include:

- Applying for social benefits.
- Paying taxes.
- Applying for government jobs.
- Enrolling children in school.
- Finding court proceedings.
- Submitting zoning board information.
- Requesting planning permits.
- Searching property and assessor databases.

- Taking driver's education programs.
- Applying for permits.
- Scheduling appointments.
- Paying fees.
- Completing numerous other government functions online (Bertot et al., 2006a, 2006b; Jaeger, 2009).

As a result of a longer and more concentrated emphasis on e-government than most other nations, the United States federal government is the largest producer of online content (Evans, 2007).

E-government services, however, are often limited by difficulties in searching for and locating the desired information, as well as a lack of availability of computers and Internet access for many segments of the general population (Bertot and Jaeger, 2008; Singh and Sahu, 2008). Such problems are exacerbated by a general lack of familiarity with the structure of government—for example, not knowing which agencies to contact—and a certain skepticism toward technology and government among many citizens (Jaeger and Thompson, 2003, 2004). Also, because many e-government sites place more emphasis on presenting political agendas rather than on promoting democratic participation, some users are becoming less trusting of the sites themselves (Jaeger, 2005, 2007). Further complications arise from the fact that many government agencies are ambivalent about direct citizen participation in the political process (Roberts, 2004).

Unequal Access to E-government

Many citizens, however, lack the individual means to access e-government and need to find an outlet to engage it to accomplish necessary educational, economic, social, and political functions. In most cases, they have no choice but to turn to the public library. People predominantly seek access to e-government information to fulfill an important personal need—for example, to secure unemployment benefits, register to vote, renew a license, make tax payments, or enroll children in school (Gibson, Bertot, and McClure, 2009; McClure, Jaeger, and Bertot, 2007). And access to e-government content is not just an issue of public benefit but is also a central premise of self-government. Democratic governance relies on access to the information of governance; otherwise, discourse about governance by the public has no content (Schudson, 1997).

Lack of access to technology is far from the only barrier to universal usability of e-government, however. Many members of the public seek assistance with e-government because they lack the technical skills to use the online functions or simply are uncomfortable engaging in online interactions without guidance (Bertot et al., 2006a, 2006b). Even for technology-savvy users, e-government services are often limited by lack of familiarity with the terminology and structures of government (Jaeger and Thompson, 2003, 2004). Because awareness of political information and how to use it depends heavily on the awareness of the people that an individual interacts with (Lake and Huckfeldt, 1998), it is likely that e-government awareness and usage function in a similar social manner. And if individuals are ultimately successful in locating the e-government information or service they need, there may still be difficulties, as many members of the public who actively seek government information are still not prepared to fully interact with it due to issues of government literacy, terminology, transparency, understandability, and timeliness, among other factors (Fenster, 2006). For these reasons, "even if Americans had all the hardware they needed to access every bit of government information they required, many would still need the help of skilled librarians whose job it is to be familiar with multiple systems of access to government systems" (Heanue, 2001, p. 124).

Thus, while many members of the public may struggle with accessing or using e-government information and services, government agencies have come to focus on it more as a means to save money than as a way to increase access for members of the public (Jaeger and Bertot, 2010a). The lack of access for certain groups reveals the inherent tension between e-government's capacity to facilitate citizen empowerment and participation and their reinforcing the current status quo by only providing greater access to those that already have it (Rubaii-Barrett and Wise, 2008). As the importance of e-government continues to grow, the cost of exclusion gets increasingly higher for groups with limited access (Holden, Norris, and Fletcher, 2002). Exclusion from e-government will lead to a "democratic divide" for those who are left out (Mossberger, Tolbert, and Stansbury, 2003). Perhaps no group faces greater hurdles in their participation in e-government than persons with disabilities.

E-government and Inaccessibility

The accessibility of government websites has been studied in more detail than the accessibility of many other parts of the Internet. This is likely due to two reasons. First, a number of governments have established clear guidelines that their agencies are supposed to implement in terms of Internet accessibility. In the United States, all federal agencies—along with all state and local agencies receiving federal technology dollars—are supposed to be in compliance with the Section 508 guidelines for Internet accessibility. Other nations have also created guidelines based on either Section 508 or the WCAG, with which government agencies are supposed to comply. The second reason is tied to the sheer importance of e-government. Exclusion from e-commerce is unfair and inconvenient, but it will not likely impair functioning in society. Exclusion from e-government, however, threatens to cut someone off from civic participation, from social services, and from their social obligations.

The essential fact is that while participating in e-commerce is a choice, participating in e-government is not. In many states, taxes can only be paid online and social services can only be applied for online. In many communities, enrollment of children for public school can only occur online. This trend has built steadily over the past several years, with governments moving ever larger amounts of information, communication, and services primarily or exclusively online. Low levels of access to e-government leave people with disabilities unable to equally participate, or participate at all, in these online manifestations of government.

The threat of unequal access to e-government is even more significant for persons with disabilities than for other socially disadvantaged groups. As with other areas of the Internet, people with disabilities are automatically disadvantaged by their lower levels of computer use, Internet access, and broadband access. In addition, e-government is uniquely important to people with disabilities. Individuals with disabilities search for government information and services, as well as download government forms, at higher rates than the rest of the population (Dobransky and Hargittai, 2006). The increased usage of e-government by individuals with disabilities stems both from the difficulties that many people with disabilities face in traveling to government offices and from the greater need by many individuals with disabilities for social services. People with disabilities are far more likely to live in poverty, and these types of social assistance are now more likely to be available only through online forms and processes.

Studies of e-government accessibility have all found low levels of compliance with Section 508 or WCAG. As a few examples over time, Stowers (2002) found that a mere 13.5 percent of federal sites studied in 2002 were accessible, Ellison (2004) found that only 22 percent of federal home pages studied were accessible in 2003, Loiacono, McCoy, and Chin (2005) found 23 percent of federal home pages in compliance with Section 508, and Jaeger (2006a) found that all federal home pages evaluated had significant accessibility problems. A very recent study by Olalere and Lazar (2011) found more than 90 percent of federal websites to be in violation of the Section 508 guidelines. This is not a positive or reassuring trend, as accessibility of e-government shows no signs of forward progress through these studies conducted over the course of nearly a decade.

Most other studies have shown similarly low percentages of accessibility, typically ranging from the single digits to low twenties, with occasional studies reaching into the thirties, for US federal, state, and local government websites and the websites of other nations (e.g., Disability Rights Commission, 2004; Ellison, 2004; Fagan and Fagan, 2004; Jackson-Sanborn, Odess-Harnish, and Warren, 2002; Jaeger, 2004a, 2004b; Jaeger and Matteson, 2009; Lazar et al. 2003; Lazar and Greenidge, 2006; Marincu and McMullin, 2004; Michael, 2004; Olalere and Lazar, 2011; Potter, 2002; Rubaii-Barrett and Wise, 2008; Stowers, 2002; West, 2003, 2004; Woolfson, 2004; World Markets Research Centre, 2001). In fact, the studies that have more detailed methods of assessing accessibility generally tend to show the lowest levels of compliance with accessibility guidelines.

The problem is by no means limited to the United States. In the United Kingdom, to help overcome failures to make accessible websites, the government set up a network of "UK Online centres" that offer free public Internet access and assistance using the Internet if it is needed; however, a great many of these locations are not physically accessible to people with disabilities (Clear and Dennis, 2009). This situation reflects a larger problem with compliance and enforcement of disability rights laws in the United Kingdom (Carvin, Hill, and Smothers, 2004). One study of 150 United Kingdom government agencies found that none of them had accessible websites, while other studies have found levels of accessibility to United Kingdom government sites to be not that much higher (Disability Rights Commission, 2004; Marincu and McMullin, 2004; Woolfson, 2004). These accessibility problems in the United Kingdom are paralleled in most other EU nations (e-Government Unit, 2005).

The types and levels of accessibility problems of e-government are far-ranging, touching every disability. For example, one study of the accessibility of federal government websites (Jaeger, 2006a) identified the following accessibility barriers across the sites examined:

• For persons with visual impairments: font size too small; incompatibility with screen readers; incompatibility with alternate color schemes; incompatibility with screen enlargements; uses flash and moving images to convey content; uses graphics and color to convey content; lack of alt tags; color scheme hard to read; use of mouse-over menus.

• For persons with mobility impairments: incompatibility with alternate input devices; font size too small; links and accompanying descriptors too small; spacing between lines not large enough; tables too closely spaced; use of mouse-over menus; too much scrolling required; pages cluttered, busy, and poorly organized.

• For persons with cognitive impairments and specific learning disabilities: navigation elements confusing and hard to use; insufficient navigation elements; lack of redundant navigation elements; inconsistent layout; inconsistent navigation; lack of clear language; use of mouse-over menus; too much scrolling required; font size too small; links and accompanying descriptors too small; spacing between lines not large enough; tables too closely spaced; pages cluttered, busy, and poorly organized.

• For persons with hearing impairments: lack of closed captioning and audio equivalents of content.

These barriers are representative of the accessibility problems identified, with some resulting in many specific problems with usage. The barriers were not all present on every site, though some sites examined did include all of these barriers.

Increasing E-government Accessibility

With government agencies required to have accessible websites and with clear guidelines being readily available, it seems quite reasonable to wonder why problems with accessibility would be so rampant in e-government. The most significant reason may be that accessibility requirements are usually unfunded mandates, meaning that government agencies are told to implement a policy without receiving additional funding. In the case of accessibility, the requirements were created after many agencies already had a website, meaning that they would have to spend more money to retrofit a site to be accessible than to design a site to be accessible from the outset. Between the lack of financial support for accessibility and the larger costs of making an existing site accessible, many agencies have written off accessibility as costing too much.

A second challenge to accessibility is the culture within government agencies. Accessibility initiatives were not accompanied by large-scale education programs for government employees about the importance of Internet accessibility, nor were meaningful efforts made to teach agency directors and managers about accessibility to ensure managerial buy-in within the agencies (Jaeger and Matteson, 2009). Without managerial leadership on the issue, it is not perceived to be an agency priority by many agency employees.

A third challenge relates to the people who are in the position of designing and implementing accessible websites. Studies of government website developers and webmasters have found a widespread lack of knowledge of accessible design and requirements, with many being unsure about the Section 508 requirements or ways to educate themselves about Section 508 years after the law was to have been implemented (Jaeger, 2006a; Lazar et al., 2003; Lazar, Dudley-Sponaugle, and Greenidge, 2004; Lazar and Greenidge, 2006). This claim is particularly baffling given that the guidelines and guidance are readily available on www.section508.gov, and www.buyaccessible.gov has a "buy accessible wizard" to help build compliant requirements and solicitations in developing and acquiring technology.

Other developers are dismissive of the importance of the Section 508 requirements, believing that accessibility only benefits a small number of people served by the agency, that accessibility features will ruin the site, and that people with disabilities do not matter as a population to the agency (Jaeger, 2006a; Lazar et al., 2003; Lazar, Dudley-Sponaugle, and Greenidge, 2004; Lazar and Greenidge, 2006). Additionally, training materials available to website developers and webmasters do not necessarily sufficiently reinforce the importance of website accessibility (Law, Jaeger, and McKay, 2010).

A further challenge is the fact that the WCAG and Section 508 guidelines both focus more on the technology than on the user. Government efforts to make e-government accessible have focused primarily on technical accessibility, rather than making e-government actively inclusive of persons with disabilities or easy for them to use (Stienstra and Troschuk, 2005). This is a significant difference, as it is technically possible to create a website that complies with all of the Section 508 guidelines that is still inaccessible (Slatin, 2001; Slatin and Rush, 2003).

For all of these various reasons for lower levels of accessibility, the impacts have been obvious to persons with disabilities. In spite of their increased need to use e-government, many people with disabilities have come to distrust e-government as a source of information or services as a result of these accessibility barriers (Cullen and Hernon, 2006). For many people with disabilities, the accessibility problems make online government—and thereby the government as a whole—seem disinterested in them and their needs. As a message to a group of people, it is one thing for the website of a department store to be inaccessible, but it is an entirely more profound message for government websites to be inaccessible. Not being included by a chain bookstore online is wrong and annoying, but not being included in a state tax website is cutting people out of basic functions as citizens.

The key insight from the lack of adoption of government accessibility standards is that the creation of a law or policy asserting the requirement of website accessibility is not enough. No one can claim it was an issue of insufficient time to prepare for Section 508—the law was passed in 1998 and implementation was supposed to occur in 2001. Agencies had three years to prepare but for the most part they did not. In addition to the requirement of e-government accessibility, the research indicates that governments need to consider the following:

- Providing funding specifically for the accessibility of e-government.
- Crafting clear articulations of who will benefit from the requirements and the importance of accessibility to those populations.
- Drafting specific guidance and instructions for website developers and webmasters.
- Establishing monitoring, testing, and compliance-oriented technical assistance programs.

- Creating enforcement mechanisms and sanctions for failure to provide accessible sites.
- Educating managers and employees of agencies about the importance of accessibility to agency staff and to members of the public (Jaeger, 2004b; Jaeger and Matteson, 2009; Rubaii-Barrett and Wise, 2008).

Amazingly, more than a decade after the intended implementation of Section 508 in the United States, the focus is still on encouraging basic compliance.

When Section 508 requirements were supposed to be implemented across federal government agencies, the National Council on Disability (2001) issued a report warning that "the costs of doing nothing may be greater than the costs of any reasonably foreseeable measures" in the implementation of Section 508 (p. 28). Ironically, this statement has become more profound than could have been envisioned in 2001. The massive and ongoing increase in the size and scope of e-government makes accessibility an ever more difficult target, because every increase in the amount of information and services available through e-government means more content that has to be made accessible and a greater backlog of inaccessible content. Moving forward, governments will need to much better "consider how to balance the accessibility needs of all Americans as more civic engagement goes digital" (Howard, 2011, n.p.).

Information Worlds and Life Online

Returning to the concepts of the information worlds theoretical framework, there exist in the contexts of employment and education several key interactions between small worlds—the immediate social worlds in which individuals live—that shape the access ultimately available to persons with disabilities. The Internet offers many opportunities to strengthen the information available in the small worlds of students with disabilities and of employees with disabilities. The ways in which members of these groups can use online communication to support one another and exchange information about succeeding in the role of student or employee demonstrate the ability of the Internet to provide new benefits to the small worlds of persons with disabilities. The Internet, in providing access to information that was previously difficult to reach or was in an inaccessible form in employment contexts, also serves to expand the range of information behavior of persons with disabilities by making more information available.

However, the different employment and education contexts previously discussed show how several other small worlds react, through their own use of the Internet, to the inclusion of persons with disabilities. On one side, the small world of professional librarians is using the Internet to extend its long-running efforts to include people with disabilities as individuals and as a group in library services. On the opposite side, the small world of postsecondary educators is replicating resistance to persons with disabilities in the face-to-face classroom by adopting exclusionary approaches to websites and virtual classrooms. In both of these cases, the social norms, information value, and information behavior of each small world toward persons with disabilities is being continued in the online environment.

For persons with disabilities, the individual has unique experiences with information and information technology access, but also has experiences with access tied to larger perceptions of the small worlds of persons with disabilities. In these broad social contexts of education and employment, the technological benefits and challenges for persons with disabilities hinge on the social norms and social types of those who design and implement the technologies. For libraries, there is a historical social norm of actively providing access to information widely and a social type that classifies persons with disabilities as valued patrons. In postsecondary education, the social norms of access are much more privileged, and persons with disabilities have historically not shared much in those privileges; also, social types of postsecondary education historically have not typically classified persons with disabilities as welcome members of the small world of the school.

The online social activities of persons with disabilities in terms of communication, interaction, and entertainment further reveal issues between the small worlds of persons with disabilities and other small worlds. In online social interactions, people with disabilities are generally drawn to engage other people with disabilities. The peer support and engagement serve to strengthen the ties between people with disabilities in their own small worlds by allowing people with disabilities to share experiences with both individuals with similar disabilities and individuals with different disabilities. Through interactions with people they would never likely meet in the physical world, the small worlds of individuals with disabilities can include individuals from a much more dispersed geographic area.

Online social interactions also allow people with disabilities to connect with others from outside the small world of disabilities. The places online that allow for interactions with different groups of people serve as boundary objects, where people from diverse small worlds can engage one another. Online games are an example of such places, but any site that allows communication and interaction with a broad population of users serves to connect different small worlds.

The choice of many people with disabilities to not reveal their disability somewhat confounds the interactions between small worlds. Some people with disabilities are only comfortable engaging members of other small worlds by representing themselves as not belonging to a small world of disability. Thus, many of the linkages that the small worlds of persons with disabilities could be making with other small worlds are limited, as the people in the other worlds may be unaware that they are interacting with a person with a disability.

Such circumstances may benefit the individual with a disability by increasing the likelihood of their acceptance into other worlds, especially if the norms and information value of the other small world perceive people with disabilities in a negative light. However, for persons with disabilities as a group, the hiding of a disability in interactions with others limits the progress that people with disabilities can make in changing any negative norms and values of other worlds toward people with disabilities. A person who views people with disabilities as objects of pity and tragedy or as having little to contribute might have a much altered perspective if a close online friend had a disability and was open about the disability in their interactions.

Within the information worlds framework, many of the issues with e-government parallel the issues with employment and education online. E-government offers a great number of opportunities for increased access to information and services for the small worlds of persons with disabilities, creating new abilities to be part of civic discourse in ways that were not previously possible for persons with disabilities. Just as telecommuting and online classes offer greater means of involvement for persons with disabilities in work and education by alleviating the need to physically travel and to be in a particular location, e-government provides the same possibilities in terms of engaging government and getting government services without having to go to a particular physical location.

However, just as in the contexts of education and employment, the barriers to e-government reveal negative perceptions about persons with disabilities by those in other small worlds who make the decisions about access to e-government. Broader perceptions of the small worlds of persons with disabilities are reflected in decisions made by those who design and implement e-government sites and by those who manage government agencies—specifically, decisions not to emphasize or prioritize making e-government accessible. The social norms, information value, and information behavior of these small worlds regarding persons with disabilities is demonstrated by the lack of focus on issues of accessibility.

A third parallel to the contexts of education and employment is found in the lack of control the small world of persons with disabilities has over e-government access. While people with disabilities can identify and lobby for agencies to correct instances of inaccessibility, they cannot actively address the situation themselves.

One significant difference between access to education and employment and access to e-government is that the latter includes more than issues of inclusion in communication, services, and opportunities. E-government is also becoming central to participating in civic life and having a voice in democracy. From its inception, the existence of a public that was informed of government decisions and was able to provide input has been the cornerstone of American democracy (Quinn, 2003; Relyea, 2008). To have only limited access to e-government can have serious consequences for the individual members of the small world of people with disabilities, but for the small world of people with disabilities to be collectively limited in their ability to participate in societal-level democratic discourse means having a reduced voice in the lifeworld of the nation and the governing decisions it makes.

A limited voice in the discourse of the lifeworld could lead to a further marginalization of persons with disabilities. Without proper voice in national discourse, the needs and goals of people with disabilities will be less discussed and represented in decisions than they already are. The social media platforms that are now being used to convey e-government content raise these concerns even more, as they bridge the concerns of access to e-government with the concerns of access to entertainment. Social media companies fall outside the requirements of Section 508, yet the Obama administration is strongly encouraging agencies to use social media as means to provide information, communicate with citizens, and distribute services (Bertot, Jaeger, and Hansen, forthcoming; Jaeger and Bertot, 2010b; Jaeger, Paquette, and Simmons, 2010). The use of social media as a conduit of e-government may make e-government convenient for other small worlds, but it demonstrates yet another case of the small worlds of persons with disabilities not being sufficiently considered in the process of making decisions about e-government services. The next chapter considers the roles of accessibility evaluation and policy reform in shifting levels of access online for persons with disabilities.

4

Improving Accessibility: Technology Evaluation and Policy Reform

This chapter explores accessibility evaluation and policy reform and their roles in the future of the Internet. The greatest challenge to equal access online is the pace of technological development. Because of the rapid rate of technological change, most technology design processes do not include considerations of accessibility. Even if it were commonly considered in design processes, developers often evidence limited understanding of testing for or achieving accessibility, while policymakers struggle to create guidelines that remain relevant to rapidly changing technologies. This chapter examines the methods of evaluating information technologies to ensure that they are accessible to persons with disabilities and to promote the development of born-accessible technologies.

Along with technology evaluation, the policy context of Internet accessibility is central to any long-term changes in Internet access for persons with disabilities. Establishing meaningful guarantees of equal access online for persons with disabilities requires the creation of clear, achievable accessibility guidelines that can adapt to rapid technological change and the political will to enforce these guidelines in all contexts. I propose and examine in this chapter specific changes to law and policy that would be required and the political issues that such changes would raise.

The Nature of Evaluations

Evaluation studies are testing approaches to determine if policies, requirements, guidelines, or standards are being properly implemented. Such evaluations determine if, and under what conditions, a policy and its components are effectively meeting programmatic, ethical, social, economic, and intellectual goals (Chen, 1990; Sanders, 2001). Evaluation "may confirm uncertain prior findings, provide new understandings about how programs work, or fundamentally question assumptions about particular interventions" (Ginsburg and Rhett, 2003, p. 490). Evaluation is intended to produce social betterment by improving conditions for users, offering prescriptions for improvement, or providing new perspectives (Grob, 2003; Henry, 2003; Henry and Mark, 2003; Lafond et al., 2000; Mabry, 2002; Wagenaar et al., 2005). "Evaluation has, now more than ever before, become an integral part of how policies, decisions, reforms, programs, and projects are undertaken to try to achieve credibility and trust" (Segerholm, 2003, p. 353).

All public policies have implications for democracy and society; as such, evaluations of these policies do as well (Hansberger, 2001). Evaluations examine policies in terms of how they affect democratic society and how they contribute to or enhance democratic values (Hansberger, 2001). Ideally, evaluations can identify gaps in access to social institutions, ensure distribution, and alleviate disadvantages and access gaps in the networked environment (Stake, 2004). Such evaluations help foster democracy by involving people often left out of the policymaking process (MacNeil, 2002; Stake, 2004).

As the use of information technologies has blossomed over the past two decades, the evaluation of information technologies and the Internet has grown increasingly important. Evaluation can play both a formative role, helping to continually refine and update policies, and a summative role, helping to ascertain whether the policy goals and objectives are being met (Thompson, McClure, and Jaeger, 2003). A key part of ensuring the development of a more accessible Internet in the future is the use of evaluation studies to document current levels of accessibility and the ways in which accessibility can be improved.

Website Evaluations

There have been numerous suggestions of specific methodologies that could be used to evaluate websites for different purposes and from different perspectives, though a great many hinge on the approach of using automated testing programs—such as Bobby, WAVE, and WebXact—to have the software checked for coding compliance with a set of accessibility guidelines, usually either the WCAG or Section 508. As a result of the Section 508 guidelines and other government requirements, a particular focus of investigations has been the accessibility of e-government websites at national, state/provincial, and local levels (e.g., Ellison, 2004; Fagan and Fagan, 2004; Jackson-Sanborn, Odess-Harnish, and Warren, 2002; Jaeger, 2006a, 2008; Jaeger and Matteson, 2009; Marincu and McMullin, 2004; Michael, 2004; Olalere and Lazar, 2011; Rubaii-Barrett and Wise, 2008; Stowers, 2002; West, 2003; World Markets Research Centre, 2001). An early suggestion for evaluating websites was in terms of compliance with laws related to security, privacy, and information access (Eschenfelder et al., 1997; Smith, Fraser, and McClure, 2000). Eschenfelder et al. (1997) provide an extensive list of more than sixty evaluation criteria in two major categories: information content and ease of use. This methodology was originally proposed for United States federal government websites but has since been extended to other national e-governments, such as New Zealand (A. G. Smith, 2001).

More broadly, studies of the accessibility of websites have also focused on education, employment, academics, retail, tourism, airlines, and distance learning, among others (e.g., Coonin, 2002; Gutierrez, Loucopoulos, and Reinsch, 2005; Jackson-Sanborn, Odess-Harnish, and Warren, 2002; King et al., 2004; Klein et al., 2003; Milliman, 2002; Ritchie and Blanck, 2003; Schmetzke, 2003; Shi, 2006; Sloan et al., 2002; Thompson, Burgstahler, and Comden, 2003; Witt and McDermott, 2004). While the quality and depth of these evaluation studies vary considerably, they work together to give a general understanding of the accessibility of the Internet.

Accessibility studies are part of a larger set of different evaluation approaches that can be used online. Huang and Chao (2001) suggest that websites should be evaluated based on usability principles, specifically that websites should employ a user-centered design that allows users of the websites to effectively reach the information they seek. Holliday (2002) created a set of evaluation criteria for the level of usefulness of websites, including factors such as amount of information about the government, contact information, feedback options, search capabilities, and related links. The Value Measuring Methodology encourages evaluation of websites based on cost/benefit, social, and political factors (Booz Allen Hamilton, 2002). Gupta and Jana (2003) suggest evaluating sites in terms of the tangible and intangible economic benefits the sites produce.

Some of these methods for evaluating websites have been created with specific populations in mind. Ritchie and Blanck (2003) assert that websites should be evaluated in relation to the users of human services that are provided on the site, such as everyday life information, referral services, peer counseling, and advocacy. Fenton (2004), in examining websites of adoption agencies, also focuses on the evaluation factors that impact users of human services provided through e-government.

User-Centered Evaluations

While the evaluation of websites can be approached from many directions, a particularly robust approach is user-centered evaluation, which focuses on the implementation of the website from the perspective of the user (Bertot and Jaeger, 2006; Bertot et al., 2006; Jaeger and Bertot, 2010a). This type of user-centered evaluation can include three interrelated elements, of which accessibility is an essential component:

- Functionality evaluation, examining how well the website and its implementation fulfill the functions that they are intended to perform.
- Usability evaluation, examining how well users are able to use and interact with the implementation of a website.
- Accessibility evaluation, examining how inclusive a website and its implementation are for all users, including persons with disabilities (Bertot and Jaeger, 2006; Bertot et al., 2006; Jaeger and Bertot, 2010a).

User-centered testing focuses on the needs of users of websites and includes users directly in the testing process.

The goal of functionality testing is to determine if the website works as intended and provides the desired results. Quite literally, this method finds whether a website and its elements objectively function according to its goals (Wallace, 2001). Functionality testing is often used to make comparisons between separate, comparable websites with similar goals (Bertot et al., 2003). In functionality testing, issues that should be considered include the types of functions that are tested, the perspectives on the functions tested, the needs of potential users of those functions, the goals of the program, and the scale of the functions (Gibbons, Peters, and Bryan, 2003). Perhaps most significant, functionality evaluation of a website can help determine if the functions of a website meet policy goals. This approach can be particularly important if employed during the implementation process while it can still be modified if necessary.

The most significant drawback to functionality testing is likely the general lack of involvement of typical users of the program. Regardless of the design of a functionality evaluation, researchers will probably not be able to anticipate all of the experiences and potential difficulties of diverse users, particularly unskilled ones (Gibbons, Peters, and Bryan, 2003). Functionality testing may have no way of getting at the impressions of users, such as level of satisfaction. These sorts of issues are better addressed by usability evaluation.

Usability evaluation examines how users react to and interact with a website. Usability may be regarded as "the extent to which the information technology affords (or is deemed capable of affording) an effective and satisfying interaction to the intended users, performing the intended tasks within the intended environment at an acceptable cost" (Sweeney, Maguire, and Shackel, 1993, p. 690). Usability can be frustrated by system complexity and poor interfaces, which create challenges in function and use of the technology (Baecker et al., 2000). Usability evaluation can elicit user input at many points in design and implementation and can iteratively employ a range of techniques (Thompson, McClure, and Jaeger, 2003). Although user participation in usability testing has been criticized as being too labor intensive (Norman and Panizzi, 2006), it provides detailed information from the perspective of the user.

Usability metrics employed in evaluation tend to focus on two specific aspects of the experience of the user—user perceptions and user interactions with the system (Hert, 2001). The first type of metric allows the user to express personal impressions of the resource, such as satisfaction, utility, value, helpfulness, benefits, frustration, and self-efficacy (Dalrymple and Zweizig, 1992; Hert, 2001). The second type of metric provides a portrait of the user's interaction with the resource by monitoring the number of errors, the time necessary to complete specified tasks, and similar measures of the efficiency and effectiveness of the resource when being used (Hert, 2001). Through the combination of these two types of data, usability testing can catch many issues that developers may have missed. By employing protocols that encourage the user to articulate immediate impressions about the website while actively using it, usability analysis can offer insight into the perspectives of the user about the resource at issue that might not otherwise be available in the course of the evaluation (Hert, 2001).

Accessibility testing is the assessment of a website based on whether or not it provides equal access to all users, particularly in terms of the website accessibility requirements of Section 508 of the Rehabilitation Act or of the WCAG. As previously noted, accessibility evaluations have investigated the accessibility of e-government, retail, airline, tourism, employment, academic, library, distance learning, and popular websites, among others. Many of these studies have relied primarily on automated testing software (i.e., Bobby, Ask Alice, WAVE, WebXact) and do not involve users in the evaluation.

More user-centered studies of online accessibility are less common, though a few studies have taken a more comprehensive approach to accessibility evaluation. In two studies examining the accessibility of educational websites in the United Kingdom, the authors argue for using a combination of automated testing, expert testing, and user testing (King et al., 2004; Sloan et al., 2002). A study of educational websites in Iowa also used a more complex method to evaluate accessibility by employing automated testing and expert testing, though not user testing (Klein et al., 2003).

In considering evaluations, it is important to understand that accessibility cannot be equated directly with usability (Theofanos and Redish, 2003). Accessibility means that a website, software application, or operating system can technically be accessed by someone using assistive technologies. Technical accessibility, however, does not necessarily equate to an interface that is easy to use. Often, there is a significant gap between accessibility and usability of interfaces for people with disabilities, with technologies that are designed to be accessible not also being usable (Theofanos and Redish, 2003). A perfect example of the gap between accessibility and usability are Web-based human-interaction proofs (HIPs), which are also commonly called CAPTCHAs. A HIP is a test to determine whether someone is a human or a computer, intended to help avoid bots and viruses from automatically signing up for thousands of accounts and log-ins. The most common type of HIP is text that appears twisted or otherwise distorted. The human user has to decipher the text to log in, but the assumption is that a computer bot could not similarly decipher the text. However, someone with a visual impairment obviously cannot use a HIP, as it would be technically impossible. Some websites now offer audio HIPs, which offer the same idea, except that the words read are provided in garbled audio. Once again, the assumption is that a human could listen to the sounds and decipher the text, but a computer bot could not.

The reality is that multiple studies have shown that blind users are successful with audio HIPs less than 50 percent of attempts (Bigham and Cavender, 2009; Sauer et al., 2010). This is an example of an interface that may be technically accessible, but, because the rate of success is below 50 percent, it is clearly not usable (Lazar, 2006). There are numerous other examples of technologies that are accessible and not usable. User-based testing, where representative users attempt to perform representative tasks, is the best way to determine the usability and accessibility of the websites. Of these types of user-centered evaluations, accessibility may be the least widely used—likely due in no small part to a lack of awareness of issues related to persons with disabilities among developers and evaluators of information technologies (Jaeger, 2008). However, for a site to be fully accessible to users with disabilities, it should be functional, usable, and accessible.

Designing and Conducting Accessibility Evaluations

To illustrate the options in conducting an accessibility evaluation, I discuss here expert testing, user testing, automated testing, and webmaster surveys as elements of accessibility testing. Each method of evaluation plays a specific role in evaluation, complementing one another and increasing the amount of information available. In the accessibility evaluation of sites, the use of a multimethod approach to evaluation is optimal and can bring more attention to an issue than single-evaluation methods could alone (Gordon and Heinrich, 2004; Thompson, McClure, and Jaeger, 2003). Because functionality and usability—as necessary underlying elements to ensure full accessibility—have already been widely documented and are more frequently used than accessibility evaluation, this discussion emphasizes issues of accessibility evaluation.

The different methods of accessibility evaluation have both benefits and limitations as part of an evaluation. Exploring the inherent value to the study of each of the methods allows for consideration of which methods are best suited to accessibility evaluation. Below, the three user-centered methods—expert testing, user testing, and webmaster questionnaires—and automated testing are examined in terms of factors such as effectiveness, efficiency, feasibility, and impact on the overall study. To contextualize the discussion, they are framed in reference to an evaluation of the requirements of Section 508, but the methods can just as easily be applied using the WCAG or other accessibility criteria.

Expert testing is the evaluation by persons knowledgeable about the design and development of websites, and it is a method by which to identify a broad range of issues. To engage in expert testing, one or more people with the skills to conduct it should be available, and they need to have an established system or rubric from which to work (Lazar, 2006). With these conditions, expert testing is a very valuable method for evaluating the accessibility of websites. The key obstacle in conducting expert testing for accessibility is that it requires persons who understand and can identify the barriers to accessibility in design and the impacts of these barriers on users with diverse disabilities, and who also have an understanding of the guidelines for accessibility and how they should be properly implemented. Table 4.1 presents selected expert testing questions that have been used to evaluate the accessibility of sites through expert testing in previous studies (Jaeger, 2006a, 2008). These kinds of questions are representative of the types of questions that are necessary for achieving a broad understanding of the accessibility of the site. The testing should be conducted to ensure as wide an analysis of the sites as possible. Sites should be tested through different operating systems and multiple browsers to see if there were significant differences in levels of accessibility and tested for compatibility with a range of assistive technologies related to different types of disabilities, including narrators and screen readers, screen enlargement software, magnifiers, alternate color schemes, and alternate input devices, among others. By using questions like those in Table 4.1 and by testing using a range of assistive technologies, expert testing can identify major accessibility barriers on sites such as the following:

- Incompatibility with assistive technologies.
- Use of flash and moving images to convey content.
- Cluttered layout and organization.
- Audio content without a text equivalent.
- Lack of alt tags.
- Difficult drop-down, mouse-over menus and other difficult navigation elements.

• Problems with consistency and clarity of context, orientation, and navigation.

One study found that the use of multiple experts was a considerably more effective method for identifying accessibility problems than a single expert working alone (Mankoff, Fait, and Tran, 2005).

Expert testing is particularly important because it is very unlikely that the accessibility evaluation of a site could be conducted so thoroughly as to include user tests that represented people who have all the different types and levels of disabilities that should be accounted for in designing for accessibility. Such representativeness in the user tests would likely require a great number of user tests involving people with an array of disabilities—visual impairments, hearing impair-

Table 4.1 Sample Questions for Expert Testing

1. Provides an audio/video/textual equivalent for every element related to content and services?

2. Alternative formats of elements of multimedia presentations synchronize to the appropriate parts of the presentation?

3. All information conveyed through color also conveyed without color?

4. Content clear and organized so as to be readable to any user?

5. Provides context and orientation information at all times?

6. Provides clear navigation mechanisms?

7. Identifies row and column headers on tables?

8. Does not rely on moving pictures or flash to convey content?

9. Designs pages to avoid flicker rates above 2 Hz or below 55 Hz?

10. Works comprehensively with assistive technologies?

11. All electronic forms allow users with assistive technologies to access the information, field elements, and functionality required for completion and submission of the forms, including directions and cues?

12. Text-only equivalent page available for every page that cannot otherwise be made completely compliant with all other requirements?

13. Ensures user control of time-sensitive content changes?

14. Users not timed out of applications?

15. Ensures direct accessibility of embedded user interfaces?

ments, mobility impairments, specific learning disabilities, cognitive disabilities, and others—and with a range of severity of impairment within each type of disability. It is unlikely that all those people could be found for testing, even if there were time and financial resources to accommodate that many user tests.

Expert testing, fortunately, allows for fewer user tests by identifying the potential issues for people with different disabilities without needing representative users from each group. Though the expert testing does not reach the same depth or granularity in identifying problems for any particular disability as a user with that disability would, expert testing does identify the major accessibility issues on each site (Jaeger, 2008). User testing enriches the findings of the expert testing—the expert testing provides breadth, while the user testing provides depth. As such, expert testing can be used to reduce the burden of user testing.

User testing, the testing of a website by users under the guidance of a researcher, provides a great depth of information from the perspective of each user who is tested. Conducting user testing creates a detailed portrait of the accessibility of a website from the perspective of people who have the same disability as the person testing the site. Though a poorly designed element of a site will sometimes cause accessibility problems to people with different kinds of disabilities, that will not always be the case. People with different levels of severity of the same kind of disability will often experience different accessibility issues on the same site. A person involved in user testing, then, can best provide information related to the experiences of people like themselves.

Because user testing provides unparalleled richness of detail for those disabilities represented in the user population, it is an extremely important method for evaluating accessibility. However, it is also labor intensive and time consuming. The first and most pressing difficulty with user testing is finding users. Users with the types of disabilities that are being tested not only have to be located, but they should also be interested in participating, have time to participate, and have the requisite computer skills. Also, the right assistive technologies should be on hand so that the users can operate the computer as they normally would. Once users are identified and recruited, the actual user testing procedures can be lengthy, especially if certain users have special requirements—such as needing frequent breaks.

Table 4.2 includes sample questions that can be used during the course of user testing to elicit the thoughts of users with disabilities about the site being evaluated. Background information on the

Table 4.2 Sample Questions for User Testing

1. What assistive technologies are you currently using (if any)?

2. Are you able to navigate the site without difficulty? If not, what accessibility problems did you face in navigating?

3. Are you able to read the text on the site without difficulty? If not, what accessibility problems did you face in reading?

4. Are you able to use the search function on the site without difficulty? If not, what accessibility problems did you face in searching?

5. Are you able to use particular applications (i.e., download forms, view audio or video, fill out forms) on the site without difficulty? If not, what accessibility problems did you face in using these applications?

6. Do you feel that the site as a whole is working well with the assistive technology you are using? Please specify.

7. Do you notice problems that might affect people with other types of disabilities? Please specify.

---

impacts of each participant's disability on the use of the Internet in general is also essential information to gather in understanding the barriers to accessibility on the sites that are being tested. Depending on the size of the site being tested, thorough user testing can take anywhere between fifteen minutes and two hours. Analyzing the results of user testing requires effort, as data need to be extracted and made sensible from a large number of comments that each user will make during the course of the testing. However, user testing generally identifies more detailed accessibility barriers than expert testing does; Table 4.3 shows a sampling of major accessibility problems identified through the user testing in one study (Jaeger, 2008).

The levels of effort to conduct user testing are extremely worthwhile. Because the depth of detail provided by user testing demonstrated in Table 4.3 is not available through any other methodology, the impact of conducting user testing on an evaluation is sizable. However, given the intense time requirements and other constraints, it is unlikely that too many user tests could feasibly be conducted in a typical accessibility evaluation. The combination of user testing and expert testing is therefore particularly valuable, because the latter provides breadth and the former provides depth.

User testing can be conducted either face-to-face or remotely (i.e., via telephone and Internet communication), with the verbal script for the face-to-face testing converted to an interactive script

Table 4.3 Types of Findings from User Testing

Elements do not enlarge	Some buttons not working
Compatibility problems with screen readers	Search function problems
	Tables too closely spaced
Compatibility problems with alternate color schemes	Small font on deeper pages
	Tabs too small
Compatibility problems with screen enlargements	Insufficient navigation elements
	Poor use of available space
Compatability problems with alternate input devices	Color scheme hard to read
	Insufficient spacing between lines and individual words
Uses flash and moving images to convey content	Inconsistent navigation
Font size too small	Navigation elements too small
Lack of alt tags	Mouse-over menus difficult to use
Spacing between lines not large enough	Too much scrolling required
Inconsistent layout	Lack of text equivalents for audio content
Header text too small	
Problems with printer-friendly version of site	Pages cluttered, busy, and poorly organized
Navigation elements confusing and hard to use	Links and accompanying descriptors too small
Uses graphics and color to convey content	

conveyed electronically. Remote testing data are usually more reflective and thoughtful, while face-to-face data are generally more spontaneous (Jaeger, 2006a, 2008). Remote user testing seems particularly vital to accessibility testing, as it allows the participation of persons with very significant disabilities who might have difficulty reaching a lab setting or participating in a limited period of time; it also allows the researcher to involve participants with disabilities who are locally unavailable for testing and allows participants with very specific technology needs to work at a computer they are comfortable with and that has all the assistive technologies they need. However, it has also been suggested that remote studies identify a smaller range of accessibility issues than face-to-face testing (Mankoff, Fait, and Tran, 2005).

Accessibility evaluations can also include sending a questionnaire to webmasters to gauge their perceptions of the accessibility of the websites being studied. The webmaster questionnaire, distributed through e-mail, provides very valuable data without too much difficulty. Compared to expert testing and user testing, a questionnaire is not time consuming or labor intensive, even taking into account the time needed to find contact information and send follow-up e-mails and reminders. If you are conducting an evaluation of the site of your own organization, gathering information from webmasters and website developers should be very straightforward.

Table 4.4 includes sample questions that can be asked of webmasters and website developers to assess the considerations of disability and accessibility in the development of their sites (Jaeger, 2008). In the context of a multimethod evaluation, a webmaster questionnaire can prove insightful, exposing issues that might otherwise have been missed in the study. Responses to these questionnaires can reveal the organizations' perceptions of the accessibility of their websites, which can be compared with the findings from the user testing and the expert testing.

A fourth kind of testing that can be used in accessibility evaluations is automated testing. Unlike the other methods discussed, it is a method that focuses on the coding of the site rather than on the user. While automated usability software tools—such as Bobby, WebXact, Watchfire, InFocus, and Deque RAMP, among others—claim to replace the need for other types of inspections, these claims fall short, because the software tends to give limited results (Jaeger, 2006b, 2008; Mankoff, Fait, and Tran, 2005). In fact, automated testing

Table 4.4 Sample Questions for Webmasters and Website Developers

1. Do you feel that the accessibility of your website for persons with disabilities is a priority within your agency?

2. When working to make your website accessible for persons with disabilities, where do you turn for resources and guidelines?

3. Do you perform accessibility testing on your website to test how well it can be used by persons with disabilities? If so, at what point in the website development process is this testing done?

4. What factors (i.e., staff time, staff skills, funding, agency mission, etc.) influence the priority accorded to the accessibility of your website for persons with disabilities?

5. Have you received any feedback from users of your site regarding its accessibility? If so, were the comments generally positive or negative?

6. If you feel that the accessibility of your website could be improved, what resources would you find beneficial in working to improve it?

reveals far less than either expert testing or user testing alone (Jaeger, 2006a; Providenti and Zai, 2007b). Automated usability software often misses true problems, while simultaneously flagging other interface features as poor when in fact they are both accessible and usable for people with disabilities (Lazar, Feng, and Hochheiser, 2010). The W3C maintains a list of automated tools, but do not endorse the use of any of these tools to automatically check websites for accessibility (Adam and Kreps, 2006).

The government of Norway, however, may have found a way to make automated tools more effective, at least in certain contexts. They have created an e-government monitoring system (www.egovmon.no) that is designed to check features of government websites, including accessibility, against government regulations. Although no studies yet exist of the effectiveness of this new tool, a government-designed accessibility checker specifically for government sites raises the possibility of a more targeted, but potentially more successful, kind of automated accessibility evaluation tool.

Generally, the other accessibility evaluation options are better than automated tools, but if no other options are available, it is better to evaluate the sites using the automated tools than to skip evaluating a site. Automated testing tools are free, but they will provide the least amount of usable information to improve the accessibility of a site. They also cannot account for functionality and usability issues, which are covered by comprehensive expert and user testing. When a human being is testing a site to ascertain whether it is accessible, checking for accessibility will reveal functionality and usability problems through the process of testing. Although automated testing has been used far more frequently than other methods in accessibility evaluations, other methods tend to provide much more information.

Evaluations and the Future of Internet Accessibility

Better awareness of the methods of accessibility testing—and user-centered testing in general—and the more widespread use of these methods are key to expanding the accessibility of the Internet today and ensuring a more accessible Internet in the future. Creating a greater awareness of the current state of accessibility through evaluation, including specific barriers to accessibility, can serve as feedback to the developers of information technologies and Internet content.

Hopefully, such evaluations can lead to positive changes in current technologies and also demonstrate the interest in accessibility to encourage greater attention to accessibility in the creation of new technologies.

Although these methods can be easily adopted within industries that develop new information technologies and new Internet content, the general resistance to accessibility limits their use in the design process. Companies and organizations that engage in accessibility testing during the design process greatly increase the likelihood of developing born-accessible products, and accessibility evaluation as an interactive process can ensure that products remain accessible as new versions are created. Yet, as discussed in detail in earlier chapters, most companies and organizations do not test for accessibility. This resistance and claims of accessibility being too burdensome are all the more curious given that the types of accessibility evaluation detailed here are not cost-intensive, time-consuming, or difficult to plan or carry out. There are many studies that can provide references and guidance on creating an accessibility evaluation that is appropriate for the technology and the audience.

For companies and organizations interested in improving accessibility of existing technologies and in developing accessible new technologies, the methods suggested in this discussion can be an extremely important aspect of creating accessible products. For researchers and advocates, these methods are equally important for examining the current state of accessibility and identifying the specific types of inaccessibility that exist. Such identification can serve to alert unaware creators of technologies and to shame those that are aware of inaccessibility in their products but are not inclined to address it. All of the attention that has been focused on the problems with accessibility evaluation of e-government has served to shift mentalities about accessibility within government agencies (Jaeger and Matteson, 2009). Similar attention to the accessibility evaluation of company websites could have impacts in other areas of the Internet.

The common use of these methods of evaluation ultimately would benefit all users. If a site or a technology is functional, usable, and accessible, it will benefit any individual who uses that site or technology. Testing and evaluating a site or a technology to ensure that it is fully accessible will improve the experience for all users of that site or technology by making the functions clearer, content easier to find and interact with, and layout and navigation more intuitive. If the future Internet is to be a place of equal access for persons with disabilities, accessibility evaluation should be embraced as a means by which to campaign for greater accessibility in design, redesign, implementation, and adoption of information technologies. It is important that accessibility evaluation be built into the policy processes related to Internet access.

Who's Minding the Accessibility?

Although the United States has a robust slate of laws related to online accessibility, the laws have not had the effect of making the Internet widely accessible to the more than 54 million persons with disabilities in the country. A large part of the explanation of this seemingly dichotomous situation is that the existence of laws and regulations is not sufficient; there also should be established mechanisms to develop guidelines, monitor compliance, promote innovation, and possess meaningful enforcement powers to ensure compliance. In the United States, no such agency exists. In fact, issues related to online accessibility are spread across agencies and often no group has monitoring or enforcement roles with the laws and regulations, which often include large loopholes to avoid compliance anyway.

For example, the Department of Transportation (DOT) has a requirement that people with disabilities cannot be discriminated against in the pricing of airlines tickets. As many airlines provide their best prices online and also charge an extra fee for placing an order via the phone, the regulation requires that airlines give the lowest price to any person with a disability who orders a ticket via phone because the website is inaccessible. Under the regulation, all that callers have to do to receive the lowest fare is to identify themselves as having a disability that prevents equal access to the airline's website. A recent study found that 40 percent of airline call center workers were not even aware of this requirement, while two major airlines were aware but did not honor it (Lazar et al., 2010). This study was conducted at the same time that airlines were being sued by travelers with disabilities for the inaccessibility of their airport kiosks (Standen, 2010). One could be forgiven for thinking that no one in government is minding the online accessibility.

The Kafkaesque nature of government oversight of Internet accessibility was prominently displayed in the summer of 2010 when the federal government announced that the Department of Justice (DOJ) would be engaging in efforts to promote Internet access for persons with disabilities (Gordon and Kundra, 2010). These announced efforts included the very worthy goals of increasing accessibility of government and educational websites. However, considering that Section 508 was passed in 1998 and was to have been fully implemented by 2001, it is a bit confusing that these efforts would be the first attention given to Section 508 compliance since 2004, many years after agencies were supposed to have been in compliance. On the one hand, it is great to see the DOJ paying attention to the issue; on the other hand, it is maddening and confusing that it took so long.

Perhaps more surprisingly, the DOJ planned to query the government agencies as to the accessibility of their sites (Gordon and Kundra, 2010). They did not plan to evaluate the accessibility of the sites but instead to ask the agencies to tell them how accessible the sites are. Apparently, the DOJ will be trusting agencies that have predominantly inaccessible websites after nine years of mostly ignoring the issue to be honest in their assessments of their own sites. This approach seems much like asking people what they had for breakfast after telling them that you expect that they have been eating healthily. Even if breakfast really consisted of a box of chocolate donuts and a six-pack of beer, the response is more likely to be soy milk, granola, and a fresh apple.

This one situation points to a series of key problems with the current legal approach of online accessibility. The most fundamental problem is that no one is in charge. The Access Board issues regulations to promote accessibility but lacks the power to do anything to monitor or enforce the regulations. The NCD can issue reports about the status of online accessibility but has even less power than the Access Board. The FCC simply encourages accessibility. The General Services Administration (GSA) can purchase accessible technologies for agencies but not make them use the technologies. The National Science Foundation (NSF), the Department of Education (DOE), the National Institutes of Health (NIH), and the Institute for Museum and Library Services (IMLS) all fund some accessibility research, but it is not their main focus. The DOJ has some power to enforce compliance but has not been that interested in using it. Other government agencies and officials could give more attention to the issue but do not. Nobody at the federal government level is really in charge of accessibility, much less overall issues of disability.

The next problem is the main enforcement mechanism that was chosen. People with disabilities have the responsibility to monitor accessibility and bring complaints and claims against agencies and companies that violate accessibility laws. This approach puts the burden on people with disabilities to enforce their own rights in a way that no other minority or traditionally disadvantaged group does. Persons with disabilities are usually relied upon to file complaints about inaccessibility, but these processes can be cumbersome, complicated, and expensive for a person filing such a complaint. A person with a disability who encounters an inaccessible technology or website is supposed to contact the responsible party. If nothing happens within a certain period of time, that person is then required to file a complaint in administrative law courts for public entities and in civil court for private entities. In both cases, this requires the person being discriminated against to hire an attorney—which can be very expensive—and invest the time and effort to pursue the claim. If the claim is in an administrative law court, the person will have to travel to the nearest one, which might be some distance away. Then, for all of the efforts of the person with the disability, courts will rule against him or her in the crushing majority of cases (Davis, 2002; Lee, 2003).

The reason that people with disabilities usually lose their cases is the third major problem with the current approach. Under all of the disability laws, covered entities, both public and private, can claim that the requested accommodation is not financially or practically reasonable and thereby an undue burden under the law. If the accommodation is an undue burden, the entity does not need to provide the accommodation. The intent of the concept under the law was that undue burden would be measured against the overall budget of the program or entity (Fulton, 2011). However, as discussed earlier, both public and private entities tend to make very wide claims about what constitutes an undue burden, and courts tend to believe pretty much any claim of an undue burden. Until these undue burden loopholes are closed, inaccessibility will remain a legally supported position (Lazar and Jaeger, 2011).

The fourth problem is that the law itself is not written to be proactive, and it struggles even to be reactive. In most nations, policies about information and technology are traditionally based on the premise that technology is static, leaving policies unable to adapt to the rapid changes in technology shaping both the physical and virtual environments (Burgelman, 2000; Crawford, 2003; R. Frieden, 2003). Accessibility is no exception, with the requirements running far behind the developments. For example, in the summer of 2010, Congress passed the Twenty-first Century Communications and Video Accessibility Act of 2010. The law does the following:

- Authorizes the FCC to require seven hours per week of video description on the top four network channels and top five cable channels nationwide.
- Allocates up to $10 million per year for equipment used by individuals who are deaf-blind.
- Requires televised emergency information to be accessible to individuals who are blind or have low vision.
- Requires accessible user controls for televisions and set-top boxes and easy access to closed captioning and video description.
- Requires captioned television programs to be captioned when delivered over the Internet.
- Requires accessible advanced communications equipment and services, such as text messaging and e-mail.
- Requires access to Internet services that are built into mobile telephone devices, like smartphones, if achievable.
- Requires devices of any size to be capable of displaying closed captioning, delivering available video description, and making emergency information accessible.

The focus on emergency information is especially important. The Internet and particularly mobile devices have made it easier to receive emergency information, such as crime alerts and weather alerts, specific to an individual's location, and to send requests for help. A lack of inclusion in this area of the Internet-enabled information exchange leaves those without access more vulnerable in emergency situations.

However, a careful reading of these elements also reveals that more than half of them are focused on television (which has been widely used for decades), one is focused on e-mail and instant messaging (which have been widely used for more than a decade), and only two focus on recent technologies. And the requirements for smartphones are not really requirements. If these requirements are ever successfully implemented, many of the technological issues at hand may no longer be relevant due to rapid technological change.

The final major problem is that the laws focus on the technologies, not the users of the technologies or the reasons that people use the technologies. Without a clear focus on the information and communication needs of the users with disabilities, the laws will permanently be far behind the current technologies. This lack of focus on users and their needs is reflected in the fact that the advisory boards that government agencies establish for the creation of accessibility regulations tend to have limited representation of people with disabilities and disability rights groups, instead having their membership composed mostly of technology companies and other corporations (Jaeger, 2006a; Jaeger and Bowman, 2005).

It is true, in general, that "discrimination law has a weak history of enforcement" due to budgetary, bureaucratic, and administrative constraints (O'Connell, 1991, p. 124). However, the situation with the monitoring and enforcement of online accessibility seems to have been intentionally designed to fail. As a result, most of the online entities that should be accessible under these laws "remain inaccessible and apparently blissfully unaware" (Riley, 2005, p. 205).

During the course of 2010, there were clear signs of hope that accessibility was beginning to be treated more seriously under the law. The Departments of Education and Justice took the unusual step of issuing a joint statement to educational institutions to say that the use of inaccessible e-book readers and similar devices by elementary, secondary, and postsecondary institutions was a violation of the ADA and Section 504 (US Department of Education and US Department of Justice, 2010). This statement followed a series of settlement agreements in which universities agreed to desist in the use of inaccessible e-book readers for course readings, such as the agreement that ended the lawsuit filed by the NFB, the American Council of the Blind (ACB), and other organizations against Arizona State University, which had been using the inaccessible Kindle e-book reader in courses (*Settlement Agreement*, 2010).

In March 2010, the Access Board announced that it would begin a major revision of Section 508 and the accessibility provisions of the Telecommunications Act to harmonize, update, clarify, and refocus the requirements by the functionality of technologies instead of by product type to account for the range of features in many products (Access Board, 2010b). These updated guidelines—if implemented as intended—will cover telephones, cell phones, mobile devices, PDAs, computer software and hardware, websites, electronic documents, and media players (Access Board, 2010a). The guidelines will also expand the ADA requirements to include self-service machines used for retail transactions, as well as incorporate the principles of the revised WCAG (Access Board, 2010a). If these guidelines are implemented as intended, the principles of accessibility would be strengthened considerably under the law, though they continue to focus primarily on sensory and mobility impairments.

The DOJ simultaneously pursued a series of revisions to the ADA to account for changes in technology and society since the passage of the law. These updates include accessibility of movie theaters, design of furniture, access to 911, and website accessibility (US Department of Justice, 2010a, 2010b, 2010c, 2010d). The last of these is the most significant change, as it extends the coverage of the ADA to the websites of all entities covered by the ADA: local governments, state governments, and places of public accommodation. In such a case, the requirements of the ADA will be applied widely to entertainment and commerce online, resolving the disagreements in the courts about the applicability of the ADA to e-commerce. All of these strengthened regulations, however, will be of value only if they are actually complied with, monitored, and enforced.

Making Online Accessibility Work

Renowned computer scientist Ben Shneiderman (2008) has suggested that the technological revolutions of the past twenty years are so all-encompassing and significant in shaping society that traditional scientific methods need to be reconceptualized. The same type of fundamental reconceptualization is definitely needed in the area of policy related to information access online. It has been suggested that the most effective Internet policy might be that which learns from core principles of the online environment, one of which is equity (Margetts, 2009). For persons with disabilities, equity is missing from both the policy and the practice of the Internet. In order for online accessibility to truly be guaranteed for persons with disabilities, the key problems detailed here need to be addressed in ways that have not been a part of accessibility law and regulation to this point.

The solution to these problems would begin with the creation of a centralized government organization to oversee accessibility for persons with disabilities—one organization that would be charged with drafting and monitoring accessibility requirements, conducting accessibility research, supporting innovation in accessibility, and enforcing accessibility requirements. Perhaps it could be called the Office of Information and Technology Accessibility or something similar. Such an organization could be located in any of a number of agencies, although being a part of the DOJ would probably be a real source of strength.

By bringing together the drafting, monitoring, and enforcement of requirements, there would be no question of who was minding online accessibility. It would be the clear responsibility of one organization to ensure equal access to the Internet for persons with disabilities. Public and private entities would know where to turn for requirements and who to pay attention to in terms of meeting those requirements. This approach would also remove the responsibility, expense, and effort from people with disabilities of trying to enforce their own civil rights. A responsible organization would serve as the place to receive accessibility complaints and pursue those complaints as the party charged with enforcement. The new organization would have its own testing and research facilities to perform comprehensive evaluations of technologies and websites that are the focus of accessibility complaints. This approach would also remove the role of the courts, preventing limitations of the accessibility requirements by the judiciary.

To accompany the consolidation of online accessibility responsibilities into a single government organization, the existing requirements for accessibility would need to be reconsidered and strengthened. These new requirements would need to be developed with the direct input from people with disabilities and disability rights organizations that represent the spectrum of different disabilities. The starting point for newly conceived regulations would be to focus on the information and communication needs of users with disabilities rather than on specific technologies.

Requirements developed from this perspective would account for the physical, intellectual, and social dimensions of accessibility and the range of needs of people with different kinds of disabilities. While definitions of disability that involve these three dimensions have been previously suggested (e.g., Jaeger and Bowman, 2002, 2005), refocusing the laws to articulate awareness of and protections for these three levels of access is needed. Following on a broader, more inclusive understanding of disability and all of the access needs that are essential components of participation in society in an age of rapid technological change, requirements should explicitly account for the full range of physical and cognitive disabilities and the physical, intellectual, and social access needs that accompany this full range of disabilities. These types of requirements would focus on accessibility and social justice outcomes rather than on technical standards, avoiding the problem of the requirements being far behind the current technologies. The access goals would remain the same as the technologies changed.

The requirements would need to cover both hardware and content. As online social networks and other online interactions are becoming a pillar of interpersonal communication, education, employment, and civic participation, persons with disabilities need to be included in these tools. The move toward a focus on communication and interaction as the primary uses of the Internet requires that social networks and other forms of online communication should also be explicitly accountable under the new requirements. Additionally, the requirements would need to create protections for people with disabilities in terms of certain kinds of content. For example, many online communities for persons with disabilities have protections of the identities of members to prevent others from engaging in discriminatory behaviors based on the online content, but much information about an individual's disability can still be put online by other people and organizations. While in some cases it may be well intentioned, such as a parent of a child with a disability seeking support from other parents, such information could lead to long-term discrimination. These new requirements also need to involve the creation of affirmative rights for persons with disabilities in contexts such as making available online only that information about disabilities that each person with disabilities is comfortable with having revealed.

The most basic change this approach would result in is the firm requirement that technologies be designed to be inherently accessible from the outset, with nothing inaccessible being allowed to reach the market. Mandating that information technologies address the physical, intellectual, and social dimensions of accessibility for individuals with disabilities would mean that to be made available, all technologies related to the Internet would have to be accessible. These requirements would apply both to new versions of existing technologies and to ones that have not yet been developed. The average multiyear gap between an information technology being introduced and an accessible version being made available renders most accessible versions of information technologies so far out-of-date as to be utterly useless. The current "disappointingly low rate of Internet connectivity by those who in many senses most need it, in one of the world's most technologically advanced countries, is evidence that market mechanisms alone are not sufficient for achieving equitable access" (Warschauer, 2003b, p. 29). Clearly, this situation is untenable for the inclusion of persons with disabilities in access to information technologies. New requirements would need to change the overall approach to the development of accessible technologies.

The requirements would not be without clear technical standards, however. The requirements would need to include clear articulations of who will benefit from the requirements and the importance of accessibility to those populations; specific guidance and instructions for website developers and webmasters; monitoring, testing, and compliance-oriented technical assistance programs; and explanations of enforcement mechanisms and clear sanctions for failure to provide accessible technologies. As part of this new set of requirements, the possibility of claiming undue burden would disappear. If an Internet-related technology is to be available to the public, it should be equally available to all members of the public. Meaningful enforcement of the new accessibility requirements needs to be a central consideration for this organization. To ensure that the laws and guidelines are actually complied with, such an agency should be given meaningful monitoring and enforcement powers over both government and corporations.

The development emphasis on portability and miniaturization would also need to be addressed in the requirements. Current trends emphasize the need for the law to require the development of Internet-enabled mobile devices, like smartphones, that are available in multiple versions by size and design to make them usable to many different populations. While many users clearly enjoy the ever-smaller devices, without equivalent larger versions, many persons with disabilities will be excluded from these new Internet-enabled devices. Because these newest versions also usually contain the latest and most efficient software and capabilities, creating equivalent, larger versions would help to ensure that people with disabilities were included in these latest developments. This inclusion can be very important in certain contexts, such as the ability to send and receive emergency information.

The organization would need authority to promote accessibility to help entities deal with the stricter online accessibility requirements. To promote innovation and new designs in accessibility, the organization would need funding to support research. Currently, research spending on disability is woefully inadequate, with only small amounts of grant money available for Internet-related accessibility research. Also, the organization would need to have a set of other inducements at its disposal to promote and reward the focus on Internet accessibility in the public and private sector, such as merit recognitions, seals of approval, and tax credits.

The organization would also support accessibility development by providing best practice guides, developer handbooks, and other instructional materials for including accessibility in the design, development, and implementation processes. In addition, the organization would try to reach managers and developers, as well as the public in general, to provide meaningful education about the social importance of Internet accessibility and the benefits to individual companies and government agencies and to society as a whole. An educational campaign promoting the benefits of accessibility to all users and the overall savings to taxpayers from integrating persons with disabilities more fully into the Internet economy could be very helpful in challenging existing corporate attitudes, government complacency, and societal indifference toward online accessibility.

The changes that could derive from such a government agency with this mandate would likely extend far beyond increased accessibility online. The increased access would create greater opportunities in education, employment, communication, social interaction, entertainment, and civic participation, which could greatly improve the opportunities for and the inclusion of people with disabilities in physical and virtual society. The greater opportunities and inclusion, in turn, would serve to give voice to the small world of people with disabilities, better integrate that small world into the larger information world, and help to change norms, types, values, and behaviors of other worlds in relation to people with disabilities. Ultimately, truly guaranteeing people with disabilities an equal place online could greatly alter the ways in which people with disabilities are perceived, treated, and included in society, in both the physical world and the online world.

The Political Realities of Change

Disability "results, in part, from choices society makes" (Field and Jette, 2008, n.p.). Better efforts to mitigate controllable risks can reduce the impacts of disability, but the failure to address systematic barriers to people with disabilities will result in ever increasing social costs (Field and Jette, 2008; McGinnis, 2003). The current levels of Internet accessibility for persons with disabilities are the direct result of choices made in terms of the levels of accessibility expected and the levels of effort put into enforcement.

The government accessibility organization detailed here presents a radical re-envisioning of the approach to promoting, monitoring, and enforcing Internet accessibility, far more robust than the approach taken anywhere in the world. While such an approach would create accessibility to the Internet and related technologies and content for persons with disabilities, the concept would face enormous opposition from industry, government agencies, and the conservative members of Congress who previously argued that the ADA would destroy the country.

People with disabilities could overcome such opposition, as they have in the past to battle for the major improvements in their civil rights brought about by the implementations of Section 504, IDEA, and the ADA. The enjoyment of the rights secured under those laws—to equal participation in education, employment, civic engagement, and entertainment—now mainly rely on equal access to the Internet. The same Internet for which equal access is the goal could facilitate campaigns to educate members of the public and to coordinate advocacy efforts among people with disabilities and disability rights organizations. And, given that people with disabilities are the largest minority group in the United States, there certainly should be plenty of members of this minority group ready and excited to participate in a campaign to secure this vital civil right.

Traditionally, government has treated disability law as a separate issue from larger civil rights concerns. A majority of the general population does not believe that individuals with disabilities have faced comparable social exclusion to the exclusions previously face by women, racial minorities, religious minorities, and people of certain national origins (Francis and Silvers, 2000). The largest problem in recognizing people with disabilities as a distinct minority may be that other minority groups are extremely hesitant to have people with disabilities seen as part of diversity. "Previously legitimized groups . . . have been reluctant to admit disability into the multicultural arena" (Davis, 2002, p. 36). Even in higher educational contexts, where there is usually greater attention to general inclusiveness, disability is not usually seen as part of diversity (Banard, Stevens, Siwatu, and Lan, 2008; Banks, 2009; Clark and Gorski, 2001; Dona and Edmister, 2001; Izzo, Murray, and Novak, 2008).

In spite of these perceptions, however, disability is a very natural part of diversity. It is, fittingly, "the most diverse of all minority groups" (Mates, 2010, n.p.). Not only is there a great diversity among people with disabilities, who represent every background and walk of life, but as a group, people with disabilities constitute the largest, most inclusive minority group in the United States. To build greater public awareness and understanding of the importance of civil rights in general and equal access online in particular for persons with disabilities, individuals with disabilities could use the capacities of the Internet to present their realities and interests as a means to articulate and advocate for their place within the larger picture of diversity, civil rights, and human rights in society. Advocating for disability as a social aspect of larger diversity concerns has the potential to help connect the importance of equal access online for persons with disabilities to the current understanding of people in other social populations focused on equality.

5

Identity and Advocacy: Possibilities and Impacts

In this chapter, I address issues of identity, representation, and advocacy online. For many individuals with disabilities, identity in society is heavily influenced by exclusions—from work, from school, from social activities. Here I discuss the roles of the Internet in both challenging and reinforcing established roles of identity for persons with disabilities and the issues of identity tied to overcoming or working around exclusions. I also examine the impact of the Internet on identity in light of representations of disability in media that can shape perceptions of disability in wider society and among persons with disabilities themselves. I further discuss the potential for disability rights organizations to positively influence identity and representations of disability through the Internet.

Through direct communication, through the creation of online profiles, and through social media, the Internet offers many opportunities for persons with disabilities to paint a realistic portrait of disability that is often not otherwise available. People with disabilities are able to use the technology to present a picture that humanizes individuals with disabilities and reveals them to have more facets to their personalities than having a disability. Interactions online can even overcome the social distancing that people with disabilities often experience in physical settings. However, these opportunities to convey realistic identities of people with disabilities run counter to the established representations in media and language that have become ensconced in the discourse of the Internet.

The ability to present realistic identities online also feeds directly into the power of the Internet as an organizing tool for persons with disabilities. The roles of Internet communication and interaction are discussed as a means for organizing for change among persons with disabilities and by those close to them. The Internet offers many opportunities for persons with disabilities to connect with those with similar conditions, seek advice and friendship, share experiences, and socialize more freely than they may be able to in other contexts. Similarly, those close to persons with disabilities are able to use the Internet to establish communities to help them to support the people in their lives with disabilities. As a result, the Internet would seem to be well positioned to support the growth of a more robust disability rights movement to campaign for equality online and in the physical world. Such extensive organizing and advocacy have yet to develop, however.

Disability in the Media

When people with disabilities attempt to counter the representations of disability in the media, it is an enormous challenge, given that people with disabilities have long been the subjects of terrible media portrayals. Disability "is shamefully misrepresented in the fun-house mirror of the mass media" (Riley, 2005, p. 1). Many in the United States associate disability with charity campaigns, poster children, and telethons that depict people with disabilities as objects of pity and tragedy (Charlton, 1998). If they somehow manage not to conceive of disability through the lens of a child in a wheelchair being exploited to garner sympathy and thereby donations, the stories and images in magazines, television, movies, and the Internet have primarily been there to reinforce the tragedy and pity narrative or to promote the equally unhelpful image of disability as heroic triumph over adversity. Media portrayals of disability are a stark and incessant reminder that disability is "a condition imposed on individuals by society" (Charlton, 1998, p. 8).

It is a rare person with an obvious disability whose personal interactions with new acquaintances aren't dictated by the expectations of being viewed as a pathetic wretch burdened by the disability, or an amazing overachiever who can serve as an inspiring story. "In order to be disabled, one must narrate one's disability for others in sweeping strokes or hushed private tones. And this narration must inevitably show how we conquer our disabilities or how they conquer us. The lack of other options refuses us the pursuit of anonymity in ordinary involvements" (Mitchell and Snyder, 2003, p. xii). One strange manifestation of this awkward social situation can be seen in many interactions where someone speaks not to a person with a disability but to a companion of the person with a disability, as if the person with a disability was not even there. It is really hard to take people seriously when you continually experience reactions that indicate that others have no expectations for you or that others expect you to be uplifting and serve to remind them how fortunate they are to not have a disability.

In a sense, though, people who have limited exposure to disability really can't be held entirely at fault for these foolish attitudes, considering that they have been exposed to a steady diet of media images that establish these biased parameters for people with disabilities in society. Consider the roles of characters with disabilities in movies and television. Such roles usually do not go to actors with disabilities. The list of successful working actors with disabilities is fairly short, with Oscar winner Marlee Matlin, who has a hearing impairment, and Emmy winner Michael J. Fox, who has Parkinson's disease, being probably the most prominent examples. The fact that real-life wheelchair user Daryl "Chill" Mitchell has starred in two primetime network televisions shows—*Ed* and *Brothers*—as a character who uses a wheelchair is nothing short of astounding. And although disability has appeared more on television in the past decade than in previous times—blindness on *Becker*, wheelchair use on *Joan of Arcadia* and *Glee*, and deafness and multiple sclerosis on *West Wing*, as well as the aforementioned *Ed* and *Brothers*—realistic portrayals of disability are still few and far between in the media. The primary message that media still send about people with disabilities in an economic sense is that they should be viewed as dependent on the charity of others and as an economic drain on their families (Pfeiffer, 2000; Ware, 2002).

Typically, characters with disabilities are played by actors without disabilities, but usually to the benefit of the actors in terms of critical acclaim. Actors portraying characters with disabilities can be seen as playing in "disability drag" (Siebers, 2008, p. 114). For example, the character on *Glee* who uses a wheelchair is played by an actor who does not use a wheelchair off of the set. The Oscars can barely contain their enthusiasm to reward actors without disabilities decked out in this disability drag. In just roughly the past twenty-five years, the following actors have won Academy Awards through pretending to have disabilities or disorders that are frequently perceived as disabilities: Daniel Day Lewis in *My Left Foot*, Dustin Hoffman in *Rain Man*, Al Pacino in *Scent of a Woman*, Tom Hanks in *Forrest Gump* and *Philadelphia*, Jack Nicholson in *As Good as It Gets*, Nicolas Cage in *Leaving Las Vegas*, Geoffrey Rush in *Shine*, Billy Bob Thorton in *Sling Blade*, Russell Crowe in *A Beautiful Mind*, Jamie Foxx in *Ray*, and Colin Firth in *The King's Speech*; Sean Penn was nominated, but did not win, for a portrayal of a person with cognitive disabilities in *I Am Sam*.

And the rewards for dressing up in a maudlin show of faux disability are not limited to the movies. Claire Danes spent much of 2010 and 2011 gathering awards—including Golden Globe, Emmy, and Screen Actors Guild awards—for her depiction of an engineer and inventor with autism in the eponymous HBO movie *Temple Grandin*. In most cases, these portrayals set up the person with the disability in the heroic, triumph-over-adversity mode, either finding happiness and redemption or helping those close to them find happiness and redemption. These portrayals also emphasize difference, with the heroic portrayal turning disability into a type of magical exotica. Ultimately, these portrayals of disability reinforce a narrative that disability is an isolated and sanitized phenomena, best addressed one case at a time, while also serving as an assurance that disability is well removed from the life of the viewer (Longmore, 1997).

Newspapers, magazines, and television news really don't do much better. Most limit their coverage of disability to health issues and the occasional heroic story (Riley, 2005). These heroic stories often focus on a famous person with a disability, such as cancer-surviving cyclist Lance Armstrong; journalist Bob Woodruff, who recovered from a severe brain injury; and late actor/director Christopher Reeve, who was paralyzed from the neck down as the result of a severe spinal cord injury. This type of coverage is paralleled by the huge market for inspiring triumph-over-disability memoirs, which sell extremely well. Whether these stories of inspiration are about a famous person or a regular person, the heroic narrative creates an expectation that people with disabilities need to be inspiring to others. Some people with disabilities refer to this as the expectation of being "an inspiration station."

When discussing disability in print, on TV, or online, news organizations often lapse into using language that is offensive. New stories frequently employ words like *wheelchair-bound, homebound,* and even *handicapped.* And rarely do news organizations use person-first terminology. Language of this sort disempowers people with disabilities and reinforces negative stereotypes about people with disabilities. Imagine the outcry if news organizations began to regularly use derogatory language about people based on gender, skin color, national origin, religion, or sexual orientation. Unfortunately, news organizations are hardly alone in their use of inappropriate language in terms of disability. Many medical terms related to disability—*lame, spastic, retarded, schizophrenic, mental, deaf,* and *blind*—have been turned into commonly used slurs in society (LaCheen, 2000). The language of medical research about disability has been corrupted into "the language of insult and disparagement," serving "to devalue and marginalize specific groups of people" (Christensen, 1996, p. 64).

These representations also remind people with disabilities that society "still generally perceives all disability as a purely internal state" (Goering, 2002, p. 375). The representations avoid acknowledging that disability is actually "an interaction between the individual and the environment" (Field and Jette, 2008, n.p.). Together, the representations and accompanying language work to undermine the sense of people with disabilities that they can have an integrated place in society and, at the same time, serve to reinforce social perceptions of the limited place of and expectations for people with disabilities.

These representations create serious problems for well-meaning people without disabilities, as well. For people who do not have a disability and are not close to someone who does, these images of people with disabilities and the language used to describe disability can seem acceptable, given the frequency with which these terms are used in society. As a result, these representations become self-perpetuating, even among people who want to be more inclusive of individuals with disabilities. People see disability represented and described in certain ways consistently, which makes the representations seem sensible and accurate.

To reach those people who want to treat persons with disabilities as human beings but are not sure how to do so, the Internet would appear to be an ideal tool. The Internet offers a place for individuals with disabilities to craft competing representations and is also a forum in which individuals with disabilities may have a better chance of getting others to acknowledge their existence. It is a space in which the small world of people with disabilities can create many opportunities for the social norms, types, and value of their small world to cross over the boundaries of other worlds, changing the perspectives of people from other small worlds. The

Internet also offers the chance to shape perceptions at the largest social levels, allowing the small world of people with disabilities to broadcast a truer image of itself into the greater information world, influencing the social norms, social types, information value, and information behavior of society at large and across the lifeworld of information in society.

Social Distancing and Disability

The trend of people socially distancing themselves from persons with disabilities has been studied for more than fifty years. Early studies first documented that people who do not have disabilities tend to be socially uncomfortable around people who have disabilities (Goffman, 1963; Kleck, Ono, and Hastorf, 1996; Richardson, 1963). Later studies began to reveal that different disabilities create different levels of social anxiety (Horne, 1985; Horne and Richardo, 1988; Jones, 1974; Tringo, 1970). The general hierarchy is that a disability is less socially awkward if it is perceived to still allow the person with the disability to be socially and economically productive or is a common enough condition that people are likely to know someone with it (Grand, Bernier, and Strohmer, 1982; Harasymiw, Horne, and Lewis, 1976; Schneider and Anderson, 1980; Westbrook, Legge, and Pennay, 1970). These feelings of less awkwardness are not necessarily particularly logical or refined, however; people without disabilities apparently are more likely to feel comfortable around wheelchair users than around persons with many other disabilities, because they surprisingly assume that using a wheelchair is just like sitting down. In short, the presence of disability "frequently short circuits the normal exchange of information and impressions about another person" (Colker and Tucker, 1998, p. 5).

Many people assume that individuals with disabilities live in a constant state of mourning due to limitations imposed by the disability, to the struggle to lead a fulfilling life, or to the inabilitity to contribute meaningfully to society (Mikas, 1988; Swain, French, and Cameron, 2003; Vash and Crewe, 2004). Efforts by people with disabilities to assure others that such assumptions are faulty frequently are not successful (Linton, 1998). Clearly, such pitying serves to distance people with disabilities, but the heroification has the same distancing effect. One writer expressed exasperation at the expectations he faced to "limp bravely into the sunset giving inspiration to all other people" (Pfeiffer, 2000, p. 98). By turning the simple act of successfully living with disability into a superhuman feat, the person with a disability is turned into something other than human again. While being seen as a hero may be better than being seen as an object of pity, most people with disabilities would appreciate being seen as people.

Additionally, much research about disability has served to reinforce the social distancing. Historically, research about disability has frequently approached it as a purely medical problem that leaves an individual in need of assistance, in line with the medical model approach (Barton, 1996; Fine and Asch, 1988; Hahn, 1997; Kitchin, 2000; Stone and Priestley, 1996). Even though disability can be studied in terms of virtually any academic discipline, research about disability is extremely limited in most fields and often serves to reflect and perpetuate negative stereotypes about disability (Turnbull and Stowe, 2001).

Combined, the negative presentations and the social distancing create significant problems for people with disabilities. "The problem of disability lies not only in the impairment of function and its effects on us individually, but also, more importantly, in the area of our relationship with 'normal' people" (Hunt, 1966, p. 146). All of these ways in which disability is represented and distanced undermines the inclination of many people with disabilities to think in terms of fighting for their own civil rights or of even *having* civil rights (Shapiro, 1994).

Consider the struggles of people with disabilities to overcome the language of discrimination. Cutesy terms like *physically challenged, differently abled,* and the unctuous *handi-capable* don't promote social inclusion or positive representations. If anything, they evoke turning people with disabilities into cartoon characters, once again making them socially distanced. Even the terms created by educators to sound more accepting of disability—*special* and *exceptional*—still put the emphasis on difference. Journalist and wheelchair user John Hockenberry may have authored the most accurate term for people with disabilities: "the chronically stared at" (Hockenberry, 1995, p. 79). Other people with disabilities have suggested terms like *the inconvenienced* and *the terminologically awkward*, which work as knowing in-jokes among people with disabilities but are not likely to change social representations or promote inclusion either.

Identity and Representations of Disability Online

Within this context, then, the Internet would seem to be the perfect platform for changing this social situation. People with disabilities can use blogs and Twitter to share the real-life experiences of disability from the perspectives of the people who live them. They can also use YouTube and Flickr to share videos and photos that accurately represent life with a disability. Profiles on Facebook can create a picture of an individual with a disability leading a fully rounded life. LinkedIn can show the professional dimensions of people with disabilities. Through these and other methods, the Internet gives people with disabilities the opportunity to create accurate representations of life with a disability that challenge the established social representations. The range of representations of disability online can be seen through the wide range of perspectives and topics covered by blogs related to disability. Several sites aggregate blogs about disability issues—Disaboom (www.disaboomlive.com/blogs), Disabled World (www.disabled-world.com/disability/blogs), and Ragged Edge (www.raggededgemagazine.com/blogindex.html). BBC News even has a blog about disability in the news, the oddly named Ouch! Blog (www.bbc.co.uk/blogs/ouch).

The Internet also provides the opportunity to challenge the social distancing of disability. People with disabilities can meet and share common interests with people who do not have disabilities in the multitude of spaces where people interact online. If people bond over a shared interest in antique model trains or common experiences as working mothers who are accountants, then the fact that one person in the friendship has a disability may be less significant in the social dynamic. The Internet also provides the opportunity to form a friendship where the disability of one of the friends is not known until that person chooses to reveal it. Once the friendship is established, a negative reaction to the disability is much less likely. In social situations where people interact via avatars, people with disabilities can mitigate negative representations of disability by using an avatar that does not have a disability. Even if the disability is revealed, the visual image of the avatar may help to put the other person at ease.

This halcyon online environment that successfully challenges and changes representations of and social distancing from persons with disabilities has not come to pass, at least not yet. While this potential outcome is still quite viable, several key factors make it difficult for representations online to have a broad social impact. The first problem is the sheer size of the Internet itself. With tens of billions of webpages, hundreds of millions of blogs, and over half a billion users of Facebook, the accurate representations of disability online are very hard to find without specifically looking for them. It seems unlikely that someone who holds negative perceptions about disability will go searching online for profiles that challenge these assumptions. As such, the positive representations of disability online will mostly be seen by people who already hold positive impressions, by people who already know the individuals who have created the content, or by a small number of people who stumble upon the content while searching for something else. Such a situation is not the making of a large social change.

The second problem is the fact that many users of the Internet only search for things that fit their established views rather than explore broadly across the diverse small worlds of the Internet (Jaeger, 2007; Prior, 2007; Sunstein, 2002, 2008). This narrowcasting leads people to read things that they already agree with, shop in stores they are already familiar with, and interact with people they already know, primarily reinforcing their physical world existence online. People tend to stick to the small worlds in which they are already comfortable and encounter the types of information with which they are already familiar. With such information behavior patterns, these people are not likely to encounter representations that challenge the established social representations of disability. The large number of websites, the mass of content, and the range of individual profiles that offer realistic portrayals of disability online cannot change the attitudes of the people who avoid ever seeing them.

A related problem is that much of the content that perpetuates negative representations and encourages social distancing exists online in the same way it does in the physical world. The movie or television show that has a negative portrayal of disability will also have a website from the company producing it, as well as a potentially large number of fan-generated sites, replicating the same negative portrayals. The news content that paints people with disabilities as heroes will provide the same story in print or video form online. The charity presenting people with disabilities as pitiful to raise money will use the same tactics online. A small world's norms and types regarding disability are generally parallel online and offline. In spite of the best efforts of people with disabilities to challenge the established representations of disability, the negative representations from the physical world have all moved online unchanged.

Some of the actions of people with disabilities do not help with challenging established representations, either. As was discussed earlier, many people with disabilities tend to primarily interact and communicate with other people with disabilities online (Anderson and Jonsson, 2005; Bowker and Tuffin, 2002; Seymour and Lupton, 2004). Such interactions have benefits of providing support, shared experiences, and the chance to learn from one another. However, they do not broadcast the real life of individuals with disabilities to people who believe the established representations of disability. By focusing on interacting with people in their own small world rather than widely across the broad range of small worlds online, many individuals with disabilities are bypassing the chance to reshape perspectives about disability in other small worlds or across the lifeworld.

A related problem comes from the opportunities that the Internet provides to be presented as not having a disability. Many people with disabilities are strongly drawn to possibilities of living life— even virtually—without a disability and thereby embrace an online life that avoids disability issues (Anderson and Jonsson, 2005; Bowker and Tuffin, 2002; Seymour and Lupton, 2004). In fact, one of the commonly purported benefits of the Internet for persons with disabilities has been the opportunity to experience life without a disability, such as through an avatar in Second Life, where "passing would be the game" (Riley, 2005, p. 199). While there once again may be individual benefits for people with disabilities, this approach to living online does not offer the opportunity to show realistic portrayals of life with a disability to other small worlds or to the nation's information world.

These issues, which have thus far limited the impact of the Internet in challenging established representations of disability and social distancing from disability, are not necessarily permanent features of the Internet. In order to harness the potential of the Internet to revise and create new representations of disability in society, people with disabilities will need to embrace their disabilities as an integral part of their online identities and broadcast life with disability beyond their own small world to increase the odds of exposing people in other small worlds to these accurate representations of disability identity. The greater the number of realistic portrayals that exist online, the greater the weight for challenging the established social representations in the lifeworld will be, and the harder social distancing online will become. Challenging negative representations also could serve as a rallying point for people with disabilities online to bring them together and create a viable online rights movement. However, the potential for such online organizing by persons with disabilities remains primarily a potential.

Built for the Internet?

Curiously, in light of the numerous barriers to Internet access and usage by people with disabilities, the personality traits that frequently go with having a disability would seem to make people with disabilities built to dominate the Internet. A psychologist who studies the characteristics that are most commonly found in people with disabilities identifies them as being:

- Accepting of difference.
- Accepting of human vulnerability and the need to help others.
- Good at handling uncertainty and unpredictability.
- Able to manage multiple tasks simultaneously.
- Oriented toward future goals and possibilities.
- Attuned to closure in personal communication.
- Able to find humor in difficulty.
- Flexible and creative in situations of limited resources (Gill, 1995).

Each of these characteristics clearly is beneficial in dealing with the chaos and uncertainty that surround a life lived with a disability. However, most of these characteristics are also of great benefit in dealing with the sprawling nature of the Internet.

The ability to multitask successfully is central to the way most people use the Internet, juggling multiple windows and activities at once. Handling uncertainty and being flexible and creative serve one well in exploring new parts of the Internet, trying new technologies and services online, and dealing with the inevitable technical glitches that one encounters online. Finding humor in difficulty is very handy for the last point as well. Skill with closure in communication is helpful in dealing with the myriad ways people communicate online. Being creative with limited resources, being attuned to future goals, and being interested in the needs of others all would indicate skill in developing new online content.

And yet, people with disabilities have not come to be a large enough presence online to even force companies and governments to make websites that are inherently accessible, much less to help guide the development of the Internet or to use the Internet to organize and advocate on a wide scale. A major part of this situation is the much lower levels of access to the Internet that people with disabilities have. Disproportionately fewer people with disabilities are online than the general population, meaning that persons with disabilities are woefully underrepresented online. Because individuals with disabilities are approximately half as likely to be online as everyone else, it is that much harder for them to be noticed.

People with disabilities have also not been able to develop a widely known and visible place online with broad name recognition. The attempts to create a primary place for people with disabilities to express their interests and their goals online—something like a Yahoo-type site for people with disabilities—have been unsuccessful. Even at the height of the dotcom investment mania when investors were throwing money at ideas, such a site could not find sufficient financial supporters (Riley, 2005).

Despite the access, technological, and other barriers, it would seem that people with disabilities should be able to become a stronger presence online. Such presence could be driven by using the technological capacities of the Internet to foster a greater commitment to organization and advocacy for disability rights in both the online environment and the physical world. Many other groups effectively organize and advocate online, so it should be possible for people with disabilities to do the same. But, as seemingly with every other element of disability and the Internet, there are challenges.

Organizing and Advocating for Disability Rights

For individuals with disabilities, true equality "incorporates the premise that all human beings—in spite of their differences—are entitled to be considered and respected as equals and the right to participate in the social and economic life of society" (Rioux, 1994, pp. 85–86). With the barriers to access and participation online, it would seem that the Internet could become a galvanizing topic for people with disabilities as an advocacy issue and as a means to increase advocacy. It can reasonably be stated that the "inaccessibility of the Internet is the most pressing civil rights problem facing people with disabilities today" (Riley, 2005, p. 207). What, then, are the impediments to organization and advocacy? Unfortunately, much of the answer lies within the approaches to organizing that people with disabilities have traditionally taken.

Each kind of disability has different impacts on the life of an individual, and different levels of the same disability can have different impacts as well. The concerns for rights and participation of a person who uses a wheelchair will be very different from those of a person with a hearing impairment. Both will want equal rights as a general principle, but the practical concerns will diverge—one will be focused on issues like curb cuts and ramps, while the other will be more concerned about translations and textual equivalents. Although a person with no vision and a person with low vision will have much closer practical concerns, there will still be different life experiences and impacts of the visual impairment. As such, people with different types of disabilities will have different access goals and issues with accommodation, empowerment, and self-sufficiency in any context, including the Internet.

Overall, these different needs and goals severely limit the ability of people with disabilities to organize and function as a collective group to argue for rights in society (McGuire, 1994). The disability rights landscape is dotted with many different organizations representing the many different kinds of disabilities. In some cases, multiple organizations with differing philosophies represent the same group, such as the ACB and the NFB. These groups logically focus on the issues most central to the lives of the people they represent. While the NFB is not going to argue against curb cuts for people who use wheelchairs, they also are not going to focus on it as a central issue in their organization.

In a 2003 study, Stroman identified eighty-nine major, national disability rights groups in the United States representing many different types of disabilities and many different agendas. In addition, there are many types of disability advocacy organizations at the local, state, and international levels (Charlton, 1998; Stroman, 2003). This large number of organizations leads to the situation where disability rights organizations truly need to better consult with one another and coordinate their efforts to increase their impact (Prince, 2001).

As a result, people with disabilities can be a much more fragmented population than groups unified by a certain gender, race, sexual orientation, national origin, or religion. It is difficult to get all or most people with disabilities to support an issue that affects only certain types of disabilities (McGuire, 1994). In fact, the cases where the collective weight of people with disabilities and their advocacy groups was most in evidence occurred in the passage of comprehensive disability rights legislation that benefited all persons with disabilities. The greatest achievement in organizing and advocacy by persons with disabilities perhaps came in the struggles to implement Section 504 of the Rehabilitation Act and IDEA.

Several years after both of these acts were passed by Congress and signed into law by Presidents Nixon and Ford, respectively, the federal government had made no attempt to implement or enforce them. The lack of effort on behalf of the laws was likely tied to the fact that Nixon tried to veto Section 504 and Ford openly mocked IDEA while signing it into law (Jaeger and Bowman, 2002). A lawsuit led to a court order against the federal government to implement Section 504, with the court wryly noting that the law would not likely implement itself (*Cherry v. Matthews*, 1976).

Nevertheless, the entire Nixon and Ford administrations elapsed without progress on implementing or enforcing the laws, and the first year of the Carter administration was no better (Fleischer and Zames, 2001; Longmore, 2003; Shapiro, 1993). When the Carter administration announced it planned to implement Section 504 by removing virtually all of the requirements and enforcement mechanisms of the law, people with disabilities began to organize a very public and effective series of protests. Government offices were occupied by people with a wide range of disabilities, while wheelchair blockades appeared around government buildings and obstructing the driveway of the secretary of Health, Education, and Welfare (HEW), who was behind the plan to remove the power from the law (Fleischer and Zames, 2001; Shapiro, 1993). The bigotry of the HEW officials was flagrantly displayed during the protests, offering punch and cookies as an incentive to get protestors to leave (Heumann, 1979; Shapiro, 1993).

It was the occupation of the San Francisco office of HEW that drew the greatest public and media attention—sixty people with a range of disabilities occupied the office, only leaving when the order was signed on April 28, 1977, to implement Section 504 as the law had been passed. The secretary of HEW decided that the protestors would not be allowed food, water, or communication but sent in a nurse because he believed that the protestors would not be able to look after themselves (Fleischer and Zames, 2001). Not surprisingly, the protestors quickly gained many prominent supporters, with San

Francisco mayor George Moscone and members of Congress Phillip Burton and George Miller organizing the flow of supplies to the protestors, who received assistance from McDonald's, Safeway markets, the Black Panthers, the California Department of Health, and a number of prominent unions, among others. During a televised congressional hearing during the protest, HEW sent a low-ranking assistant to answer the questions of Burton and Miller (Longmore, 2003). Widespread support for the protestors and the increasingly untenable position of the Carter administration finally forced the implementation of Section 504 and IDEA.

The other big organizing success of the disability rights movement revolved around the much less eventful passage and implementation of the ADA in 1990. Learning from the events surrounding Section 504 and IDEA, the disability community lined up in vocal and active support of the ADA during its consideration by Congress (Fleischer and Zames, 2001). The ADA was opposed by a broad, motley group of organizations, including the US Chamber of Commerce, the National Restaurant Association, the National Federation of Independent Businesses, Greyhound Bus and most other public transportation companies, the *New York Times*, and the *Wall Street Journal*. In reaction to the ADA, one conservative commentator declared that "the disabled lobby is waging war against every other citizen" (Howard, 1994, p. 148). Nevertheless, the law passed overwhelmingly and was immediately signed by President George H. W. Bush, a prominent supporter of the law. A major part of the success of the process of passage and implementation—as well as the overall strength of the law itself—was "the concerted and organized efforts by a range of disability rights and advocacy groups to ensure its success" (Jaeger and Bowman, 2005, p. 41).

If these two periods of activism and organization represent the high-water mark for disability rights, the time since the passage of the ADA has been defined by an erosion of organization and advocacy by disability rights groups. Further, the amount of attention paid to the disability rights movement by the public, media, and politicians has steadily declined since the passage of the ADA (Barnartt and Scotch, 2001; Scotch, 2001). A key part of the dwindling attention has been an increased total number of protests and advocacy efforts that have been staged by people with a specific type of disability rather than larger actions for collective disability rights (Barnartt and Scotch, 2001).

Organizing and Advocating Online

To make a significant, positive impact to improve online accessibility, people with disabilities will need to work together to organize and advocate across types of disability. In the battles to pass and implement key civil rights legislation—Section 504, IDEA, and the ADA—people with all types of disabilities were unified by the fact that the laws addressed threats that all people with disabilities faced equally (McGuire, 1994). Since the passage of the ADA, disability rights groups have placed much more emphasis on the issues that affect individual types of disabilities. People with disabilities have a large number of different political organizations devoted to promoting civil rights—from local issues, like bus access and promoting the recognition of local artists with disabilities, to national organizations lobbying for legislation (Corbett, 1999; Fleischer and Zames, 2001; Stroman, 2003; Zola, 1994). For a substantive change in the accessibility of the Internet, all of these groups will need to begin working closely together for the greater good.

The trouble is that online inaccessibility is not the kind of unifying mutual threat that was addressed by IDEA, Section 504, and the ADA. Online access presents different challenges to different groups of users with disabilities. Some groups of people with disabilities actually benefit enormously from access to a device or website that is utterly inaccessible to another group of people with disabilities. Given the wide range of experiences, a concerted effort to organize and advocate for improved online accessibility will be more difficult.

A Web-enabled mobile device such as a smartphone—a hybrid telephone, Internet device, computer, camera, and media player that offers a tremendous range of very convenient and useful programs for everyday life—presents a perfect example of the divergent impacts of the Internet on different groups of people with disabilities. To an individual with a hearing, speech, or other type of communication impairment or to a person with a cognitive impairment that effects the verbalization of thoughts, a smartphone with a touch screen may prove a wondrous way to facilitate communication, with various ways of messaging and video conferencing to allow users to sign to one another over the smartphone. These same devices—with capacities to display, send, and even verbalize text—also provide enormous benefits in face-to-face communications for people with these types of impairments (Higgins, 2009).

To a user with a visual impairment, a mobility impairment, or one of many cognitive impairments, the same touch screen may be nearly or totally impossible to use (Portner, 2010). If you cannot see the screen, there are limited ways for the mobile device to guide you through the use of a touchscreen. If you have limited motor control, using a touchscreen will not be any easier in a physical sense. And many cognitive impairments will render the design of the interface something far less than intuitive. The assistive software programs that are available for some of the devices are of limited utility and cost more than the mobile devices themselves (Portner, 2010). The existing design tools to increase the accessibility of mobile devices have not been widely used by manufacturers (Burzagli et al., 2007).

Ironically, smartphones and other Web-enabled mobile devices— if they are accessible—have enormous potential to help people with sensory and mobility disabilities navigate. Through a global positioning system (GPS), the location-aware applications on mobile devices can locate the position of a user and display the location in relation to the surrounding area (Farkas, 2010). These augmented reality applications are typically used to find stores, restaurants, and people, but they can also provide people with disabilities a clearer sense of where they are heading, what obstacles may be in the path, and what the best routes are around the obstacles. A further irony is that some see Web-enabled mobile devices, particularly iPads—because of their ease of use and intuitive design for most users—as a great benefit to populations that have lower levels of computer usage (Frommer, 2010). Unfortunately, populations such as people with disabilities will not benefit from ease-of-use and intuitive design if the technology is inherently inaccessible.

While it is terrific that mobile devices have advanced to the point where they can be of enormous use to people with hearing, speech, and other types of communication impairments, the fact that these devices are so beneficial to one part of the population inhibits the likelihood of a cross-disability campaign for equal access to mobile devices or to the Internet in general. However, specific forums and groups have formed online not so much to advocate but to make changes. The problems with the varying levels of access to mobile devices have led to the growth of websites, listservs, and blogs aimed at influencing corporate behavior in the development of mobile devices (Pedlow, Kasnitz, and Shuttleworth, 2010).

An even more active form of engagement can be found in the open source communities—such as Inclusive Android—where people with disabilities are creating their own accessibility patches and accessible software platforms to increase the accessibility of currently inaccessible products (Mankoff, Hayes, and Kasnitz, 2010). Similar do-it-yourself groups have formed to create and publish freely available code and metadata that can be used to create accessible websites without altering the original source code (Blansett, 2008). The Web offers important opportunities for small groups of technology-inclined people with disabilities to begin to address the accessibility barriers that developers, governments, and corporations choose to ignore. These do-it-yourself efforts may ultimately prove to be the most effective means of achieving accessibility online.

The challenges of organizing and advocating for online access are all the more ironic considering that the incessant usage of computers and other technologies hooked to the Internet may actually increase the number of disabilities by exacerbating existing conditions in some people and creating new ones in others. Excessive computer usage has been tied to carpal tunnel syndrome, repetitive stress disorders, vision loss, attention deficit disorder, attention deficit hyperactivity disorder, and even addictive behaviors.

The Internet also offers enormous opportunities to organize for a political cause. A presidential campaign obviously draws more general interest than disability rights issues, yet a great deal can be learned about organizing online and focusing attention on issues from the efforts of the Obama campaign in 2008. Through their creative use of the many, many channels of social media to raise funds, bring awareness to issues, and organize both in physical and virtual spaces, the Obama campaign can inform the efforts of any political cause through their methods (Jaeger, Paquette, and Simmons, 2010).

There are many indications that people with disabilities could have great success with advocating online. Some disability scholars and advocates have been finding uses for the Internet since the dawn of the Web. For example, the first disability research listserv was established in 1995 at the University of Leeds (Barnes, Mercer, and Shakespeare, 1999). Virtually all disability rights groups have an active Web presence with websites and e-mail lists to disseminate positions and findings as well as to organize members. The more technologically advanced organizations have embraced the reach of social media, using Facebook, Twitter, Flickr, YouTube, and other social media and networking outlets to advocate and organize.

These social media outlets are particularly effective for disability rights organizations that focus on all types of disabilities—such as the American Association for People with Disabilities (AAPD) and the National Organization on Disability (NOD)—to encompass people with different disabilities and to engage broader audiences that may otherwise be unaware of disability issues. Research indicates that online communities engaged in civic and political issues are likely to be particularly focused in addressing issues (Cullen and Sommer, 2011). These broad efforts to bring together different types of disability and to emphasize the common goals across types of disability will be essential in efforts to make the Internet an inclusive environment. To be effective going forward, people with disabilities will need to "build coalitions not on the basis of natural identification but on the basis of healthcare needs, information sharing, and support groups" (Siebers, 2008, p. 72).

The creation of online grassroots campaigns—also known as "netroots" campaigns—can facilitate making major statements that harness the size of the population of persons with disabilities. As the largest minority group in the United States, people with disabilities could create a very sizable, coordinated voice on specific issues through online petitions, e-mail campaigns, and other uses of social media and networking to bring attention to issues that affect a large number of Americans. If, in the course of a few weeks, every member of Congress received e-mails from millions of people with disabilities demanding action to improve Internet accessibility, it would likely get their attention.

The Internet also opens the possibility of greater support from nongovernmental organizations (NGOs) in the struggle for equal access online. Certain educational and research organizations—such as the Trace Research and Development Center at the University of Wisconsin—are working to develop technologies and interfaces to make the Internet more accessible to persons with disabilities. More broadly, the issue of equal access online impacts many different populations. Advocacy and research groups interested in access for these diverse populations have greater ability to coordinate their efforts between organizations representing a range of access needs.

People with disabilities collectively could focus on Internet accessibility as the new great civil rights frontier, bringing the power of mass movement to rallying for equal access online. Rather than conceiving of Internet access in terms of the small world of their own particular disability, people with disabilities need to consider the issue as one that affects the small worlds of all disabilities—what can be seen as the information world of people with disabilities.

Comprehensive, sustained online accessibility matters to every person with a disability, given that the types of disabilities benefiting from the current generation of technologies may be badly disadvantaged by the next generation of technologies.

People with disabilities also need to approach online access as a long-term, sustained issue. Because the technology changes so rapidly, the process of advocating for access will be continual until the system of conceiving, developing, and implementing new technologies changes to produce exclusively born-accessible technologies. To permanently change the thinking in corporations and government agencies, people with disabilities need to make a concerted effort to position themselves to change the system from within. One way to help ensure such long-term changes is for more people with disabilities to enter careers in science, technology, and engineering fields with the expressed goal of improving accessibility. Despite the significant barriers that persons with disabilities face in education—particularly in higher education—more people with disabilities working as programmers, Web developers, knowledge managers, industrial designers, and engineers will have enormous impacts on the development of accessible products. Otherwise, advocacy organizations will be trapped in a permanent loop of trying to advance accessibility to catch up with the newest technologies.

As with the ADA, Section 504, and IDEA, people with disabilities need to use their collective voice to call for the concerted enforcement of existing regulations, the clarification of contested areas of current regulations, and the creation of stronger, broader regulations for online accessibility. People with disabilities need to find ways to take this message outside their own small worlds and work until it is successfully conveyed to the broader lifeworld of information. More ambitiously, this same collective voice needs to argue for an entirely new approach to monitoring and enforcing online accessibility. Although a wheelchair blockade is not possible in cyberspace, people with disabilities have plenty of ability to use the Internet to organize and advocate for changes to the laws and policies related to disability and the Internet.

6

Toward an Inclusive Internet

As is hopefully clear by this point, online accessibility is increasingly necessary for involvement in technologically advanced societies. Internet accessibility for persons with disabilities is an issue of social justice, civil rights, and human rights, given that equal access to the Internet is becoming essential for participation in education, employment, entertainment, communication, and civic engagement. It also offers a means for people with disabilities to socially connect in new ways and to interact in ways that remove barriers. To ensure that individuals with disabilities are socially included, the barriers and challenges created by online inaccessibility and the rapid developments of new technologies related to the Internet need to be limited and removed through changes in approaches to disability rights laws, the assessment of existing technologies, and the creation of new technologies.

This final chapter synthesizes the themes from the book and offers a discussion of the ways in which individuals with disabilities, disability rights organizations, policymakers, technology developers, and researchers can all contribute to improving the accessibility of the Internet to promote the inclusion of persons with disabilities in the broad range of worlds online.

Accessibility and the Internet

Over time, advances in technology have helped people with disabilities in communication, education, employment, civic participation, and many other areas while also helping them secure a greater presence in society. As a result of technological advancements, individuals with disabilities are "more familiar and less frightening" now than even not that many years ago (Mairs, 1996, p. 127). Thankfully, people with disabilities in technologically advanced societies do not have to worry about being locked away, burned at the stake, banished, or asexualized as they did in the past. However, all of the gains of previous civil rights laws guaranteeing equal access to education, employment, and so many other aspects of society will have been for naught if all of these types of interactions rely on an inherently inaccessible Internet.

Given the overall prevalence of people with disabilities in society—approximately 54 million out of the 320 million people in the United States—it seems counterintuitive to need to argue for them to even be considered in the development of technologies. When a group includes more than 15 percent of the population of the United States, one would think that it would be attended to without intervention. As the baby boom generation ages, both the percentage of the population with a disability and the total number of people with disabilities will increase substantially. Internet accessibility is a major social problem and one that will grow in social significance as age swells the ranks of people with disabilities.

There is no way to avoid potentially joining this minority group. It is a minority that includes people of all ages, genders, socioeconomic strata, races, religions, national origins, and sexual orientations. For that reason alone, all people should be deeply concerned about ensuring equal online access for individuals with disabilities. Because it is not only a matter of social justice on the national level but also a matter that might affect any individual, it is in the best interest of everyone for the Internet to be fully inclusive. Issues of disability and the Internet matter to everyone.

Promoting Online Accessibility

As befits the fact that online accessibility matters to everyone, there are many opportunities that people have to work to improve and sustain equal access to the Internet. First, people with disabilities can begin to be more vocal and active on an individual level to educate others about the importance of online accessibility. Each person with a disability can actively explain to friends, family, and colleagues about the importance of online accessibility. People with disabilities who are online also can use the platform of cyberspace to broadcast the message of accessibility and to reach out to those who may not be aware of accessibility issues across different small worlds and throughout the larger lifeworld of information. If a site or technology is not accessible, instead of reflexively deciding not to use it, individuals with disabilities can let the government agency or company responsible for that technology know about the problem and how it should be addressed. This may help educate government agencies and companies as well.

Individuals with disabilities can also vote with their wallets if a case of inaccessibility is not corrected. The number of people with disabilities is large, and these people have many friends and family members. If a company is not providing an accessible service and is not correcting the problem, individuals with disabilities can boycott the company and try to convince others to do so as well. That may change the minds of corporations that do not consider people with disabilities an important demographic. In the case of government agencies that refuse to become accessible, there will not likely be the option of boycotting the agency. There will, however, be the option of informing the elected officials who oversee the agency about the problems and let them know that they will lose votes and campaign contributions if the situation is not addressed.

Disability rights organizations can work more closely to promote online accessibility. The same determination and coordination that were brought to the fights for Section 504, IDEA, and the ADA can be brought to the fight for guarantees of equal access online. This will mean a coordinated effort to change the law and to increase attention to enforcement of accessibility by the government. Disability rights organizations also can be a part of broad public campaigns about the importance of online accessibility. They can be centrally engaged in efforts to educate others about the importance of accessibility and in efforts to boycott companies that refuse to mend their inaccessible ways.

Managers and technology developers in both the public and private sectors can drop their self-serving excuses about the difficulty of accessibility. These myths have been disproved, and there is no sane reason to continue making inherently inaccessible products at this point. Not only is inaccessibility unethical and often illegal, but inaccessible products cut out a large part of the potential market for any new technology. If concerns of morality and justice are not persuasive, the sheer drive for market share should be enough incentive to create accessible technologies. An accessible product will promote usage by persons with disabilities and by many other users who will benefit from the clarity and ease of use provided by the accessible design, without negatively affecting—or even being noticeable in— the experiences of current users from other populations. Accessible technologies are readily designable and testable, so the recalcitrant avoidance of accessibility is simply inexplicable.

Chapter 4 outlined in detail the actions that can be taken in the policy arena by politicians and public servants to radically improve online accessibility. Underlying all those changes that would guarantee equal access online is the principle that public servants—both elected officials and career civil servants—have an obligation to ensure that all members of the public have the ability to participate equally in government, in elections, and in civic discourse. "Information is power, and a healthy democracy must guarantee access to this information and power equally for all of its citizens" (Hawthorne, Denge, and Coombs, 1997, n.p.). Failing to adequately promote private sector online accessibility harms all individuals with disabilities, but failing to adequately promote public sector online accessibility not only infringes on the civil rights of individuals with disabilities but also harms democracy itself by curtailing the participation of a large part of the population. Online accessibility is important to nearly one-fifth of the population of this democracy. It is long past time that government officials took it more seriously.

Researchers also can pay greater attention to issues of accessibility. In the worlds of corporate and government research, developers of technologies can commit themselves to iteratively testing for accessibility in a meaningful way through the processes of creation, refinement, and implementation of technologies. The design principles and evaluation methodologies exist and can be implemented in the development of any technology. More corporate and government researchers can also contribute to expanding the body of resources that can be used in creating and testing accessible technologies.

In the academic sector, scholars can pay greater attention to accessibility as a key area of research. Issues of online accessibility can provide important research topics in fields as diverse as information studies, computer science, law, history, public policy, critical studies, sociology, communication, media studies, political science, anthropology, and education, among many others. However, accessibility research is primarily left to small numbers of researchers scattered across these fields, with only a small number of scholarly outlets being interested in publishing such research. Accessibility research also needs to become more inclusive, focusing greater attention on the information and access needs of persons with cognitive disabilities.

Because of their status outside the government and corporate worlds, academics are especially well positioned to provide research that realistically portrays the true levels of accessibility online, the interventions that could improve accessibility, and the best ways in which to achieve increased accessibility. Academic researchers have an important role to play in bringing attention to issues of social injustice and finding new ways to address the injustices. It is time academia made more contributions to addressing this vital social problem.

Even members of the general population can consider finding ways to contribute to the promotion of online accessibility. They can join campaigns to increase awareness of online accessibility issues and participate in boycotts of companies that refuse to provide accessible technologies. An average member of the general public who does not have a disability has a pressing reason to become involved, because "the majority of US residents will experience disabilities or will have a family member who does" (Field and Jette, 2008, n.p.). Given this high likelihood of experiencing disability or having a family member who does, individuals without a disability would be wise to consider themselves only temporarily without a disability. To avoid being on the wrong side of discrimination one day, campaigning for online accessibility now seems like sensible planning for the future.

The Accessible Future

The human urge to create and invent has long been producing assistive technologies. Archaeologists have discovered canes, prostheses, and other mobility devices that date to thousands of years before the Common Era. The desire of persons with disabilities to use technologies to improve integration in society is as old as human society itself. Yet, people with disabilities tend to have ambivalent attitudes toward technology, due primarily to the fact that a single technology can be simultaneously liberating and isolating (Lupton and Seymour, 2000).

A very basic example of this phenomenon is the mobility cane. For a person with a visual impairment, a white cane can make navigating through the world significantly easier by offering important information about everything in and around a walking path. However, the same white cane can also be stigmatizing, as it is a clear symbol to everyone else that the person using the cane has a visual impairment. The cane thus serves simultaneously as a tool to facilitate opportunities for social interaction and as a symbol that reinforces a sense of difference and that short-circuits social interactions.

In most cases, the isolating aspects of the technologies have nothing to do with the technologies themselves or their functions; the isolation is tied directly to the perceptions of others. Most people with visual impairments, for example, find that the social reactions to their walking with a mobility cane and walking with a guide dog are extremely different experiences (Lupton and Seymour, 2000). The cane is often stigmatizing as a foreign instrument, but the guide dog does not carry a stigmatizing value because other people can relate to, and usually are quite fond of, dogs. A guide dog can actually facilitate inclusion, based on the positive connotations of the dog itself.

The Internet, then, stands as perhaps the ultimate collision of the promises and pitfalls of technology for persons with disabilities. With its tumultuous mix of the potential to generate previously impossible levels of inclusion and the realities of massive inequalities of access to technology and content, the Internet is simultaneously an emblem of the promises of inclusion and the pitfalls of exclusion for persons with disabilities. On the one hand, an accessible Internet can facilitate previously difficult or impossible social interactions, create new communities of people with disabilities, broadcast and humanize the experiences of persons with disabilities to others, and open new opportunities for participation and inclusion in education, employment, government, and society at large. On the other hand, an inaccessible Internet creates new barriers to education, employment, government, communication, and society as a whole at a time when it is providing new opportunities to everyone else, causing people with disabilities to become further isolated and disenfranchised as technology speeds away from their reach.

If most technologies are a double-edged sword of inclusion and exclusion to people with disabilities, the Internet hangs precipitously over people with disabilities like the sword of Damocles. While exclusion from most technologies would result in some level of isolation or distancing, a predominantly inaccessible Internet likely means a future with limited access to every aspect of society. In contrast, a predominantly accessible Internet has the potential to produce unprecedented levels of opportunity and inclusion for people with disabilities.

The question of whether the Internet will ultimately be a force primarily of inclusion or of exclusion for persons with disabilities remains to be answered. While such a decision continues to be pending, the gravity of the answer grows exponentially. By interlinking cultures, economies, industries, and communities across the globe in ways that were unimaginable twenty years ago, the Internet is becoming a central element of life in even the poorest, most rural corners of the planet. Farmers in less developed nations can rely on Web-enabled phones to increase the profits from their harvests. I believe that people with disabilities in developed nations should at least be able to have equal access to online education and equal ability to complete online job applications. To be a part of the global economy and the workforce, persons with disabilities need an accessible Internet.

The notion of inclusion as a global issue points to the fact that equal access to Internet-related technology and content truly is a matter of human rights. The right to receive and share information as a civil right and as a human right has been formally recognized in the United States for nearly a half century. In 1969, the United States Supreme Court explicitly stated, "The Constitution protects the right to receive information and ideas" (*Stanley v. Georgia*, 1969, p. 564). Often an unspoken aspect of the freedom of expression, this protected right to receive and to have access to information is essential; without it, many avenues for participation in society would not exist (Jaeger and McClure, 2004; Mart, 2003; McIver, Birdsall, and Rasmussen, 2003). Being a general guarantee in the United States, it clearly applies to persons with disabilities. In recent years, many other nations—either through national law or as signatories to international declarations—have also articulated similar assertions of information access as a civil rights or human rights issue for persons with disabilities.

I have previously detailed accessibility issues and actions that can be taken by governments, industries, Web developers, advocacy groups, employers, and educators to ensure that these rights are actually guaranteed to persons with disabilities in the age of the Internet. Beyond the necessary contributions of these groups, there are also important contributions that can be made in schools through research and education.

Researchers working in areas of computer science, engineering, information science, communication, industrial design, and related areas have the ability to make the most obvious and immediate impacts through research into the creation of new accessible technologies, the conversion of existing inaccessible technologies, and the facilitation of processes to ensure future born-inclusive technologies. These fields can apply their knowledge and creativity to helping governments, industries, Web developers, advocacy groups, employers, and educators develop and implement accessible technologies and content for the Internet.

However, educators and academics in these fields and all other fields can make other significant contributions in the promotion of an accessible and inclusive Internet. Much of the progression toward born-inclusive technologies depends on people beyond those with disabilities understanding the importance of and demanding the use of accessible technologies. At elementary and secondary levels, accessibility and its importance could be a core part of all computer science classes so that an inclusive attitude toward technology is encouraged from a young age.

In higher education, educators and administrators could move beyond the traditional biases against students and faculty with disabilities to create environments that are much more inclusive for people with disabilities and that share the significance of accessibility with all other students. By teaching acceptance of disability, encouraging accessibility research, accepting students and hiring faculty inclusively, making accessibility a part of the curriculum of relevant courses, and using only accessible texts and technologies, colleges and universities can demonstrate to all students the value of accessibility. Not only should universities know better than to use electronic systems that inherently exclude students and faculty with disabilities, but they should also follow the lead of the California State University system and demand accessible technologies from vendors. A positive sign in 2011 for disability awareness in higher education was the announcement of the opening of a Disability Cultural Center at Syracuse University that will coordinate educational, cultural, and social activities related to disability, a first in higher education.

Such emphatic demonstrations will encourage an expectation on the part of all students that the products they use in the future should be accessible to all. Expectations for accessibility from college students will translate into the future leaders of business and government working toward the creation of accessible technologies, workplaces, and community spaces. Future designers and developers of technology will be ready to make born-inclusive technologies. Future educators who are attuned to accessibility will enter elementary and secondary classrooms. All of these attitudinal changes would go a long way to force corporations, schools, and governments to create and use accessible technologies online; if they don't, there will be a much larger demand and outcry than is currently possible.

The field of disability studies has unique responsibilities in engaging issues of disability and the Internet. As noted near the beginning of this book, the vast majority of discourse and research about the intersections of disability and the Internet is being produced by the fields of information studies, computer science, law, communication, education, and universal design. It behooves disability studies to become more directly engaged in these discourses. Currently, the practical orientation of the fields most directly working on the issues of accessibility and the Internet define the parameters of what can be accomplished. Active involvement in the discussions of these issues by the scholars who best understand the sociological, historical, and broader contextual issues of disability would ineluctably result in technologies that better served the needs of and more strongly promoted societal inclusion of persons with disabilities.

The unthinking optimism of the early days of the World Wide Web is long gone. Technology developers still need to be reminded that technologies "should be designed to be readily, equally, and equitably accessible to all users" (Fleischmann, 2010, p. 96). If the future Internet is truly to be accessible for persons with disabilities, a great deal of effort will be required. Large-scale improvements will only come with committed efforts for education, advocacy, organizing, and campaigning for reconceptualizations of the law of online accessibility. As with previous battles for equal rights for people with disabilities, it will be a long process that will require real dedication.

Such dedication is very necessary, however. A lack of equal access on the Internet is not a problem that will decrease in seriousness. As more activities in the areas of communication, interaction, employment, education, and civic participation move primarily and then exclusively online, the impacts of unequal access on persons with disabilities will multiply and mushroom. Inaccessible online education alone could seriously erode the ability of people with disabilities to have a place in society. The virtual world has the potential to revive the physical exclusions of the past with compound interest.

Fortunately, there is no reason to believe that a fully accessible Internet is not achievable. If one stops to consider the miracle and wonder of the commonly used information technologies of 2011, most technologies that we use for communication would be unimaginable in the science fiction of 1991. If the same innovative thinking and dedication is brought to the design of inherently accessible technologies, it seems that online accessibility can be easily accomplished for websites, for computers, for smartphones and mobile devices, and for whatever other Internet-related technologies the future holds. And creating a culture that is accustomed to inherently accessible technologies will create a self-perpetuating expectation for all new products to be inherently accessible when introduced.

Information technology has long helped to integrate and include people with disabilities into society. An accessible Internet has the genuine potential to be the greatest tool of integration and inclusion of people with disabilities. An accessible Internet would mean equal access to communication, interaction, education, employment, entertainment, government, and civic contexts online. When signing the ADA into law in 1991, President George H. W. Bush proclaimed, "Let the shameful wall of exclusion finally come tumbling down." Twenty years on, it is long past time for the virtual walls of exclusion to be torn down as well, and it is in everyone's best interests to help bring these walls down.

Concluding on a Personal Note

In Chapter 1 of this book, I drew into the discussion my personal experiences to help contextualize the parallel changes to technology and disability in society over the past few decades. As such, it seems not unreasonable to return to the first-person perspective to emphasize the central threads of the book. If you, the reader, carry away nothing else from what you have read, please remember that equal access to the Internet for people with disabilities is essentially the quest to be given equal opportunity.

Every goal from the disability rights movement could be described the same basic way: the equal opportunity to get an education, the equal opportunity to have a job, the equal opportunity to ride the bus, and on and on. In this world of the Internet, the issue moves to the equal opportunity to access the Internet and all the educational, employment, social, civic, and other possibilities it offers. It should not be viewed as an issue of the cost or effort to make things accessible, nor should people with disabilities be dismissed as unwelcome in the information society. The need for equal access to the Internet is the most pressing of civil rights issues that people with disabilities now face, and it is the biggest challenge they must overcome.

Not that the previous efforts to achieve equal opportunities have all been resounding successes. Tremendous progress has been made, of course—public schools can no longer refuse to admit students with disabilities, employers can no longer openly refuse to hire a qualified candidate because of disability, and many public places and spaces are equally open to people with disabilities. The throwing off of millennia of oppression will not be easily accomplished in a handful of decades. However, the numbers showing the extremely high levels of unemployment and poverty faced by persons with disabilities, as well as the much lower levels of educational attainment, are a harsh but vital reminder that much more progress is still needed.

It also reminds me, as a person with a disability, how fortunate I have been in the equal opportunities that have been presented to me in education and employment. Thankfully, these have outweighed the opportunities that I have been denied. For most individuals with disabilities, life has probably been heavily shaped by the tensions between the people who saw a person and the people who saw a disability.

When I was born, my parents' careers had primarily been as educators and community organizers, so they were prepared and not the least bit deterred by having a newborn with a disability. My mother quit working to attend to my early education, meaning that my already financially strained family sacrificed a great deal for me. I'll never be able to fully articulate my gratitude to them. I also benefited greatly from the thoughtful elementary and secondary educators who were able to see me as a smart kid rather than a broken one. For every teacher that consigned me to a limited future, there were the teachers who saw potential and gave me opportunities to succeed, from the elementary school principal who had me in both gifted and special education classes, to the principal of the high school I graduated from who pushed me to become a student who was academically ready for graduate school before going to college. My mentor has been my closest collaborator—and a dear friend—for nearly a decade, who somehow unfailingly puts up with the occasional oddities of working with a scholar of little vision. And there have been so many other great friends and colleagues who have refused to relegate me to being interchangeable with my disability.

Yet, the other perspective was always present as well. When I was in law school, one of my professors asked me to stay after class one day. He then offered the sage advice that although I was an excellent student, I should never become a lawyer, as juries would never find in favor of clients who could only afford to hire "a defective." Several years later, while interviewing for faculty positions, one of the full professors at a particular school told me—in front of most of her colleagues—that she would never be in favor of hiring me, both because of my disability and because I studied issues of accessibility. She explained that making things accessible "ruins the experience for real people." Yes, she actually referred to people without disabilities repeatedly as "real people." Her colleagues obviously approved of her comments. Needless to say, I am not a practicing lawyer, nor did I get a job offer from that university.

And new challenges always present themselves. I constantly struggle against the perceptions in much of academia that studying issues of disability is not a worthy research endeavor or that people with disabilities should not be researching the topic of disability. Opportunities gained, opportunities lost. For people with disabilities, the opportunities being sought are of the type that involves the equal chance to succeed in spite of disability. Opportunities that are presented out of pity are as unwelcome as no opportunities being presented at all.

The balance of opportunities and challenges is not unique to people with disabilities, of course. The truth is that everyone relies on opportunities that are provided by others. The star quarterback cannot be a star if no team drafts him. The powerful member of Congress is not powerful if no one votes for her. Any job requires someone else taking a chance on you. Simply put, no one succeeds alone. But in the case of people with disabilities, the opportunities were so lacking for so long, and the discrimination is still so acceptable to so many people, that the need for equal opportunities remains bloody, raw, and pronounced.

Given the ways in which the Internet is reshaping work, education, civic participation, social interaction, and communication, equal access to the Internet is a civil rights issue, it is a human rights issue, it is an employment rights issue, it is an educational rights issue, and it is an issue of justice and fairness. Equal access to the Internet now is as important to people with disabilities as equal access to education and employment were three decades ago. And, in the end, all we are asking for is an opportunity to be an equal part of the Internet age.

References

Abram, S. 2003. "The Americans with Disabilities Act in Higher Education: The Plight of Disabled Faculty." *Journal of Law and Education* 32: 1–20.

Abrar, A., and K. Dingle. 2009. "From Madness to Method: The Americans with Disabilities Act Meets the Internet." *Harvard Civil Rights–Civil Liberties Law Review* 44: 133–157.

Access Board. 2002. *FY 2001 Annual Report.* http://www.access-board.gov/publications/01AnnualRept.txt.

———. 2010a. *Board Releases Draft Refresh of Section 508 Standards and Section 255 Guidelines.* http://www.access-board.gov/news/ict-draft-rule.htm.

———. 2010b. *Americans with Disabilities Act (ADA) Accessibility Guidelines for Buildings and Facilities; Telecommunications Act Accessibility Guidelines; Electronic and Information Technology Accessibility Standards: Advance Notion of Proposed Rulemaking.* http://www.access-board.gov/sec508/refresh/notice.htm.

Access Now, Inc. v. Southwest Airlines Co. Case No. 02-21734-CIV-SEITZ/BANDSTRA U.S.D.C. S.D. FL. (Oct 18, 2002).

Adam, A., and D. Kreps. 2006. "Enabling or Disabling Technologies? A Critical Approach to Web Accessibility." *Information Technology and People* 19: 203–218.

———. 2009. "Disability and Discourses of Web Accessibility." *Information, Communication and Society* 12: 1041–1058.

Albrecht, G. L. 1992. *The Disability Business: Rehabilitation in America.* Newbury Park, CA: Sage.

Albrecht, G. L., and L. M. Verbugge. 2000. "The Global Emergence of Disability." In G. L. Albrecht, R. Fitzpatrick, and S. C. Scrimschaw (eds.), *The Handbook of Social Studies in Health and Medicine.* London: Sage, pp. 293–307.

American Library Association. 2000. *Access to Electronic Information, Services, and Networks*. Chicago: American Library Association.

———. 2001. *Library Services for People with Disabilities Policy*. Chicago: American Library Association.

———. 2009. *The State of America's Libraries*. Chicago: American Library Association. www.ala.org/ala/newspresscenter/mediapresscenter/presskits/2009stateofamericaslibraries/2009statehome.cfm.

———. 2010. *Libraries Connect Communities: Public Library Funding and Technology Access Study 2009–2010*. Chicago: American Library Association. http://www.ala.org/plinternetfunding.

Americans with Disabilities Act. 1990. 42 USC section 12101 et seq.

Anderson, B. 2007. "Social Capital, Quality of Life, and ICTs." In B. Anderson, M. Brynin, J. Gershung, and Y. Raban (eds.), *Information and Communication Technologies in Society: E-Living in a Digital Europe*. London: Routledge, pp. 162–174.

Anderson, J., J. C. Bricout, and M. D. West. 2001. "Telecommuting: Meeting the Needs of Businesses and Employees with Disabilities. *Journal of Vocational Rehabilitation* 16: 97–104.

Anderson, P. 2007. "Peer Assistance for Personal Assistance: Analysis of Online Discussions About Personal Assistance from a Swedish Web Forum for Disabled People." *Disability and Society,* 22: 251–265.

Anderson, P., and B. Jonsson. 2005. "Being There." *Disability and Society* 20: 719–733.

Anderson, R. C. 2007. "Faculty Members with Disabilities in Higher Education." In M. L. Vance (ed.), *Disabled Faculty and Staff in a Disabling Society: Multiple Identities in Higher Education*. New York: Association on Higher Education and Disability, pp. 183–200.

Annam, S. L. Reid, and J. Kaki. 2009. "Gmail Accessibility: A Case Study of Accessibility for AJAX Applications." Presented at the 2009 International Technology and Persons with Disabilities Conference, Boston, MA.

Architectural Barriers Act. 1968. 42 USC section 12101 et seq.

Auld, H., and N. B. Hilyard. 2005. "That All May Read…" *Public Libraries* 44, 2: 69–76.

Baecker, R., K. Booth, S. Jovicic, J. McGrenere, and G. Moore. 2000. "Reducing the Gap Between What Users Know and What They Need to Know." *Proceedings of the 2000 ACM Conference on Universal Usability*, pp. 17–23.

Bagenstos, S. R. 2009. *Law and the Contradictions of the Disability Rights Movement*. New Haven: Yale University Press.

Baker, D. L. 2006. "Autism as Public Policy." In D. Pothier and R. Devlin (eds.), *Critical Disability Theory: Essays in Philosophy, Politics, Policy, and Law*. Vancouver: University of British Columbia Press, pp. 177–194.

Baker, P. M. A. 2001. "Policy Bridges for the Digital Divide: Assessing the Landscape and Gauging the Dimensions." *First Monday* 6: 5. http://www.firstmonday.org.

Baker, P. M. A., and N. W. Moon. 2008. "Wireless Technologies and Accessibility for People with Disabilities: Findings from a Policy Research Instrument." *Assistive Technology* 20: 149–156.

Baker, P. M. A., N. W. Moon, and A. C. Ward. 2006. "Virtual Exclusion and Telework: Barriers and Opportunities of Technocentric Workplace Accommodation Policy." *Work* 27: 4212–4230.

Baker, S. M. 2006. "Consumer Normalcy: Understanding the Value of Shopping Through Narratives of Consumers with Visual Impairments." *Journal of Retailing* 81: 37–50.

Baldridge, D. C., and J. F. Veiga. 2006. "The Impact of Anticipated Social Consequences on Recurring Disability Accommodation Requests." *Journal of Management* 32: 158–179.

Baldwin, M. 1997. "Can the ADA Achieve Its Employment Goals?" *Annals of the American Academy of Political and Social Science* 549: 37–52.

Ballas, J. L. 2005. "Does Your Library's Website Pass the Usability Test?" *Computers in Libraries* 25, 9: 36–39.

Banard, L., T. Stevens, K. O. Siwatu, and W. Lan. 2008. "Diversity Beliefs as a Mediator to Faculty Attitudes Toward Students with Disabilities." *Journal of Diversity in Higher Education* 1: 169–175.

Banks, K. H. 2009. "A Qualitative Investigation of White Students' Perceptions of Diversity." *Journal of Diversity in Higher Education* 2: 149–155.

Barnartt, S., and R. Scotch. 2001. *Disability Protests: Contentious Politics 1970–1999*. Washington, DC: Gallaudet University Press.

Barnes, C., and G. Mercer. 2003. *Disability*. Cambridge, UK: Polity.

Barnes, C., G. Mercer, and T. Shakespeare. 1999. *Exploring Disability: A Sociological Introduction*. Cambridge, UK: Polity.

Barr, S. 2007. "Public Less Satisfied with Government Websites." *Washington Post,* March 21. http://www.washingtonpost.com/wp-dyn/content/article/2007/03/20/AR2007032001338.html.

Barton, L. 1996. "Sociology and Disability: Some Emerging Issues." In L. Barton (ed.), *Disability and Society: Emerging Issues and Insights*. London: Addison Wesley Longman, pp. 3–17.

Bashaw, J. 2008. "Applying the Americans with Disabilities Act to Private Websites After *National Federation of the Blind v. Target*." *Shidler Journal of Law, Commerce, and* Technology 4: 3–25.

Batavia, A. I., and K. Schriner. 2001. "The Americans with Disabilities Act as Engine of Social Change: Models of Disability and the Potential of a Civil Rights Approach." *Policy Studies Journal* 29: 690–702.

Baynton, D. C. 2001. "Disability and the Justification of Inequality in American History." In P. K. Longmore and L. Umansky (eds.), *The New Disability History: American Perspectives*. New York: New York University Press, pp. 33–57.

Bell, L., and T. Peters. 2005. "Digital Library Services for All." *American Libraries* 36, 8: 46–49.

Berkowitz, E. D. 1987. *Disabled Policy: America's Programs for the Handicapped*. Cambridge: Cambridge University Press.

Bertot, J. C. 2003. "The Multiple Dimensions of the Digital Divide: More than Technology 'Haves' and 'Have-nots.'" *Government Information Quarterly* 20: 185–191.

———. 2009. "Public Access Technologies in Public Libraries: Impacts and Implications." *Information Technology and Libraries* 28, 2: 84–95.

Bertot, J. C., and P. T. Jaeger. 2006. "User-Centered E-government: Challenges and Benefits for Government Websites." *Government Information Quarterly* 23, 2: 163–168.

———. 2008. "The E-government Paradox: Better Customer Service Doesn't Necessarily Cost Less." *Government Information Quarterly* 25: 149–154.

Bertot, J. C., P. T. Jaeger, and D. Hansen. Forthcoming. "The Impact of Polices on Government Social Media Usage: Issues, Challenges, and Recommendations." *Government Information Quarterly.*

Bertot, J. C., P. T. Jaeger, L. A. Langa, and C. R. McClure. 2006a. "Drafted: I Want You to Deliver E-government." *Library Journal* 131, 13: 34–39.

———. 2006b. "Public Access Computing and Internet Access in Public Libraries: The Role of Public Libraries in E-government and Emergency Situations." *First Monday* 11, 9. http://www.firstmonday.org/issues /issue11%209/bertot/index.html.

Bertot, J. C., P. T. Jaeger, C. R. McClure, C. B. Wright, and E. Jensen. 2009. "Public Libraries and the Internet 2008–2009: Issues, Implications, and Challenges." *First Monday* 14, 11. http://firstmonday.org/htbin/cgiwrap /bin/ojs/index.php/fm/article/viewArticle/2700/2351.

Bertot, J. C., P. T. Jaeger, J. A. Shuler, S. N. Simmons, and J. M. Grimes. 2009. "Reconciling Government Documents and E-government: Government Information in Policy, Librarianship, and Education." *Government Information Quarterly* 26: 433–436.

Bertot, J. C., C. R. McClure, and P. T. Jaeger. 2008. "The Impacts of Free Public Internet Access on Public Library Patrons and Communities." *Library Quarterly* 78: 285–301.

Bertot, J. C., C. R. McClure, K. M. Thompson, P. T. Jaeger, and L. A. Langa. 2003. *Florida Electronic Library: Pilot Project Functionality Assessment for the Florida Division of Library Services.* Tallahassee: Information Use Management and Policy Institute.

Bertot, J. C., J. T. Snead, P. T. Jaeger, and C. R. McClure. 2006. "Functionality, Usability, and Accessibility: Iterative User-entered Evaluation Strategies for Digital Libraries." *Performance Measurement and Metrics* 7, 1: 17–28.

Bessis, S. 1995. *From Social Exclusion to Social Cohesion: A Policy Agenda.* Paris: UNESCO.

Bias, R. G., and D. J. Mayhew (eds.). 1994. *Cost-justifying Usability.* Boston, MA: Academic Press.

Bigham, J., and A. Cavender. 2009. "Evaluating Existing Audio CAPTCHAs and an Interface Optimized for Non-visual Use." *Proceedings of the ACM Conference on Human Factors in Computing Systems (CHI),* pp. 1829–1838.

Black, R. 2004. "Feature Films: Public Perceptions of Disability." In C. A. Bowman, and P .T. Jaeger (eds.), *A Guide to High School Success for Students with Disabilities*. Westport, CT: Greenwood Press, pp. 36–44.

Blanck, P. D., E. Hill, C. D. Siegal, and M. Waterstone. 2003. *Disability Civil Rights Law and Policy*. St. Paul, MN: Thomson/West.

Blansett, J. 2008. "Digital Discrimination: Ten Years After Section 508, Libraries Still Fall Short of Addressing Disabilities Online." *Library Journal* 133, 13: 26–29.

Board of Trustees of the University of Alabama v. Garrett. 2001. 531 U.S. 356.

Booz Allen Hamilton. 2002. *International E-economy Benchmarking: The World's Most Effective Policies for E-government*. Washington, DC: Booz Allen Hamilton.

Bound, J., and T. Waidmann. 2002. "Accounting for Recent Declines in Employment Rates Among Working-aged Men and Women with Disabilities." *Journal of Human Resources* 37: 231–250.

Bourke, A. B., K. C. Strehorn, and P. Silver. 2000. "Faculty Members' Provision of Instructional Accommodations to Students with LD." *Journal of Learning Disabilities* 33, 1: 26–32.

Bowe, F. G. 1993. "Access to the Information Age: Fundamental Decisions in Telecommunications Policy." *Policy Studies Journal* 21, 4: 765–774.

Bowker, N., and K. Tuffin, K. 2002. "Disability Discourse for Online Identities." *Disability and Society* 17: 327–344.

Bowman, C. A., and P. T. Jaeger. 2007. "Academic Interviews and Persons with Disabilities." In M. L. Vance (ed.), *Disabled Faculty and Staff in a Disabling Society: Multiple Identities in Higher Education*. New York: Association on Higher Education and Disability, pp. 225–234.

Boyd, P., and M. Berejka. 2009. *Consolidated Comments of Microsoft Corporation Before the Department of Commerce, National Telecommunications and Information Administration, Department of Agriculture, Rural Utilities Service, and the Federal Communications Commission in the Matter of American Recovery and Reinvestment Act of 2009 Broadband Initiatives, the Commission's Consultative Role in the Broadband Provisions of the Recovery Act*. Redmond, WA: Microsoft Corporation. http://www.ntia.doc.gov/broadbandgrants /comments/78A.pdf.

Boyle, J. 1996. *Shamans, Software, and Spleens: Law and the Construction of the Information Society*. Cambridge: Harvard University Press.

Bradbard, D. A., C. Peters, and Y. Caneva. 2010. "Web Accessibility Policies at Land-grant Universities." *Internet and Higher Education* 13: 258–266.

Braddock, D. L., and S. L. Parish. 2001. "An Institutional History of Disability." In G. L. Albrecht, K. D. Seelman, and M. Bury (eds.), *Handbook of Disability Studies*. Thousand Oaks, CA: Sage, pp. 11–68.

Bradley, N., and W. Poppen. 2003. "Assistive Technology, Computers and Internet May Decrease Sense of Isolation for Homebound and Disabled Persons." *Technology and Disability* 15: 19–25.

Bragg, L. 1997. "From the Mute God to the Lesser God: Disability in Medieval Celtic and Old Norse Literature." *Disability and Society* 12: 165–177.

Brandt, E., and A. Pope. 1997. *Enabling America: Assessing Disability and Rehabilitation in America.* Washington, DC: National Academy Press.

Branson, J., and D. Miller. 2002. *Damned for Their Difference: The Cultural Construction of Deaf People as Disabled.* Washington, DC: Gallaudet University Press.

Bricout, J. C. 2004. "Using Telework to Enhance Return to Work Outcomes for Individuals with Spinal Cord Injuries." *NeuroRehabilitation* 19: 147–159.

Brown, E. F. 1971. *Library Services to the Disadvantaged.* Metuchen, NJ: Scarecrow Press.

Brown, T. J. 1988. *Dorothea Dix: New England Reformer.* Cambridge: Harvard University Press.

Bruyère, S., W. E. Erickson, and S. Van Looy. 2005. "Information Technology and the Workplace: Implications for Persons with Disabilities." *Disability Studies Quarterly* 25, 2. http://www.dsq-sds.org.

Bryan, W. V. 1996. *In Search of Freedom: How Persons with Disabilities Have Been Disenfranchised from Mainstream Society.* Springfield, IL: Charles C. Thomas.

Bulmer, M. 2003. *Francis Galton: Pioneer in Heredity and Biometry.* Baltimore: Johns Hopkins University Press.

Burgelman, J.-C. 2000. "Regulating Access in the Information Society: The Need for Rethinking Public and Universal Service." *New Media and Society* 2: 51–66.

Burgstahler, S. A. 2002. "Universal Design of Distance Learning." *Information Technology and Disabilities* 8, 1. www.rit.edu/~easi/itd.htm.

———. 2008a. "Universal Design in Higher Education." In S. Burgstahler and R. C. Cory (eds.), *Universal Design in Higher Education: From Principles to Practice.* Cambridge: Harvard Education Press, pp. 1–20.

———. 2008b. "Universal Design of Technological Environments: From Principles to Practice." In S. Burgstahler and R. C. Cory (eds.), *Universal Design in Higher Education: From Principles to Practice.* Cambridge: Harvard Education Press, pp. 213–224.

Burgstahler, S. A., B. Corrigan, and J. McCarter. 2004. "Making Distance Learning Courses Accessible to Students and Instructors with Disabilities." *Internet and Higher Education* 7: 233–246.

Burkhauser, R. V., and M. C. Daly. 1996. "The Potential Impact on the Employment of People with Disabilities." In J. West (ed.), *Implementing the Americans with Disabilities Act.* Cambridge, MA: Blackwell, pp. 153–192.

Burnett, G., and P. T. Jaeger. 2008. "Small Worlds, Lifeworlds, and Information: The Ramifications of the Information Behavior of Social Groups in Public Policy and the Public Sphere." *Information Research* 13, 2, paper 346. http://InformationR.net/ir/13-2/paper346.html.

Burnett, G., P. T. Jaeger, and K. M. Thompson. 2008. "The Social Aspects of Information Access: The Viewpoint of Normative Theory of Information Behavior." *Library and Information Science Research* 30: 56–66.

Burzagli, L., M. Billi, E. Palchetti, T. Catarci, G. Santucci, and E. Bertini. 2007. "Accessibility and Usability Evaluation of MAIS Designer: A New Design Tool for Mobile Devices." *Lecture Notes in Computer Science* 4555: 275–284.

Burzagli, L., F. Gabbanini, F. Natalini, E. Palchetti, and A. Agostini. 2008. "Using Web Content Management Systems for Accessibility: The Experience of a Research Institute Portal." *Lecture Notes in Computer Science* 5105: 454–461.

Byerley, S. L., and M. B. Chambers. 2002. "Web-based Library Databases for Non-visual Users." *Library Hi Tech* 20, 2: 169–178.

Byerley, S. L., M. B. Chambers, and M. Thohira. 2007. "Accessibility of Web-based Library Databases: The Venders' Perspectives in 2007." *Library Hi Tech* 25: 509–527.

Camilleri, J., and A.-M. Callus. 2001. "Out of the Cellars—Disability, Politics and the Struggle for Change: The Maltese Experience." In L. Barton (ed.), *Disability, Politics, and the Struggle for Change*. London: David Fulton, pp. 79–92.

Campbell, F. K. 2009. *Contours of Ableism: The Production of Disability and Abledness*. London: Palgrave.

Carling-Jenkins, R. 2010. "A Way Forward: Presenting a Post-modern Framework for Disability." *Review of Disability Studies* 6, 1: 18–29.

Carlson, S. 2004. "Left Out Online: Electronic Media Should Be a Boon for People with Disabilities, but Few Colleges Embrace the Many New Technologies That Could Help." *Chronicle of Higher Education* 50, 40: A23.

Carlton, J. 2009. "Folks Are Flocking to the Library, a Cozy Place to Look for a Job: Books, Computers and Wi-fi Are Free, but Staffs Are Stressed by Crowds, Cutbacks." *Washington Post*, January 19, p. A1.

Carmein, S. 2004. "MAPS: Creating Socio-technical Environments in Support of Distributed Cognition for People with Cognitive Impairments and Their Caregivers." *Extended Abstract of CHI 2004*, pp. 1051–1052.

Carter, S., A. Hurst, J. Mankoff, and J. Li. 2006. "Dynamically Adapting GUIs to Diverse Input Devices." *Proceedings of the 8th International ACM SIGACCESS Conference on Computers and Accessibility*, pp. 63–70.

Carvin, A., J. Hill, and S. Smothers. 2004. *"E-government for All: Ensuring Equitable Access to Online Government Services*. London: EDC Center for Media and Community and the NYS Forum.

Charlton, J. I. 1998. *Nothing About Us Without Us: Disability Oppression and Empowerment*. Berkeley: University of California Press.

Charmaz, K. 2000. "Experiencing Chronic Illness." In G. L. Albrecht, R. Fitzpatrick, and S. C. Scrimschaw (eds.), *The Handbook of Social Studies in Health and Medicine*. London: Sage, pp. 277–292.

Chen, H. 1990. *Theory-driven Evaluations*. Newbury, CA: Sage.

Chen, Y., and A. Persson. 2002. "Internet Use Among Young and Older Adults: Relation to Psychological Well-being." *Educational Gerontology* 28: 731–744.

Cherry v. Matthews. 1976. 419 F. Supp. 922 (D.D.C. 1976).

Childers, T. L., and C. Kaufman-Scarborough. 2009. "Expanding Opportunities for Online Shoppers with Disabilities." *Journal of Business Research* 62: 572–578.

Christensen, C. 1996. "Disabled, Handicapped, or Disordered: What's in a Name?" In C. Christensen and F. Rizvi (eds.), *Disability and the Dilemma of Education and Justice*. Buckingham: Open University Press, pp. 63–78.

Church, K., C. Frazee, M. Panitch, T. Luciani, and V. Bowman. 2007. *Doing Disability at the Bank: Discovering the Work of Learning/Teaching Done by Disabled Bank Employees*. Toronto: RBC Foundation Institute for Disability Studies.

Clair, J. A., J. E. Beatty, and T. L. Maclean. 2005. "Out of Sight but Not Out of Mind: Managing Invisible Social Identities in the Workplace." *Academy of Management Review* 30: 78–95.

Clark, C., and P. Gorski. 2001. "Multicultural Education and the Digital Divide: Focus on Race, Language, Socioeconomic Class, Sex, and Disability." *Multicultural Perspectives* 3, 3: 39–44.

Clear, F., and C. Dennis. 2009. "E-government, Disability, and Inclusion." In L. Budd and L. Harris (eds.), *E-governance: Managing or Governing?* New York: Routledge, pp. 213–236.

CNN. 2009. "Hard Economic Times: A Boon for Public Libraries." *CNN.com*. http://www.cnn.com/2009/US/02/28/recession.libraries /index.html.

Colella, A. 2001. "Coworker Distributed Fairness: Judgments of the Workplace Accommodation of Employees with Disabilities." *Academy of Management Review* 26: 1001–1016.

Colella, A., R. Paetzold, and M. Belliveau. 2004. "Factors Affecting Coworkers' Procedural Justice Inferences of the Workplace Accommodation of Employees with Disabilities." *Personnel Psychology* 57: 1–23.

Colker, R. 2005. *The Disability Pendulum: The First Decade of the Americans with Disabilities Act*. New York: New York University Press.

Colker, R., and B. P. Tucker. 1998. *The Law of Disability Discrimination*. 2nd ed. Cincinnati: Anderson.

Comeaux, D., and A. Schmetzke. 2007. "Web Accessibility Trends in University Libraries and Library Schools." *Library Hi Tech* 25, 4: 457–477.

Condeluci, A. 1991. *Interdependence: The Route to Community*. 2nd ed. Winter Park, FL: GR Press.

Connell, R. S. 2008. "Survey of Web Developers in Academic Libraries." *Journal of Academic Librarianship* 34, 2: 121–129.

Coonin, B. 2002. "Establishing Accessibility for E-journals: A Suggested Approach. *Library Hi Tech* 20, 2: 207–213.

Corbett, J. 1999. "Disability Arts: Developing Survival Strategies." In P. Reitsh and S. Reiter (eds.), *Adults with Disabilities: Internal Perspectives in the Community*. Mahwah, NJ: Lawrence Erlbaum, pp. 171–181.

Corker, M., and T. Shakespeare. 2002. "Mapping the Terrain." In M. Corker and T. Shakespeare (eds.), *Disability/Postmodernity: Embodying Disability Theory*. New York: Continuum, pp. 1–17.

Cornell University. 2010. *2008 Disability Status Report*. Online Resource for US Disability Statistics. http://www.irl.cornell.edu/edi/disability statistics/index.cfm.

Council of Europe. 2003a. *Access to Social Rights for People with Disabilities in Europe*. Strasbourg: Council of Europe.

———. 2003b. *Legislation to Counter Discrimination Against Persons with Disabilities*. Strasbourg, France: Council of Europe.

Couser, G. T. 2009. *Signifying Bodies: Disability in Contemporary Life Writing*. Ann Arbor: University of Michigan Press.

Crawford, C. 2003. "Cyberplace: Defining a Right to Internet Access Through Public Accommodation Law." *Temple Law Review* 76: 225–280.

Cromby, J., and P. Standon. 1999. "Cyborgs and Stigma: Technology, Disability, Subjectivity." In A. J. Gordo-Lopez and I. Parker (eds.), *Cyberpsychology*. New York: Routledge, pp. 95–112.

Crowder, J. 2006. "Can You Repeat the Question?" *Chronicle of Higher Education*. http://www.chronicle.com.

Cullen, R., and P. Hernon. 2006. "More Citizen Perspectives on E-government." In P. Hernon, R. Cullen, and H. C. Relyea (eds.), *Comparative Perspectives on E-government: Serving Today and Building for Tomorrow*. Lanham, MD: Scarecrow Press, pp. 209–242.

Cullen, R., and L. Sommer. 2011. "Participatory Democracy and the Value of Online Community Networks: An Exploration of Online and Offline Community Networks Engaged in Civil Society and Political Activity." *Government Information Quarterly* 28: 148–154.

Culnan, M. J. 1983. "Environmental Scanning: The Effects of Task Complexity and Source Accessibility on Information Gathering Behavior." *Decision Sciences* 14, 2: 194–206.

Culnan, M. J. 1984. "The Dimensions of Accessibility to Online Information: Implications for Implanting Office Information Systems." *ACM Transactions on Office Information Systems* 2, 2: 141–150.

———. 1985. "The Dimensions of Perceived Accessibility to Information: Implications for the Delivery of Information Systems and Services." *Journal of the American Society for Information Science* 36, 5: 302–308.

Cunningham, C., and N. Coombs. 1997. *Information Access and Adaptive Technology*. Phoenix: Oryx Press.

Curran, K., I. Crawford, and L. O'Hara. 2004. "Catering to Disabled Surfers: A Case Study in Web Site Navigation for Disabled Students." *Technology and Disability* 16: 41–47.

Dalrymple, P. W., and D. L. Zweizig. 1992. "Users' Experiences of Information Retrieval Systems: An Exploration of the Relationship

Between Search Experience and Affective Measures." *Library and Information Science Research* 14: 167–181.

Daniels, M. 1997. *Benedictine Roots in the Development of Deaf Education: Listening with the Heart*. Westport, CT: Bergin and Garvey.

D'Aubin, A. 2007. "Working for Barrier Removal in the ICT Area: Creating a More Accessible and Inclusive Canada." *Information Society* 23: 193–201.

Davis, L. J. 1997. "Constructing Normalcy: The Bell Curve, the Novel, and the Invention of the Disabled Body in the Nineteenth Century." In L. J. Davis (ed.), *The Disability Studies Reader*. New York: Routledge, pp. 9–29.

———. 2000. "Dr. Johnson, Amelia, and the Discourse of Disability in the Eighteenth Century." In H. Duetsch and F. Nussbaum (eds.), *Defects: Engendering the Modern Body*. Ann Arbor: University of Michigan Press, pp. 54–74.

———. 2002. *Bending over Backwards: Disability, Dismodernism, and Other Difficult Positions*. New York: New York University Press.

Dawes, S. S. 2009. "Governance in the Digital Age: A Research and Action Framework for an Uncertain Future." *Government Information Quarterly* 26: 257–264.

DeBell, M., and C. Chapman. 2003. *Computer and Internet Use by Children and Adolescents in 2001*. Washington, DC: National Council for Education Statistics.

DePoy, E., and S. F. Gilson. 2004. *Rethinking Disability: Principles for Professional and Social Change*. Belmont, CA: Wadsworth.

———. 2006. "Universal Web Access: An Intelligent Web Interface." *International Journal of Technology, Knowledge and Society* 1: 128–131.

———. 2008. *The Human Experience: An Explanatory Legitimacy Approach*. Thousand Oaks, CA: Sage.

———. 2009. "Policy Legitimacy: A Model for Disability Policy Analysis and Change." *Review of Disability Studies* 5, 4: 37–48.

Devlin, R., and D. Pothier. 2006. "Introduction: Toward a Critical Theory of Dis-citizenship." In D. Pothier and R. Devlin (eds.), *Critical Disability Theory: Essays in Philosophy, Politics, Policy, and Law*. Vancouver: University of British Columbia Press, pp. 1–22.

Disability Rights Commission (United Kingdom). 2004. *The Web: Access and Inclusion for Disabled People*. London: Stationery Office.

Dispenza, M. L. 2002. "Overcoming the New Digital Divide: Technology Accommodations and the Undue Hardship Defense Under the Americans with Disabilities Act. *Syracuse Law Review* 52: 159–181.

Dobransky, K., and E. Hargittai. 2006. "The Disability Divide in Internet Access and Use." *Information Communication and Society* 9: 313–334.

Dona, J., and J. H. Edmister. 2001. "An Examination of Community College Faculty Members' Knowledge of the Americans with Disabilities Act of 1990 at the Fifteen Community Colleges in Mississippi." *Journal of Postsecondary Education and Disability* 14, 2: 91–103.

Dougherty, W. C. 2010. "Can Digital Resources Truly Be Preserved?" *Journal of Academic Librarianship* 36: 445–448.

Downey, G. J. 2008. *Closed Captioning: Subtitling, Stenography, and*

Digital Convergence of Text with Television. Baltimore: Johns Hopkins University Press.

———. 2010. "Teaching Reading with Television: Constructing Closed Captioning Using Rhetoric of Literacy." In A. R. Nelson, and J. L. Rudolph (eds.), *Education and the Culture of Print in Modern America*. Madison: University of Wisconsin Press, pp. 191–214.

Doyle, A. 2003. "Education Policy." In S. Quin and B. Redmond (eds.), *Disability and Social Policy in Ireland*. Dublin: University College Dublin Press, pp. 10–27.

Doyle, B. 1995. *Disability Discrimination and Equal Opportunities: A Comparative Study of the Employment Rights of Disabled Persons*. London: Mansell.

Draffon, E. A. 2009. "Assistive Technology." In D. Pollack (ed.), *Neurodiversity in Higher Education: Positive Responses to Specific Learning Strategies*. Chichester, UK: Wiley-Blackford, pp. 217–242.

Drehmer, D. E., and J. E. Borieri. 1985. "Hiring Decisions for Disabled Workers: The Hidden Bias." *Rehabilitation Psychology* 30: 157–164.

Dziedzic, D. 1983. "Public Libraries." In F. K. Cykle (ed.), *That All May Read: Library Service for Blind and Physically Handicapped People*. Washington, DC: Library of Congress, pp. 309–326.

Ebbers, W. E., W. J. Pieterson, and H. N. Noordman. 2008. "Electronic Government: Rethinking Channel Management Strategies." *Government Information Quarterly* 25:181–201.

Egan, P. M., and T. A. Guiliano. 2009. "Unaccommodating Attitudes: Perceptions of Students as a Function of Academic Accommodation Use and Test Performance." *North American Journal of Psychology* 11, 3: 487–500.

E-government Act. 2002. P.L. 107–347.

e-Government Unit (United Kingdom). 2005. "eAccessiblity of Public Sector Services in the European Union. London: e-Government Unit. http://www.cabinetoffice.gov.uk/e-government/eaccessiblity.

Ellcessor, E. 2010. "Bridging Disability Divides." *Information, Communication and Society* 13: 289–308.

Ellison, J. 2004. "Assessing the Accessibility of Fifty United States Government Web Pages: Using Bobby to Check on Uncle Sam." *First Monday* 9, 7. http://www.firstmonday.org/issues/issue9_7/ellison /index.html.

Else, S. 2008. "Courts Must Welcome the Reality of the Modern World: Cyberspace Is the Place Under Title III of the Americans with Disabilities Act." *Washington and Lee Law Review* 65: 1121–1158.

Enns, H., and A. H. Neufeldt. 2003. *In Pursuit of Participation: Canada and Disability at Home and Abroad*. Concord, CA: Captus.

Eschenfelder, K. R., J. C. Beachboard, C. R. McClure, and S. K. Wyman. 1997. "Assessing US Federal Government Websites." *Government Information Quarterly* 14: 173–189.

Esrock, S. L., and G. B. Leichty. 1998. "Social Responsibility and Corporate Web Pages: Self-representation or Agenda-setting?" *Public Relations Review* 24: 305–319.

European Union. 1996. *Resolution of the Council and the Representatives of the Governments of the Member States of Inequality of Opportunity for People with Disabilities*. Brussels: European Union (Official Journal 13.01.1997).

Evans, K. 2007. "E-government and Information Technology for the Federal Government." Presented at the Center for Information Policy and Electronic Government, University of Maryland.

Fagan, J. C., and B. Fagan. 2004. "An Accessibility Study of State Legislative Web Sites." *Government Information Quarterly* 21: 65–85.

Fairlie, R. W. 2005. "Are We Really a Nation Online? Ethnic and Racial Disparities in Access to Technology and Their Consequences." Report presented to the Leadership Conference on Civil Rights, Washington, DC.

Farkas, M. 2010. "Your Reality, Augmented." *Library Journal* 41, 9: 24.

Federal Communications Commission. 2010. *The National Broadband Plan: Connecting America*. Washington, DC: Federal Communications Commission. http://www.broadband.gov.

Feinberg, L. E. 2004. "FOIA, Federal Information Policy, and Information Availability in a Post-9/11 World." *Government Information Quarterly* 21: 439–460.

Fenster, M. 2006. "The Opacity of Transparency." *Iowa Law Review* 91: 885–949.

Fenton, R. 2004. "United Kingdom Adoption Agency Web Sites." *First Monday* 9, 2. http://www.firstmonday.org/issues/issue9_2/fenton/index.html.

Field, M. J., and A. M. Jette. 2008. "Dealing with Disability." *Issues in Science and Technology* 24, 2. http://www.issues.org/24.2/field.html.

Fine, M., and A. Asch. 1988. "Disability Beyond Stigma: Social Interaction, Discrimination, and Activism." *Journal of Social Issues* 44, 1: 3–21.

First, P. F., and Y. Y. Hart. 2002. "Access to Cyberspace: The New Issue in Educational Justice." *Journal of Law and Education* 31: 385–411.

Fkiaras, E. 2005. "Liability Under the Americans with Disabilities Act for Private Web Site Operators." *Shindler Journal of Law, Commerce and Technology* 2: 10–24.

Fleischer, D. Z., and F. Zames. 2001. *The Disability Rights Movement: From Charity to Confrontation*. Philadelphia: Temple University Press.

Fleischmann, K. R. 2010. "The Public Library in the Life of the Internet: How the Core Values of Librarianship Can Shape Human-centered Computing." In J. C. Bertot, P. T. Jaeger, and C. R. McClure (eds.), *Public Libraries and the Internet: Roles, Perspectives, and Implications*. Westport, CT: Libraries Unlimited, pp. 91–102.

Fox, S. 2004. *Older Americans and the Internet*. Washington, DC: Pew Internet and American Life Project.

———. 2006. *Online Health Search*. Washington, DC: Pew Internet and American Life Project. http://www.pewinternet.org/pdfs/PIP_Online_Health_2006.pdf.

———. 2011a. *Americans Living with Disability and Their Technology Profile*. Washington, DC: Pew Internet and American Life Project.

———. 2011b. *What People Living with Disability Can Teach Us*. Washington, DC: Pew Internet and American Life Project.

Fox, S., and G. Livingston. 2007. *Latinos Online: Hispanics with Lower Levels of Education and English Proficiency Remain Largely Disconnected from the Internet.* Washington, DC: Pew Internet and American Life Project. http://www.pewinternet.org.

Fox, S., and M. Madden. 2005. *Generations Online.* Washington, DC: Pew Internet and American Life Project. http://www.pewinternet.org/pdfs /PIP_Generations_Memo.pdf.

Francis, L. P., and A. Silvers (eds.). 2000. *Americans with Disabilities: Exploring Implications of the Law for Individuals with Disabilities.* New York: Routledge.

Frank, G. 1998. "Beyond Stigma: Visibility and Self-empowerment of Persons with Congenital Limb Deficiencies." *Journal of Social Issues* 44: 95–115.

French, R. S. 1932. *From Homer to Helen Keller: A Social and Educational Study of the Blind.* New York: American Foundation for the Blind.

Frieden, L. 2003. *When the Americans with Disabilities Act Goes Online: Application of the ADA to the Internet and the World Wide Web.* Washington, DC: National Council on Disability.

Frieden, R. 2003. "Adjusting the Horizontal and Vertical in Telecommunications Regulation: A Comparison of the Traditional and a New Layered Approach." *Federal Communication Law Journal* 55: 207–250.

Fromer, D. 2010. "The iPad Is for Grandparents, Not Just Geeks. *CNN.* http://www.cnn.com.

Fullmer, S., and R. Walls. 1994. "Interests and Participation on Disability-related Computer Bulletin Boards." *Journal of Rehabilitation* 60, 1: 24–30.

Fulton, C. 2011. "Web Accessibility, Libraries, and the Law." *Information Technology and Libraries* 30, 1: 34–43.

Furlong, M. S. 1989a. "Crafting an Electronic Community: The SeniorNet Story." *International Journal of Technology and Aging* 2: 125–134.

Furlong, M. S. 1989b. "An Electronic Community for Older Adults: The SeniorNet Network." *Journal of Communication* 39, 3: 145–153.

Gabel, D. 2007. "Broadband and Universal Service." *Telecommunications Policy* 31, 6/7: 327–346.

Ghai, A. 2001. "Marginalization and Disability: Experiences from the Third World." In M. Priestley (ed.), *Disability and the Life Course: Global Perspectives.* Cambridge: Cambridge University Press, pp. 26–37.

———. 2002. "Disability in the Indian Context: Post-colonial Perspectives." In M. Corker and T. Shakespeare (eds.), *Disability/Postmodernity: Embodying Disability Theory.* New York: Continuum, pp. 88–100.

Gibbons, S., T. A. Peters, and R. Bryan. 2003. *E-book Functionality: What Libraries and Their Patrons Want and Expect from Electronic Books.* Chicago: Library and Information Technology Association.

Gibson, A. N., J. C. Bertot, and C. R. McClure. 2009. "Emerging Role of Public Librarians as E-government Providers." In R. H. Sprague Jr. (ed.), *Proceedings of the 42nd Hawaii International Conference on System Sciences,* pp. 1–10.

Gibson, M. 1977. "Preparing Librarians to Serve Handicapped Individuals." *Journal of Education for Librarianship* 18: 123.

Gill, C. 1995. "A Psychological View of Disability Culture." *Disability Studies Quarterly* 15, 4: 16–19.

Ginsburg, A., and N. Rhett. 2003. "Building a Better Body of Evidence: New Opportunities to Strengthen Evaluation Utilization." *American Journal of Evaluation* 24: 489–498.

Goering, S. 2002. "Beyond the Medical Model? Disability, Formal Justice, and the Exception for the 'Profoundly Impaired.'" *Kennedy Institute of Ethics Journal* 12, 4: 373–388.

Goffman, E. 1963. *Stigma: Notes on the Management of Spoiled Identity.* Englewood Cliffs, NJ: Prentice Hall.

Goggin, G., and C. Newell. 2000. "An End to Disabling Policies? Toward Enlightened Universal Service." *Information Society* 16: 127–133.

———. 2003. *Digital Disability: The Social Construction of Disability in New Media.* Lanham, MD: Rowman and Littlefield.

———. 2007. "The Business of Digital Disability." *Information Society* 23: 159–168.

Golbeck, J. 2008. "Introduction to Computing with Social Trust." In J. Golbeck (ed.), *Computing with Social Trust*. London: Springer, pp. 1–5.

Gordon, D. I., and V. Kundra. 2010. *Memorandum for Chief Acquisitions Officers and Chief Information Officers: Improving the Accessibility of Government Information.* Washington, DC: Office of Management and Budget. http://www.whitehouse.gov.

Gordon, R., and C. J. Heinrich. 2004. "Modeling Trajectories in Social Program Outcomes for Performance Accountability." *American Journal of Evaluation* 25: 161–189.

Grand, S. A., J. E. Bernier, and D. C. Strohmer. 1982. "Attitudes Toward Disabled Persons as a Function of Social Context and Specific Disability." *Rehabilitation Psychology* 27: 165–174.

Grimes, J. M., K. R. Fleischmann, and P. T. Jaeger. 2010. "Research Ethics in Virtual Worlds." In C. Wankel and S. Malleck (eds.), *Emerging Ethical Issues of Life in Virtual Worlds*. Charlotte, NC: Information Age, pp. 73–99.

Grob, G. F. 2003. "A Truly Useful Bat Is One Found in the Hands of a Slugger." *American Journal of Evaluation* 24: 499–505.

Gross, E. F., J. Juvonen, and S. L. Gable. 2002. "Internet Use and Well-being in Adolescence." *Journal of Social Issues* 58, 1: 75–90.

Grubesic, T. H. 2008. "The Spatial Distribution of Broadband Providers in the United States: 1999–2004." *Telecommunications Policy* 32, 3/4: 212–233.

Gulliksen, J., H. Alexson, H. Persson, and B. Goransson. 2010. "Accessibility and Public Policy in Sweden." *Interactions* 17, 3: 26–29.

Guo, B., J. C. Bricout, and J. Huang. 2005. "A Common Open Space or a Digital Divide? A Social Model Perspective on the Online Disability Community in China." *Disability and Society* 20, 1: 49–66.

Gupta, M. P., and D. Jana. 2003. "E-government Evaluation: A Framework and Case Study." *Government Information Quarterly* 20: 365–387.

Gutierrez, C. F., C. Loucopoulos, and R. W. Reinsch. 2005. "Disability-accessibility of Airlines' Web Sites for U.S. Reservations Online." *Journal of Air Transport Management* 11: 239–247.

Hackett, S., and B. Parmanto. 2009. "Homepage Not Enough When Evaluating Website Accessibility." *Internet Research* 19, 1: 78–87.

Hackett, S., B. Parmanto, and X. Zeng. 2004. "Accessibility of Internet Websites Through Time." *Proceedings of the ACM Conference on Assistive Technology (ASSETS)*, pp. 32–39.

Hahn, H. 1997. "New Trends in Disability Studies: Implications for Educational Policy." In D. K. Lipsky and A. Gartner (eds.), *Inclusion and Social Reform: Transforming America's Classrooms*. Baltimore: Paul H. Brooks, pp. 315–328.

———. 2001. "Adjudication or Empowerment: Contrasting Experiences with a Social Model of Disability." In L. Barton (ed.), *Disability, Politics, and the Struggle for Change*. London: David Fulton, pp. 59–78.

Halchin, L. E. 2004. "Electronic Government: Government Capability or Terrorist Resource." *Government Information Quarterly* 21: 406–419.

Hansberger, A. 2001. "Policy and Program Evaluation, Civil Society, and Democracy." *American Journal of Evaluation* 22: 211–228.

Hanson, E. C. 2008. *The Information Revolution and World Politics*. Lanham, MD: Rowman and Littlefield.

Harasymiw, S. J., M. D. Horne, and S. C. Lewis. 1976. "Disability Social Distance Hierarchy for Population Subgroups." *Scandinavian Journal of Rehabilitation Medicine* 8: 33–36.

Harper, K. A, and J. DeWaters. 2008. "A Quest for Website Accessibility in Higher Education Institutions." *Internet and Higher Education* 11: 160–164.

Harris, J. 2010. "The Use, Role and Application of Advanced Technology in the Lives of Disabled People in the UK." *Disability and Society* 25: 427–439.

Hawke, C., and A. Jannarone. 2002. "Emerging Issues of Web Accessibility: Implications for Higher Education." *West's Education Law Reporter* 160, 3: 715–727.

Hawthorne, S., J. Demge, and N. Coombs. 1997. "The Law and Library Access for Persons with Disabilities." *Information Technology and Disabilities* 4, 1. www.rit.edu/~easi/itd.htm.

Hayes, T. L., and T. H. Macan. 1997. "Comparison of the Factors Influencing Interviewer Hiring Decisions for Applicants with and Those Without Disabilities." *Journal of Business and Psychology* 11: 357–371.

Hazard, B. 2008. "Separate but Equal? A Comparison of Content on Library Web Pages and Their Text Versions." *Journal of Web Librarianship* 2, 2/3: 417–428.

Heanue, A. 2001. "In Support of Democracy: The Library Role in Public Access to Government Information." In N. Kranich (ed.), *Libraries and Democracy: The Cornerstones of Liberty*. Chicago: American Library Association, pp. 121–128.

Hearing Aid Compatibility Act. 1988. P.L. 100-394.

Heidegger, M. 1977. "The Question Concerning Technology." In D. Krell (ed.), *Martin Heidegger Basic Writings*. New York: Harper and Row, pp. 284–317.

Henry, G. T. 2003. "Influential Evaluations." *American Journal of Evaluation* 24: 515–524.

Henry, G. T., and M. M. Mark. 2003. "Beyond Use: Understanding Evaluations' Influence on Attitudes and Action." *American Journal of Evaluation* 24: 293–314.

Heres, J., and F. Thomas. 2007. "Civic Participation and ICTs." In B. Anderson, M. Brynin, J. Gershung, and Y. Raban (eds.), *Information and Communication Technologies in Society: E-living in a Digital Europe*. London: Routledge, pp. 175–188.

Hert, C. A. 2001. "User-centered Evaluation and Its Connection to Design." In C. R. McClure and J. C. Bertot, *Evaluating Networked Information Services: Techniques, Policy, and Issues*. Medford, NJ: Information Today, pp. 155–174.

Hesse, B. W. 1995a. "Curb Cuts in the Virtual Community: Telework and Persons with Disabilities." *Institute of Electrical and Electronics Engineers* 36: 418–425.

———. 1995b. "Using Telework to Accommodate the Needs of Employees with Disabilities." *Journal of Organizational Computing and Electronic Commerce* 6: 327–343.

Heumann, J. E. 1979. "Handicap and Disability." In J. P. Hourihan (ed.), *Disability: Our Challenge*. New York: Teachers College Press, pp. 7–32.

Heyer, K. C. 2002. "The ADA on the Road: Disability Rights in Germany." *Law and Social Inquiry* 27: 723–762.

Hibbert, C. 1975. *The House of Medici*. New York: William Morrow.

Higgins, C., Jr. 2009. "Insurers Shun Multitasking Speech Devices." *New York Times*, September 14. www.nytimes.com/2009/09/15/technology/15speech.html.

Higgins, P. C. 1992. *Making Disability: Exploring the Social Transformation of Human Variation*. Springfield, IL: Charles C. Thomas.

Hindes, Y., and J. Mather. 2007. "Inclusive Education at the Postsecondary Level: Attitudes of Students and Professors." *Exceptionality Education Canada* 17, 1: 107–128.

Hinton, C. A. 2003. "The Perceptions of People with Disabilities as to the Effectiveness of the Americans with Disabilities Act." *Journal of Disability Policy Studies* 13: 210–220.

Hockenberry, J. 1995. *Moving Violations: War Zones, Wheelchairs, and Declarations of Independence*. New York: Hyperion.

Hoffman, D. L., and T. P. Novak. 1998. "Bridging the Racial Divide on the Internet." *Science* 280, 5362: 390–391.

Holden, S. H., D. F. Norris, and P. D. Fletcher. 2002. "Electronic Government at the Grassroots." *Proceedings of the 36th Hawaii International Conference on Systems Sciences*.

Holliday, I. 2002. "Building E-government in East and Southeast Asia: Regional Rhetoric and National (In)action." *Public Administration and Development* 22: 323–335.

Holt, C., and W. Holt. 2003. "Training Rewards and Challenges of Serving Library Users with Disabilities." *Library Media Connection* 23, 6: 17–19.

Horne, M. D. 1985. *Attitudes Toward Handicapped Students: Professional, Peer and Parent Reactions.* Hillsdale, NJ: Erlbaum.

Horne, M. D., and J. L. Richardo. 1988. "Hierarchy of Response to Handicaps." *Psychological Reports* 62: 83–86.

Horrigan, J. B. 2004. *How Americans Get in Touch with Government.* Washington, DC: Pew Internet and American Life Project.

———. 2006. *Politics Online.* Washington, DC: Pew Internet and American Life Project.

———. 2008. *Home Broadband Adoption 2008: Adoption Stalls for Low-income Americans Even as Many Broadband Users Opt for Premium Services That Give Them More Speed.* Washington, DC: Pew Internet and American Life Project. http://www.pewinternet.org/~/media//Files/Reports/2008/PIP_Broadband_2008.pdf.

———. 2009. *Obama's Online Opportunities II: If You Build It, Will They Log On?* Washington, DC: Pew Internet and American Life Project. http://www.pewinternet.org/~/media//Files/Reports/2009/PIP_Broadband%20Barriers.pdf.

———. 2010. *Broadband Adoption and Use in America.* Washington, DC: Federal Communications Commission.

Horrigan, J. B., and L. Rainie. 2002. *Counting on the Internet.* Washington, DC: Pew Internet and American Life Project.

Howard, A. 2011. "Pew: Disability or Illness Hinders Many Americans from Using the Internet." http://Gov20.govfresh.com.

Howard, P. K. *The Death of Common Sense: How Law Is Suffocating America.* New York: Warner.

Huang, C. J., and M.-H. Chao. 2001. "Managing WWW in Public Administration: Uses and Misuses." *Government Information Quarterly* 18: 357–373.

Huang, J., and B. Guo. 2005. "Building Social Capital: A Study of the Online Disability Community." *Disability Studies Quarterly* 25, 2. http://www.dsq-sds.org.

Hughes, P., and K. Paterson. 1997. "The Social Model of Disability and the Disappearing Body." *Disability and Society* 12: 325–340.

Hunt, P. 1966. *Stigma: The Experience of Disability.* London: Geoffrey Chapman.

Imrie, R. 1996. *Disability and the City: International Perspectives.* London: Paul Chapman.

Individuals with Disabilities Education Act. 1974. 20 U.S.C.A. section 1400 et seq.

Ingstad, B. 2001. "Disability and the Developing World." In G. L. Albrecht, K. D. Seelman, and M. Bury (eds.), *Handbook of Disability Studies.* Thousand Oaks, CA: Sage, pp. 772–792.

Izzo, M. V., A. Murray, and J. Novak. 2008. "The Faculty Perspective on Universal Design for Learning." *Journal of Postsecondary Education and Disability* 21, 2: 60–72.

Jacko, J. A., and V. L. Hanson. 2002. "Universal Access and Inclusion in Design." *Universal Access in the Information Society* 2: 1–2.

Jackson, T. A. 1999. "Web Page Design: A Study of Three Genres." Master's thesis, University of North Carolina–Chapel Hill.

Jackson-Sanborn, E., K. Odess-Harnish, and N. Warren. 2002. "Web Site Accessibility: A Study of Six Genres." *Library Hi Tech* 20, 3: 308–317.

Jaeger, P. T. 2002. "Section 508 Goes to the Library: Complying with Federal Legal Standards to Produce Accessible Electronic and Information Technology in Libraries." *Information Technology and Disabilities* 8, 2. www.rit.edu/~easi/its.htm.

———. 2003. "The Endless Wire: E-government as Global Phenomenon." *Government Information Quarterly* 20, 4: 323–331.

———. 2004a. "Beyond Section 508: The Spectrum of Legal Requirements for Accessible E-government Websites in the United States." *Journal of Government Information* 30, 4: 518–533.

———. 2004b. "The Social Impact of an Accessible E-democracy: Disability Law in the Development of the E-government." *Journal of Disability Policy Studies* 15, 1: 19–26.

———. 2005. "Deliberative Democracy and the Conceptual Foundations of Electronic Government." *Government Information Quarterly* 22, 4: 702–719.

———. 2006a. "Assessing Section 508 Compliance on Federal E-government Websites: A Multi-method, User-centered Evaluation of Accessibility for Persons with Disabilities." *Government Information Quarterly* 23, 2: 169–190.

———. 2006b. "Telecommunications Policy and Individuals with Disabilities: Issues of Accessibility and Social Inclusion in the Policy and Research Agenda." *Telecommunications Policy* 30, 2: 112–124.

———. 2007. "Information Policy, Information Access, and Democratic Participation: The National and International Implications of the Bush Administration's Information Politics." *Government Information Quarterly* 24: 840–859.

———. 2008. "User-centered Policy Evaluations of Section 508 of the Rehabilitation Act: Evaluating E-government Websites for Accessibility." *Journal of Disability Policy Studies* 19, 1: 24–33.

———. 2009. "Persons with Disabilities and Intergenerational Universal Usability." *Interactions* 16, 3: 66–67.

Jaeger, P. T., and J. C. Bertot. 2010a. "Designing, Implementing, and Evaluating User-centered and Citizen-centered E-government." *International Journal of Electronic Government Research* 6, 2: 1–17.

———. 2010b. "Transparency and Technological Change: Ensuring Equal and Sustained Public Access to Government Information." *Government Information Quarterly* 27: 371–376.

———. 2011. "Responsibility Rolls Down: Public Libraries and the Social and Policy Obligations of Ensuring Access to E-government and Government Information." *Public Library Quarterly* 30: 1–25.

Jaeger, P. T., J. C. Bertot, C. R. McClure, and M. Rodriguez. 2007. "Public Libraries and Internet Access Across the United States: A Comparison by State from 2004 to 2006." *Information Technology and Libraries* 26, 2: 4–14.

Jaeger, P. T., J. C. Bertot, and J. A. Shuler. 2010. "The Federal Depository

Library Program (FDLP), Academic Libraries, and Access to Government Information." *Journal of Academic Librarianship* 36: 469–478.

Jaeger, P. T., and C. A. Bowman. 2002. *Disability Matters: Legal and Pedagogical Issues of Disability in Education.* Westport, CT: Bergin and Garvey/Praeger.

———. 2005. *Understanding Disability: Inclusion, Access, Diversity, and Civil Rights.* Westport, CT: Praeger.

Jaeger, P. T., and G. Burnett. 2010. *Information Worlds: Social Context, Technology, and Information Behavior in the Age of the Internet.* London: Routledge.

Jaeger, P. T., and M. Matteson. 2009. "E-government and Technology Acceptance: The Implementation of Section 508 Guidelines for E-government Websites." *Electronic Journal of E-government* 7, 1: 87–98. http://www.ejeg.com/volume-7/vol7-iss1/v7-i1-art8.htm.

Jaeger, P. T., and C. R. McClure. 2004. "Potential Legal Challenges to the Application of the Children's Internet Protection Act (CIPA) in Public Libraries: Strategies and Issues." *First Monday* 9, 2. http://www .firstmonday.org/issues/issue9_2/jaeger/index.html.

Jaeger, P. T., C. R. McClure, and J. C. Bertot. 2005. "The E-rate Program and Libraries and Library Consortia, 2000–2004: Trends and Issues." *Information Technology and Libraries* 24, 2: 57–67.

Jaeger, P. T., S. Paquette, and S. N. Simmons. 2010. "Information Policy in National Political Campaigns: A Comparison of the 2008 Campaigns for President of the United States and Prime Minister of Canada." *Journal of Information Technology and Politics* 7: 1–16.

Jaeger, P. T., M. Subramaniam, C. B. Jones, and J. C. Bertot. 2011. "Diversity and LIS Education: Inclusion and the Age of Information." *Journal of Education for Library and Information Science* 52: 166–183.

Jaeger, P. T., and K. M. Thompson. 2003. "E-government Around the World: Lessons, Challenges, and New Directions." *Government Information Quarterly* 20, 4: 389–394.

———. 2004. "Social Information Behavior and the Democratic Process: Information Poverty, Normative Behavior, and Electronic Government in the United States." *Library and Information Science Research* 26, 1: 94–107.

Jaeger, P. T., and B. Xie. 2009. "Developing Online Community Accessibility Guidelines for Persons with Disabilities and Older Adults." *Journal of Disability Policy Studies* 20: 55–63.

Johnson, A. D. 2004. "Assistive Technology Changes Lives: Opening a Window to the World." *Diversity Inc* 3, 3: 23–32.

Johnson, C. A. 2010. "Do Public Libraries Contribute to Social Capital? A Preliminary Investigation into the Relationship." *Library and Information Science Research* 32: 147–155.

Johnson, H. M. 2006. *Too Late to Die Young: Nearly True Tales from a Life.* New York: Holt.

Jones, R. L. 1974. "The Hierarchical Structure of Attitudes Toward the Exceptional." *Exceptional Children* 40: 430–436.

Jongbloed, L. 2003. "Disability Policy in Canada." *Journal of Disability Policy Studies* 13: 203–209.

Kanayama, T. 2003a. "Ethnographic Research on the Experience of Japanese Elderly People Online." *New Media and Society* 5, 2: 267–288.

———. 2003b. "Leaving It All Up to Industry: People with Disabilities and the Telecommunications Act of 1996." *Information Society* 19: 185–194.

Karasik, J. 2005. "Steven Jacobs and THE IDEAL Group: Think Globally and Be Patient!" National Center for Technology Innovation. http://www.nationaltechncenter.org.

Keates, S., and P. J. Clarkson. 2003. "Countering Design Exclusion: Bridging the Gap Between Usability and Accessibility." *Universal Access in the Information Society* 2: 215–225.

Kelderman, E. 2010. "Technology Gives Blind Students Better View of Music." *Chronicle of Higher Education.* http://www.chronicle.com.

Keller, J. 2010. "Cal State's Strong Push for Accessible Technology Gets Results." *Chronicle of Higher Education.* http://www.chronicle.com.

Kennard, W. E., and E. E. Lyle. 2001. "With Freedom Comes Responsibility: Ensuring That the Next Generation of Technologies Is Accessible, Usable, and Affordable." *CommLaw Conspectus* 10: 5–22.

Kennaway, J. R., J. R. W. Glauret, and I. Zwitserlood. 2007. "Providing Signed Content on the Internet by Synthesized Animation." *ACM Transactions on Computer-Human Interaction* 14: Article 15.

Kessling, N. D. 2008. "Why the Target 'Nexus Test' Leaves Disabled Americans Disconnected: A Better Approach to Determine Whether Private Commercial Websites Are 'Places of Accommodation.'" *Houston Law Review* 45: 992–1029.

Kiernan, V. 2006. "Sign of the Times." *Chronicle of Higher Education* 52, 36: A37–A38.

King, N., T. H.-Y. Ma, P. Zaphris, H. Petrie, and F. Hamilton. 2004. "An Incremental Usability and Accessibility Evaluation Framework for Digital Libraries." In P. Brophy, S. Fisher, and J. Craven (eds.), *Libraries Without Walls 5: The Distributed Delivery of Library and Information Services.* London: Facet, pp. 123–131.

Kingi, J., and A. Bray. 2000. *Maori Concepts of Disability.* Dunedin, NZ: Donald Bailey Institute.

Kinney, B. 2010. "The Internet, Public Libraries, and the Digital Divide." *Public Library Quarterly* 29, 2: 104–161.

Kitchin, R. 2000. "The Researched Opinions on Research: Disabled People and Disability Research." *Disability and Society* 15: 343–356.

Kleck, R., H. Ono, and A. H. Hastorf. 1996. "The Effects of Physical Deviance on Face-to-Face Interaction." *Human Relations* 19: 425–436.

Klein, D., W. Myhill, L. Hansen, G. Asby, S. Michaelson, and P. Blanck. 2003. "Electronic Doors to Education: Study of High School Website Accessibility in Iowa." *Behavioral Sciences and the Law* 21: 27–49.

Kohrman, M. 2005. *Bodies of Difference: Experiences of Disability and Institutional Advocacy in the Making of Modern China.* Berkeley: University of California Press.

Kruse, D., and T. Hale. 2003. "Disability and Employment: Symposium Introduction." *Industrial Relations* 42: 1–10.

Kruse, D., and L. Schur. 2003. "Employment of People with Disabilities Following the ADA." *Industrial Relations* 42: 31–66.

LaCheen, C. 2000. "Achy Breaky Pelvis, Lumber Lung and Juggler's Despair: The Portrayal of the Americans with Disabilities Act on Television and Radio." *Berkeley Journal of Employment and Labor Law* 21: 223–245.

Lafond, C. L., T. L. Toomey, C. Rothstein, W. Manning, and A. C. Wagenaar. 2000. "Policy Evaluation Research: Measuring the Independent Variables." *Evaluation Review* 24, 1: 92–101.

Lake, R. L. D., and R. Huckfeldt. 1998. "Social Capital, Social Networks, and Political Participation." *Political Psychology* 19: 567–584.

Lang, H. G. 2000. *A Phone of Our Own: The Deaf Insurrection Against Ma Bell*. Washington, DC: Gallaudet University Press.

Lanterman, C. S. 2007. "Universal Design as a Context for Teacher Education Programs." In M. L. Vance (ed.), *Disabled Faculty and Staff in a Disabling Society: Multiple Identities in Higher Education*. New York: Association on Higher Education and Disability, pp. 275–287.

Lathouwers, K., J. de Moor, and R. Didden. 2009. "Access to and Use of Internet by Adolescents Who Have a Physical Disability: A Comparative Study." *Research in Developmental Disabilities* 30: 702–711.

Law, C. M., P. T. Jaeger, and E. McKay. 2010. "The Need for Developer-centered Universal Access Design Resources." *Universal Access in the Information Society* 9: 327–335.

Lazar, J. 2006. *Web Usability: A User-centered Design Approach*. Boston: Addison-Wesley.

———. 2007. "Introduction to Universal Usability." In J. Lazar (ed.), *Universal Usability: Designing Computer Interfaces for Diverse User Populations*. Chichester, UK: John Wiley, pp. 1–12.

Lazar, J., A. Allen, J. Kleinman, and C. Malarkey. 2007. "What Frustrates Screen Reader Users on the Web: A Study of 100 Blind Users." *International Journal of Human-Computer Interaction* 22, 3: 247–269.

Lazar, J., P. Beere, K. Greenidge, and Y. Nagappa. 2003. "Web Accessibility in the Mid-Atlantic United States: A Study of 50 Homepages." *Universal Access in the Information Society* 2: 331–341.

Lazar, J., A. Dudley-Sponaugle, and K. Greenidge. 2004. "Improving Web Accessibility: A Study of Webmaster Perceptions." *Computers in Human Behavior* 20, 2: 269–288.

Lazar, J., J. Feng, and H. Hochheiser. 2010. *Research Methods in Human-Computer Interaction*. Chichester, UK: John Wiley.

Lazar, J., and K. Greenidge. 2006. "One Year Older, but Not Necessarily Wiser: An Evaluation of Homepage Accessibility Problems Over Time." *Universal Access in the Information Society* 4, 4: 285–291.

Lazar, J., and P. T. Jaeger. 2011. "Reducing Barriers to Online Access for People with Disabilities." *Issues in Science and Technology* 17, 2: 68–82.

Lazar, J., P. T. Jaeger, A. Adams, A. Angelozzi, J. Manohar, J. Marciniak, J. Murphy, P. Norasteh, C. Olsen, E. Poneres, T. Scott, N. Vaidya, and J.

Walsh. 2010. "Up in the Air: Are Airlines Following the New DOT Rules on Equal Pricing for People with Disabilities When Websites are Inaccessible?" *Government Information Quarterly* 27: 329–336.

Lazar, J., P. T. Jaeger, and J. C. Bertot. 2010. "Persons with Disabilities and Physical and Virtual Public Library Settings." In J. C. Bertot, P. T. Jaeger, and C. R. McClure (eds.), *Public Libraries and the Internet: Roles, Perspectives, and Implications.* Westport, CT: Libraries Unlimited, pp. 177–189.

Lazar, J., and B. Wentz. 2011. "*This* Isn't *Your* Version: Separate but Equal Web Site Interfaces Are Inherently Unequal for People with Disabilities." *User Experience* 10, 2.

Lee, B. A. 2003. "A Decade of the Americans with Disabilities Act: Judicial Outcomes and Unresolved Problems." *Industrial Relations* 42: 11–30.

Lee, B., and K. Newman. 1995. "Employer Responses to Disability: Preliminary Evidence and a Research Agenda." *Employee Responsibilities and Rights Journal* 8: 209–229

Lenhart, A. 2010. *Cell Phones and American Adults.* Washington, DC: Pew Internet and American Life Project. http://www.pewinternet.org.

Lenhart, A., L. Rainie, S. Fox, J. Horrigan, and T. Spooner. 2000. *Who's Not Online: 57% of Those Without Internet Access Say They Do Not Plan to Log On.* Washington, DC: Pew Internet and American Life Project. http://www.pewinternet.org.

Lessig, L. 2008. *Remix: Making Art and Commerce Thrive in the Hybrid Economy.* New York: Penguin.

Levy, T. 2001. "Legal Obligations and Workplace Implications for Institutions of Higher Education Accommodating Learning Disabled Students." *Journal of Law and Education* 30, 1: 85–121.

Leyser, Y. 1989. "A Survey of Faculty Attitudes and Accommodations for Students with Disabilities." *Journal of Postsecondary Education* 7, 3/4: 97–108.

Light, J. 2001. "Separate but Equal? Reasonable Accommodation in the Information Age." *Journal of the American Planning Association* 67: 263–278.

Lilly, E. B., and C. J. Van Fleet. 2000. "Measuring the Accessibility of Library Homepages." *Reference and User Services Quarterly* 40: 156–165.

Linton, S. 1998. *Claiming Disability: Knowledge and Identity.* New York: New York University Press.

Litvak, S., and A. Enders. 2001. "The Interface Between Individuals and Environments." In G. L. Albrecht, K. D. Seelman, and M. Bury (eds.), *Handbook of Disability Studies.* Thousand Oaks, CA: Sage, pp. 711–733.

Livingston, G. 2010. *The Latino Digital Divide: The Native Born Versus the Foreign Born.* Washington, DC: Pew Internet and American Life Project. http://www.pewinternet.org.

Loader, B. 1998. *Cyberspace Divide: Equality, Agency and Policy in the Information Society.* London: Routledge.

Loges, W. E., and J. Jung. 2001. "Exploring the Digital Divide: Internet Connectedness and Age." *Communication Research* 28, 4: 536–562.

Loiacono, E. T. 2003. "Improving Web Accessibility." *Computer* 36, 1: 117–119.

———. 2004. "Cyberaccess: Web Accessibility and Corporate America." *Communications of the ACM* 47, 12: 82–87.

Loiacono, E. T., and S. McCoy. 2004a. "Charity Begins at the Homepage: Providing Access to the Web for People with Disabilities." *Communications of the Association for Information Systems* 13, article 29.

———. 2004b. "Website Accessibility: An Online Sector Analysis." *Information Technology and People* 17: 87–101.

———. 2006. "Website Accessibility: A Cross-sector Comparison." *Universal Access in the Information Society* 4: 393–399.

Loiacono, E. T., S. McCoy, and W. Chin. 2005. "Federal Web Site Accessibility for People with Disabilities." *IT Professional* 7, 1: 27–31.

Loiacono, E. T., N. C. Romano Jr., and S. McCoy. 2009. "The State of Corporate Website Accessibility." *Communications of the ACM* 52, 8: 128–132.

Longmore, P. K. 1997. "Conspicuous Contribution and American Cultural Dilemmas: Telethon Rituals of Cleansing and Renewal." In D. T. Mitchell and S. L. Snyder (eds.), *The Body and Physical Difference: Discourses on Disability*. Ann Arbor: University of Michigan Press, pp. 134–158.

———. 2003. *Why I Burned My Book and Other Essays on Disability*. Philadelphia: Temple University Press.

Loprest, P., and E. Maag. 2001. *Barriers to and Support for Work Among Adults with Disabilities*. Washington, DC: Urban Institute.

Lovejoy, E. 1983. "History and Standards." In F. K. Cykle (ed.), *That All May Read: Library Service for Blind and Physically Handicapped People*. Washington, DC: Library of Congress, pp. 1–24.

Ludgate, K. 1997. "Telecommuting and the Americans with Disabilities Act: Is Working from Home a Reasonable Accommodation?" *Minnesota Law Review* 81: 1309.

Lupton, D., and W. Seymour. 2000. "Technology, Selfhood, and Physical Disability." *Social Science and Medicine* 50: 1851–1862.

Mabry, L. 2002. "Postmodern Evaluation—or Not?" *American Journal of Evaluation* 23: 141–157.

Mack, E. A., and T. H. Gruibesic. 2009. "Forecasting Broadband Provision." *Information Economics and Policy* 21: 297–311.

MacNeil, C. 2002. "Evaluator as Steward of Citizen Deliberation." *American Journal of Evaluation* 23: 45–54.

Madden, M. 2010. *Older Adults and Social Media*. Washington, DC: Pew Internet and American Life Project. http://www.pewinternet.org.

Mairs, N. 1996. *Waist-high in the World: A Life Among the Nondisabled*. Boston: Beacon Press.

Majeska, M. L. 1988. *Talking Books: Pioneering and Beyond*. Washington, DC: Library of Congress.

Maloney-Krichmar, D., and J. Preece. 2005. "A Multilevel Analysis of Sociability, Usability and Community Dynamics in an Online Health

Community." *Transactions on Human-Computer Interaction* 12, 2: 1–32.

Mandel, L. H., B. W. Bishop, C. R. McClure, J. C. Bertot, and P. T. Jaeger. 2010. "Broadband for Public Libraries: Importance, Issues, and Research Needs." *Government Information Quarterly* 27: 280–291.

Manister, M. R. 2010. "Warning: DOJ on Lookout for Inaccessible Web Pages." *Disability Compliance for Higher Education* 15, 12: 3.

Mankoff, J., H. Fait, and T. Tran. 2005. "Is Your Web Page Accessible? A Comparative Study of Methods for Assessing Web Page Accessibility for the Blind." *Proceedings of the ACM Conference on Human Factors in Computing Systems (CHI)*, pp. 41–50.

Mankoff, J., G. R. Hayes, and D. Kasnitz. 2010. "Disability Studies as a Source of Critical Inquiry for the Field of Assistive Technology." *Proceedings of the 12th International ACM SIGACCESS Conference on Computers and Accessibility*, pp. 1–8.

Mann, W. C., P. Belchior, M. R. Tomita, and B. J. Kemp. 2005. "Computer Use by Middle-aged and Older Adults with Disabilities." *Technology and Disability* 17: 1–9.

Margetts, H. Z. 2009. "The Internet and Public Policy." *Policy and Internet* 1, 1: article 1.

Marincu, C., and B. McMullin. 2004. "A Comparative Analysis of Web Accessibility and Technical Standards Conformance in Four EU States." *First Monday* 9, 7. http://www.firstmonday.org/issues/issue9_7/marincu/index.html.

Marks, D. 1999. "Dimensions of Oppression: Theorising the Embodied Subject." *Disability and Society* 14: 611–626.

Mart, S. N. 2003. "The Right to Receive Information." *Law Library Journal* 95: 175–189.

Maskery, H. 2007. "Crossing the Digital Divide: Possibilities for Influencing the Private-sector Business Case." *Information Society* 23: 187–191.

Mates, B. T. 2010. "Twenty Years of Assistive Technologies." *American Libraries,* September 14. http://www.americanlibraries.org.

McClure, C. R., and P. T. Jaeger. 2008. "Government Information Policy Research: Importance, Approaches, and Realities." *Library and Information Science Research* 30: 257–264.

McClure, C. R., P. T. Jaeger, and J. C. Bertot. 2007. "The Looming Infrastructure Plateau? Space, Funding, Connection Speed, and the Ability of Public Libraries to Meet the Demand for Free Internet Access." *First Monday* 12, 12. http://www.uic.edu/htbin/cgiwrap/bin/ojs/index.php/fm/article/view/2017/1907.

McCreadie, M., and R. E. Rice. 1999. "Trends in Analyzing Access to Information, Part 1: Cross-disciplinary Conceptions of Access." *Information Processing and Management* 35: 45–76.

McGinnis, J. M. 2003. "Toward Improved Quality of Life." *Issues in Science and Technology* 19, 4. http://www.issues.org/19.4/mcginnis.html.

McGrenere, J., J. Sullivan, and R. M. Baecker. 2006. "Designing Technology for People with Cognitive Impairments." *Proceedings of the ACM*

Conference on Human Factors in Computing Systems (CHI), pp. 1635–1638.

McGuire, J. F. 1994. "Organizing from Diversity in the Name of Community: Lessons from the Disability Civil Rights Movement." *Policy Studies Journal* 22: 112–122.

McIver, W. J., W. F. Birdsall, and M. Rasmussen. 2003. "The Internet and the Right to Communicate." *First Monday* 8, 12. http://www.firstmonday.org.

McLawhorn, L. 2001. "Leveling the Accessibility Playing Field: Section 508 of the Rehabilitation Act." *North Carolina Journal of Law and Technology* 3: 63–100.

McNulty, T. 2004. "Libraries, Media Centers, Online Resources, and the Research Process." In C. A. Bowman and P. T. Jaeger (eds.), *A Guide to High School Success for Students with Disabilities*. Westport, CT: Greenwood, pp. 117–131.

Mehra, B., C. Merkel, and A. P. Bishop. 2004. "The Internet for Empowerment of Minority and Marginalized Users." *New Media and Society* 6: 781–802.

Mendle, J. 1995. "Library Services for Persons with Disabilities." *Reference Librarian* 49/50: 105–121.

Metts, R. L. 2000. *Disability Issues, Trends, and Recommendations for the World Bank*. Washington, DC: World Bank.

Michael, S. 2004. "Making Government Accessible—Online." *Federal Computer Week*, April 19, pp. 24–30.

Mikas, E. 1988. "Positive Attitudes Toward Disabled People: Disabled and Nondisabled Persons' Perspectives." *Journal of Social Issues* 44: 49–61.

Milliman, R. E. 2002. "Website Accessibility and the Private Sector: Disability Stakeholders Cannot Tolerate 2% Access!" *Information Technology and Disabilities* 8, 2. http://www.rit.edu/~easi.itd.htm.

Mitchell, D. T., and S. L. Snyder. 1997. "Introduction: Disability Studies and the Double-blind of Representation." In D. T. Mitchell and S. L. Snyder (eds.), *The Body and Physical Difference: Discourses on Disability*. Ann Arbor: University of Michigan Press, pp. 1–31.

———. 2003. *Narrative Prosthesis: Disability and the Dependencies of Discourse*. Ann Arbor: University of Michigan Press.

Mitchell, M. 2008. "Using the Media to Teach Disability Stereotypes." *Review of Disability Studies* 4, 4: 24–32.

Moe, J. 2011. "What Are the Barriers to the Internet for People with Disabilities?" *Marketplace Tech*. http://marketplace.publicradio.org.

Moffat, K., J. McGrenere, B. Purves, and M. Klawe. 2004. "The Participatory Design of a Sound and Image Enhanced Daily Planner for People with Aphasia." *Proceedings of the SIGCHI Conference on Human Factors in Computing Systems*. New York: ACM, pp. 407–414.

Molloy, E., and M. Nario-Richmond. 2007. "College Faculty Perceptions of Learning Disabled Students: Stereotypes, Group Identity, and Bias." In M. L. Vance (ed.), *Disabled Faculty and Staff in a Disabling Society: Multiple Identities in Higher Education*. New York: Association on Higher Education and Disability, pp. 253–268.

Morton, T. G. 1897. *The History of the Pennsylvania Hospital, 1751–1895*. Philadelphia: Times Printing House.

Moser, I. 2006. "Disability and the Promises of Technology: Technology, Subjectivity, and Embodiment Within an Order of the Normal." *Information Communication and Society* 9: 373–395.

Mossberger, K., C. J. Tolbert, and M. Stansbury. 2003. *Virtual Inequality: Beyond the Digital Divide*. Washington, DC: Georgetown University Press.

Mueller, J. P. 2003. *Accessibility for Everybody: Understanding the Section 508 Accessibility Requirements*. New York: Springer-Verlag.

Murray, B., and S. Kenney. 1990. "Teleworking as an Employment Option for People with Disabilities." *International Journal of Rehabilitation Research* 13: 205–214.

Nadler, D. M., and V. M. Furman. 2001. "Access Board Issues Final Standards for Disabled Access Under Section 508 of Rehabilitation Act." *Government Contract Litigation Reporter* 14, 19: 14.

National Council on Disability. 2001. *The Accessible Future*. Washington, DC: National Council on Disability. http://www.ncd.gov.

———. 2009. *National Disability Policy: A Progress Report*. Washington, DC: National Council on Disability. http://www.ncd.gov.

National Federation of the Blind. 2010. "Penn State Discriminates Against Blind Students and Faculty." http://www.nfb.org/nfb/NewsBot.asp ?ID=702&MODE=VIEW.

National Federation of the Blind v. Target. 2006. 452 F. Supp. 2d 946.

Neufeldt, A. H., J. Watzke, G. Birch, and D. Buchner. 2007. "Engaging the Business/Industrial Sector in Accessibility Research: Lessons in Bridge Building." *Information Society* 23: 169–181.

Nicholas, D., I. Rowlands, M. Jubb, and H. R. Jamali. 2010. "The Impact of the Economic Downturn on Libraries: With Special Reference to University Libraries." *Journal of Academic Librarianship* 36: 376–382.

Nieland, R. A., and G. F. Thuronyi. 1994. *Answering the Call: Telephone Pioneer Talking-Book Machine-Repair Program, 1960–1993*. Washington, DC: Library of Congress.

Norden, M. F. 1994. *The Cinema of Isolation: A History of Physical Disability in the Movies*. New Brunswick, NJ: Rutgers University Press.

Norman, K. L., and E. Panizzi. 2006. "Levels of Automation and User Participation in User Testing." *Interacting with Computers* 18: 246–264.

Norris, P. 2001. *Digital Divide: Civic Engagement, Information Poverty, and the Internet Worldwide*. Cambridge: Cambridge University Press.

O'Connell, L. 1991. "Investigators at Work: How Bureaucratic and Legal Constraints Influence the Enforcement of Discrimination Law." *Public Administration Review* 51: 123–130.

Office of Government Services. 2002. *A Usability Analysis of Selected Federal Government Web Sites*. Washington, DC: Arthur Andersen.

Ogden, J. S., and L. Menter. 2009. "Inaccessible School Webpages: Are Remedies Available?" *Journal of Law and Education* 38: 393–408.

Olalere, A. M., and J. Lazar. 2011. "Accessibility of U.S. Federal Government Web Sites: Section 508 Compliance and Site Accessibility Statements." *Government Information Quarterly* 28: 303–309.

Oliver, K. 1997. "The Spirit of the Law: When ADA Compliance Means Overall Excellence in Service to Patrons with Disabilities." *Public Libraries* 36, 5: 294–298.

Oliver, M. 1990. *The Politics of Disablement*. Basingstoke, UK: Macmillan.

Oliver, M., and C. Barnes. 1998. *Disabled People and Social Policy*. London: Longman.

Organisation for Economic Co-operation and Development. 2000. *Understanding the Digital Divide*. http://www.oecd.org.

Ossmann, R., K. Miesenberger, and D. Archambault. 2008. "A Computer Game Designed for All." *Lecture Notes in Computer Science* 5105: 585–592.

Ostroff, E., L. Limont, and D. G. Hunter. 2002. *Building a World Fit for People: Designers with Disabilities at Work*. http://adaptive environments.org/adp/profiles/1_mace.php.

Paetzold, R., M. F. Garcia, A. Colella, L. R. Ren, M. d. C. Triana, and M. Ziebro. 2008. "Perceptions of People with Disabilities: When Is Accommodation Fair?" *Basic and Applied Social Psychology* 30: 27–35.

Parry, M. 2010. "Colleges Lock Out Blind Students Online." *Chronicle of Higher Education*. http://www.chronicle.com.

Pasquinelli, E. 2010. "The Illusion of Reality: Cogntive Aspects and Ethical Drawbacks: The Case of *Second Life*." In C. Wankel and S. Malleck (eds.), *Emerging Ethical Issues of Life in Virtual Worlds*. Charlotte, NC: Information Age, pp. 197–215.

Pedlow, R., D. Kasnitz, and R. Shuttleworth. 2010. "Barriers to the Adoption of Cell Phones for Older People with Impairments in the USA: Results from an Expert Review and Field Study." *Journal of Technology and Disability* 22: 147–158.

Peters, C., and D. A. Bradbard. 2003. "Web Accessibility: An Introduction and Ethical Implications." *Journal of Information, Communication and Ethics in Society* 8: 206–232.

Pfeiffer, D. 2000. "The Disability Paradigm." *Journal of Disability Policy Studies* 11: 98–99.

Pierce, B. 1999. "NFB Sues AOL." National Federation of the Blind. http://nfb.org/legacy/bm/bm99/bm991201.htm.

Pollack, D. 2009. "Introduction." In D. Pollack (ed.), *Neurodiversity in Higher Education: Positive Responses to Specific Learning Strategies*. Chichester, UK: Wiley-Blackford, pp. 1–12.

Poore, C. 2007. *Disability in Twentieth-century German Culture*. Ann Arbor: University of Michigan Press.

Portner, J. 2010. "Smartphones Flunk for Blind Users: Blind Users See Digital Divide in New Generation Phones." *Bay Citizen* (San Francisco, CA), June 22. www.baycitizen.org/technology/story/smartphones-fail-visually-impaired.

Potter, A. 2002. "Accessibility of Alabama Government Web Sites." *Journal of Government Information* 29: 303–317.

Powell, A., A. Byrne, and D. Dailey. 2010. "The Essential Internet: Digital Exclusion in Low-income American Communities." *Policy and Internet* 2, 2, article 7.

Preece, J. 2000. *Online Communities: Designing Usability and Supporting Sociability.* New York: John Wiley.

Premeaux, S. F. 2001. "Impact of Applicant Disability on Selection: The Role of Disability Type, Physical Attractiveness, and Proximity." *Journal of Business and Psychology* 16: 291–298.

Priestley, M. 2001. "Introduction: The Global Context of Disability." In M. Priestley (ed.), *Disability and the Life Course: Global Perspective.* Cambridge: Cambridge University Press, pp. 3–14.

Prince, M. J. 2001. "Tax Policy as Social Policy: Canadian Tax Assistance for People with Disabilities." *Canadian Public Policy* 27: 487–501.

———. 2009. *Absent Citizens: Disability Politics and Policy in Canada.* Toronto: University of Toronto Press.

Prior, M. 2007. *Post-broadcast Democracy: How Media Choice Increases Inequality in Political Involvement and Polarizes Elections.* New York: Cambridge University Press.

Providenti, M., and R. Zai III. 2007a. "Web Accessibility at Academic Libraries: Standards Legislation, and Enforcement. *Library Hi Tech* 25: 494–508.

———. 2007b. "Web Accessibility at Kentucky's Academic Libraries." *Library Hi Tech* 25: 478–493.

Puttee, A. 2002. "Federalism, Democracy and Disability Policy in Canada: An Introduction." In A. Puttee (ed.), *Federalism, Democracy and Disability Policy in Canada.* Montreal: McGill-Queen's University Press, pp. 1–10.

Qualters, S. 2009. "Blind Law Student Sues Law School Admissions Council over Accessibility." *National Law Journal.* http://www.law.com.

Quin, S., and B. Redmond. 2003. "Disability Policy in Ireland." In S. Quin and B. Redmond (eds.), *Disability and Social Policy in Ireland.* Dublin: University College Dublin Press, pp. 1–9.

Quinn, A. C. 2003. "Keeping the Citizenry Informed: Early Congressional Printing and 21st Century Information Policy." *Government Information Quarterly* 20: 281–293.

Quinn, G., and A. Bruce. 2003. "Towards Free and Inclusive Societies for People with Disabilities." In S. Quin and B. Redmond (eds.), *Disability and Social Policy in Ireland.* Dublin: University College Dublin Press, pp. 182–199.

Rainey, M. 2011. "The Digital Divide: The Importance of Gaining Broadband Access for All Americans." *Insight into Diversity* 76, 6: 8–9.

Rainie, L., and J. Anderson. 2008. *The Future of the Internet III: New Media Ecology.* Washington, DC: Pew Internet and American Life Project. http://www.pewinternet.org.

Reddick, C. G. 2005. "Citizen Interaction with E-government: From the Streets to Servers?" *Government Information Quarterly* 22: 338–357.

Rehabilitation Research and Training Center on Disability Demographics and Statistics. 2007. *2006 Disability Status Report.* Ithaca: Cornell University.

Relyea, H. C. 2008. "Federal Government Information Policy and Public Policy Analysis: A Brief Overview." *Library and Information Science Research* 30: 2–21.

Relyea, H. C., and L. E. Halchin. 2003. "Homeland Security and Information Management." In D. Bogart (ed.), *The Bowker Annual: Library and Trade Almanac 2003*. Medford, NJ: Information Today, pp. 231–250.

Rich, R. F., C. T. Erb, and R. A. Rich. 2002. "Critical Legal and Policy Issues for People with Disabilities." *DePaul Journal of Health Care Law* 6: 1–53.

Richardson, S. A. 1963. "Some Social Psychological Consequences of Handicapping." *Pediatrics* 32: 291–297.

Riley, C. A., Jr. 2005. *Disability and the Media: Prescriptions for Change*. Lebanon, NH: University Press of New England.

Rioux, M. H. 1994. "Toward a Concept of the Equality of Well-being: Overcoming the Social and Legal Construction of Inequality." In M. H. Rioux and J. M. Bach (eds.), *Disability Is Not Measles*. North York, ON: Roeher Institute, pp. 67–108.

Rioux, M. H., and M. J. Prince. 2002. "The Canadian Political Landscape of Disability: Policy Perspectives, Social Status, Interest Groups and the Rights Movement." In A. Puttee (ed.), *Federalism, Democracy and Disability Policy in Canada*. Montreal: McGill-Queen's University Press, pp. 11–28.

Ritchie, H., and P. Blanck. 2003. "The Promise of the Internet for Disability: A Study of On-line Services and Web Site Accessibility at Centers for Independent Living." *Behavioral Sciences and the Law* 21: 5–26.

Roberts, N. 2004. "Public Deliberation in an Age of Direct Citizen Participation." *American Review of Public Administration* 34: 315–353.

Rosen, G. 1968. *Madness in Society: Chapters in the Historical Sociology of Mental Illness*. Chicago: University of Chicago Press.

Rothman, W. 2011. "For the Disabled, Just Getting Online Is a Struggle." *MSNBC*, January 21. http://www.msnbc.com.

Roulstone, A. 1998. *Enabling Technology: Disabled People, Work and New Technology*. Buckingham, UK: Open University Press.

Rubaii-Barrett, N., and L. Wise. 2008. "Disability Access and E-government: An Empirical Analysis of State Practices." *Journal of Disability Policy Studies* 19: 52–64.

Russell, C. 2003. "Access to Technology for the Disabled: The Forgotten Legacy of Innovation." *Information and Communications Technology Law* 12: 237–246.

Sadon, R. 2010. "E-textbooks Starting to Turn a Page." *MSNBC*, August 23. http://www.msnbc.com.

Sanders, J. R. 2001. "A Vision for Evaluation." *American Journal of Evaluation* 22: 363–366.

Sauer, G., J. Holman, J. Lazar, H. Hochheiser, and J. Feng. 2010. "Accessible Privacy and Security: A Universally Usable Human-interaction Proof." *Universal Access in the Information Society* 9: 239–248.

Schartz, K., H. A. Schartz, and P. Blanck. 2002. "Employment for Persons with Disabilities in Information Technology Jobs: Literature Review for 'IT Works.'" *Behavioral Sciences and the Law* 20: 637–657.

Scheer, J., and N. Groce. 1998. "Impairment as Human Constant: Cross-cultural and Historical Perspectives on Variation." *Journal of Social Issues* 44, 1: 23–37.

Schmetzke, A. 2002. "Accessibility of Web-based Information Resources for People with Disabilities. *Library Hi Tech* 20, 2: 135–136.

———. 2003. "Web Accessibility at University Libraries and Library Schools: 2002 Follow-up Study." In M. Hricko (ed.), *Design and Implementation of Web-enabled Teaching Tools*. Hershey, PA: Idea Group, pp. 145–189.

———. 2005. "Access to Online Library Resources for All: Role of Policy and Policy Change." *Interface* 27, 4: 4–11.

———. 2007a. "Introduction: Accessibility of Electronic Information Resources for All." *Library Hi Tech* 25: 454–456.

———. 2007b. "Leadership at the American Library Association and Accessibility: A Critical View." *Library Hi Tech* 25: 528–537.

Schneider, C. R., and W. Anderson. 1980. "Attitudes Toward the Stigmatized: Some Insights into Recent Research." *Rehabilitation Counseling Bulletin* 23: 299–313.

Schudson, M. 1997. "Why Conversation Is Not the Soul of Democracy." *Critical Studies in Mass Communication* 14: 297–309.

Schur, L. A. 2003a. "Barriers or Opportunities? The Causes of Contingent and Part-time Work Among People with Disabilities." *Industrial Relations* 42: 589–622.

———. 2003b. "Contending with the 'Double-handicap': Political Activism Among Women with Disabilities." *Women and Politics* 25: 31–62.

Scotch, R. K. 2001. *From Goodwill to Civil Rights: Transforming Federal Disability Policy*. Philadelphia: Temple University Press.

Scotch, R. K., and K. Shriner. 1997. "Disability as Human Variation: Implications for Policy." *Annals of the American Academy of Political and Social Science* 549: 148–159.

Sears, A., V. L. Hanson, and B. Myers. 2007. "Introduction to Special Issue on Computers and Accessibility." *ACM Transactions on Computer-Human Interaction* 14: Article 11.

Section 504 of the Rehabilitation Act. 1973. 29 USC section 701 et seq.

Section 508 of the Rehabilitation Act. 1998. 29 USC section 794d.

Segerholm, C. 2003. "Researching Evaluation in National (State) Politics and Administration: A Critical Approach." *American Journal of Evaluation* 24: 353–372.

Selwyn, N. 2004. "Reconsidering Political and Popular Understandings of the Digital Divide." *New Media and Society* 6: 341–362.

Settlement Agreement Between the United States, the National Federation of the Blind, the American Council of the Blind, and Arizona State University. 2010. http://www.ada.gov/arizona_state_university.htm.

Sevilla, J., G. Herrera, B. Martinez, and F. Alcantud. 2007. "Web Accessibility for Individuals with Cognitive Deficits: A Comparative Study Between an Existing Commercial Web and Its Cognitively Accessible Equivalent." *ACM Transactions on Computer-Human Interaction* 14: Article 12.

Seymour, W., and D. Lupton. 2004. "Holding the Line Online: Exploring

Wired Relationships for People with Disabilities." *Disability and Society* 19: 291–305.

Sgroi, D. 2008. "Social Network Theory, Broadband and the Future of the World Wide Web." *Telecommunications Policy* 32, 1: 62–84.

Shakespeare, T. 1994. "Cultural Representation of Disabled People: Dustbin for Disavowal." *Disability and Society* 9: 283–299.

Shapiro, J. P. 1993. *No Pity: People with Disabilities Forging a New Civil Rights Movement*. New York: Times Books.

———. 1994. "Disability Policy and the Media: A Stealth Civil Rights Movement Bypasses the Press and Defies Conventional Wisdom." *Policy Studies Journal* 22: 123–133.

Shaw, L. H., and C. S. W. Grant. 2002. "In Defense of the Internet: The Relationship Between Internet Communication and Depression, Loneliness, Self-esteem, and Perceived Social Support." *CyberPsychology and Behavior* 5: 157–171.

Sherry, M. 2008. *Disability and Diversity: A Sociological Perspective*. New York: NOVA Science.

Shi, Y. 2006. "The Accessibility of Queensland Visitor Information Centres' Websites." *Tourism Management* 27: 829–841.

Shigaki, C. L., K. J. Hagglund, M. Clark, and K. Conforti. 2002. "Access to Health Care Services Among People with Disabilities and Higher-income Uninsured Adults." *Journal of the American Medical Association* 295, 17: 2027–2036.

Shneiderman, B. 2000. "Universal Usability." *Communications of the ACM* 43, 5: 84–91.

———. 2008. "Science 2.0." *Science* 319: 349–1350.

Shuler, J. A., P. T. Jaeger, and J. C. Bertot. 2010. "Implications of Harmonizing E-government Principles and the Federal Depository Library Program (FDLP)." *Government Information Quarterly* 27: 9–16.

Siebers, T. 2006. "Disability Studies and the Future of Identity Politics." In L. M. Alcoff, M. Hames-Garcia, S. P. Mohanty, and P. M. L. Moya (eds.), *Identity Politics Reconsidered*. New York: Palgrave Macmillan, pp. 10–30.

———. 2008. *Disability Theory*. Ann Arbor: University of Michigan Press.

Simpson, J. 2009. "Inclusive Information and Communication Technologies for People with Disabilities." *Disability Studies Quarterly* 29: 1–13. http://www.dsq-sds.org.

Singh, A. K., and R. Sahu. 2008. "Integrating Internet, Telephones, and Call Centers for Delivering Better Quality E-governance to All Citizens." *Government Information Quarterly* 25: 477–490

Slatin, J. M. 2001. "The Art of the ALT: Toward a More Accessible Web." *Computers and Composition* 18: 73–81.

Slatin, J. M., and S. Rush. 2003. *Maximum Accessibility*. Boston: Addison Wesley.

Sloan, D., P. Gregor, P. Booth, and L. Gibson. 2002. "Auditing Accessibility of UK Higher Education Websites." *Interacting with Computers* 14: 313–325.

Smith, A. G. 2001. "Applying Evaluation Criteria to New Zealand Government Websites." *International Journal of Information Management* 21: 137–149.

Smith, B., B. T. Fraser, and C. R. McClure. 2000. "Federal Information Policy and Access to Web-based Information." *Journal of Academic Librarianship* 26: 274–281.

Smith, D. D. 2001. *Special Education: Teaching in an Age of Opportunity.* Boston: Allyn and Bacon.

Smythe, I. 2010. *Dyslexia in the Digital Age: Making IT Work.* New York: Continuum.

Southeast ADA Center. 2002. "Judge Rules that Inaccessible Website Violates ADA." http://www.sedbtac.org/ed/whats_new/articles.php?id=2520.

Spindler, T. 2002. "The Accessibility of Web Pages for Mid-sized College and University Libraries." *Reference and User Services Quarterly* 42, 2: 149–154.

Spooner, T., P. Meredith, and L. Rainie. 2003. *Regional Variations in Internet Use Mirror Differences in Educational and Income Levels.* Washington, DC: Pew Internet and American Life Project. http://www.pewinternet.org.

Spooner, T., L. Rainie, and P. Meredith. 2001. *Asian-Americans and the Internet: The Young and the Connected.* Washington, DC: Pew Internet and American Life Project. http://www.pewinternet.org.

Stake, B. 2004. "How Far Dare an Evaluator Go Toward Saving the World?" *American Journal of Evaluation* 25: 103–107.

Standen, A. 2010. "Unfriendly Skies: Blind Passengers Sue United." National Public Radio. http://www.npr.org/templates/story/story.php?storyId=130921227.

Stanley v. Georgia. 1969. 394 U.S. 557.

Stapleton, D. C., B. L. O'Day, G. A. Livermore, and A. J. Imparato. 2006. "Dismantling the Poverty Trap: Disability Policy for the Twenty-first Century." *Milbank Quarterly* 84: 701–732.

Stephanidis, C., and P. L. Emailiani. 1999. "Connecting to the Information Society: A European Perspective." *Technology and Disability* 10: 21–44.

Stephanidis, C., and A. Savidis. 2001. "Universal Access in the Information Society: Methods, Tools, and Interactive Technologies." *Universal Access in the Information Society* 1: 40–55.

Stevenson, S. 2009. "Digital Divide: A Discursive Move Away from Real Inequities." *Information Society* 25: 1–22.

Stewart, R., V. Narendra, and A. Schmetzke. 2005. "Accessibility and Usability of Online Library Databases." *Library Hi Tech* 23, 2: 265–286.

Stienstra, D. 2006. "The Critical Space Between: Access, Inclusion and Standards in Information Technologies." *Information, Communication and Society* 9: 335–354.

Stienstra, D., and L. Troschuk. 2005. "Engaging Citizens with Disabilities in eDemocracy." *Disability Studies Quarterly* 25, 2. http://www.dsq-sds.org.

Stienstra, D., J. Watzke, and G. E. Birch. 2007. "A Three-way Dance: The Global Public Good and Accessibility in Information Technologies." *Information Society* 23: 149–158.

Stiker, H. J. 1999. *A History of Disability*. Trans. W. Sayers. Ann Arbor: University of Michigan Press.

Stodden, R. A. 2005. "The Status of Persons with Disabilities in Postsecondary Education." *TASH Connections* 31, 11/12: 4–7.

Stone, C. I., and B. Sawatzki. 1980. "Hiring Bias and the Disabled Interviewee: Effects of Manipulating Work History and Disability Information of the Disabled Job Applicant." *Journal of Vocational Behavior* 16: 96–104.

Stone, E. 1999. "Modern Slogan, Ancient Script: Impairment and Disability in the Chinese Language." In M. Corker and E. French (eds.), *Disability Discourse*. Philadelphia: Open University Press, pp. 136–147.

Stone, E., and M. Priestley. 1996. "Parasites, Pawns, and Partners: Disability Research and the Role of Non-disabled Researchers." *British Journal of Sociology* 47: 699–716.

Stowers, G. N. L. 2002. *The State of Federal Websites: The Pursuit of Excellence*. Washington, DC: IBM Endowment for the Business of Government. http://www.endowment.pwcglobal.com/pdfs/Stowers Report0802.pdf.

Streib, G., and I. Navarro. 2006. "Citizen Demand for Interactive E-government: The Case of Georgia Consumer Services." *American Review of Public Administration* 36: 288–300.

Stroman, D. F. 2003. *The Disability Rights Movement: From Deinstitutionalization to Self-Determination*. Lanham, MD: University Press of America.

Sullivan, M. 2001. "Disabled People and the Politics of Partnership in Aotoaroa, New Zealand." In L. Barton (ed.), *Disability, Politics, and the Struggle for Change*. London: David Fulton, pp. 93–109.

Sullivan, T., and R. Matson. 2000. "Barriers to Use: Usability and Content Accessibility on the Web's Most Popular Sites." In J. Thomas and J. Scholtz (eds.), *Proceedings of the Conference on Universal Usability*. New York: ACM, pp. 139–144.

Sunstein, C. R. 2002. "The Law of Group Polarization." *Journal of Political Philosophy* 10: 175–195.

———. 2008. "Neither Hayek nor Habermas." *Public Choice* 134: 87–95.

Suppes, P. 1974. "A Survey of Cognition in Handicapped Children." *Review of Educational Research* 44: 145–176.

Svenonious, E. 2000. *The Intellectual Foundation of Information Organization*. Cambridge: MIT Press.

Swain, J., S. French, and C. Cameron. 2003. *Controversial Issues in a Disabling Society*. Philadelphia: Open University Press.

Sweeney, M., M. Maguire, and B. Shackel. 1993. "Evaluating User-Machine Interaction: A Framework." *International Journal of Man-Machine Studies* 38: 689–711.

Switzer, J. V. 2003. *Disabled Rights: America Disability Policy and the Fight for Equality*. Washington, DC: Georgetown University Press.

Tagaki, H., S. Saito, K. Fukuda, and C. Asakawa. 2007. "Analysis of Navigability of Web Applications for Improving Blind Accessibility." *ACM Transactions on Computer-Human Interaction* 14: Article 13.

Taleo Research. 2006. *Trends in Hourly Job Application Methods.* http://www.taleo.com.

Taylor, H. 2000. "How the Internet Is Improving the Lives of Americans with Disabilities." The Harris Poll (No. 30).

Teerling, M. L., and W. Pieterson. 2010. "Multichannel Marketing: An Experiment on Guiding Citizens to the Electronic Channels." *Government Information Quarterly* 27: 98–107.

Telecommunications Accessibility Enhancement Act. 1988. P.L. 100-542.

Telecommunications Act. 1996. 47 USC section 225 et seq.

Telecommunications for the Disabled Act. 1982. P.L. 97-410.

Television Circuitry Decoder Act. 1990. P.L. 101-431.

Temkin, B., and N. Belanger. 2004. *Web Sites Are Fast but Inaccessible.* Cambridge, MA: Forrester Research.

Tennant, J. 2009. "The Reasonableness of Working from Home in the Digital Age." *Review of Disability Studies* 5, 4: 10–20.

Theofanos, M., and J. Redish. 2003. "Bridging the Gap: Between Accessibility and Usability." *Interactions* 10, 6: 36–51.

Thomas, C. 1999. *Female Forms: Experiencing and Understanding Disability.* Philadelphia: Open University.

Thomas, D. 1982. *The Experience of Handicap.* London: Methuen.

Thompson, K. M., C. R. McClure, and P. T. Jaeger. 2003. "Evaluating Federal Websites: Improving E-government for the People." In J. F. George (ed.), *Computers in Society: Privacy, Ethics, and the Internet.* Upper Saddle River, NJ: Prentice Hall, pp. 400–412.

Thompson, R. 1997. *Extraordinary Bodies.* New York: Columbia University Press.

Thompson, T., S. Burgstahler, and D. Comden. 2003. "Research on Web Accessibility in Higher Education." *Journal of Information Technology and Disabilities* 9, 2. www.rit.edu/~easi/itd.htm.

Tongia, R., and E. J. Wilson. 2007. "Turning Metcalfe on His Head: The Multiple Costs of Network Exclusion." Paper presented at the 35th Telecommunications Policy Research Conference. Vienna, VA.

Tringo, J. L. 1970. "The Hierarchy of Preference Toward Disability Groups." *Journal of Special Education* 4: 295–307.

Tung, L., and O. Rieck. 2005. "Adoption of Electronic Government Services Among Business Organizations in Singapore." *Journal of Strategic Information Systems* 14: 417–440.

Turnbull, H. R., Jr., and M. J. Stowe. 2001. "Five Models for Thinking About Disability: Implications for Policy Responses." *Journal of Disability Policy Studies* 12: 198–205.

Turmusani, M. 2003. *Disabled People and Economic Needs in the Developing World: A Political Perspective from Jordan.* Burlington, VT: Ashgate.

Turner, S. D. 2009. *Dismantling Digital Deregulation: Toward a National Broadband Strategy.* Washington, DC: Free Press. http://www.freepress.net/files/Dismantling_Digital_Deregulation.pdf.

Tusler, A. 2005. "How to Make Technology Work: A Study of Best Practices in United States Electronic and Information Technology Companies." *Disability Studies Quarterly* 25, 2.

Twenty-first Century Communications and Video Accessibility Act. 2010. S. 3304.

United Nations. 1994. *Standard Rules on the Equalization of Opportunities for Persons with Disabilities*. New York: United Nations.

———. 2007. *Convention on the Rights of Persons with Disabilities*. New York: United Nations.

University of California Los Angeles. 2003. *UCLA Internet Report: Surveying the Digital Future*. Los Angeles: Anderson Graduate School of Management. http://www.ccp.ucla.edu.

US Census Bureau. 2008. *Americans with Disabilities 2005: Household Economic Studies*. Washington, DC.

US Department of Commerce. 1995. *Falling Through the Net: A Survey of the "Have Nots" in Rural and Urban America*. Washington, DC.

———. 1998. *Falling Through the Net II: New Data on the Digital Divide*. Washington, DC.

———. 1999. *Falling Through the Net: Defining the Digital Divide*. Washington, DC.

———. 2000. *Falling Through the Net: Toward Digital Inclusion*. Washington, DC.

———. 2002. *A Nation Online: How Americans Are Expanding Their Use of the Internet*. Washington, DC.

———. 2004. *A Nation Online: Entering the Broadband Age*. Washington, DC.

US Department of Education. 2004a. "How Do Individuals with Disabilities Use the Web?" http://www.ed.gov/policy/gen/guid/disability-awareness .doc.

———. 2004b. *National Survey of Postsecondary Faculty*. Washington, DC.

———. 2010. *Digest of Education Statistics, 2009*. Washington, DC.

US Department of Education and US Department of Justice. 2010. *Electronic Book Reader Dear Colleague Letter: Questions and Answers About the Law, the Technology, and the Population Affected*. http://www.ed.gov.

US Department of Justice. 2010a. *Fact Sheet: Advance Notice of Proposed Rulemaking on Accessibility of Next Generation 9-1-1*. Washington, DC.

———. 2010b. *Fact Sheet: Advance Notice of Proposed Rulemaking on Accessibility of Web Information and Services Provided by Entities Covered by the ADA*. Washington, DC.

———. 2010c. *Fact Sheet: Advance Notice of Proposed Rulemaking on Equipment and Furniture*. Washington, DC.

———. 2010d. *Fact Sheet: Advance Notice of Proposed Rulemaking on Movie Captioning and Video Description*. Washington, DC.

Vaccarella, B. 2001. "Finding Our Way Through the Maze of Adaptive Technology. *Computers in Libraries* 21, 9: 44–47.

Valentine, J. 2002. "Naming and Narrating Disability in Japan." In M. Corker and T. Shakespeare (eds.), *Disability/Postmodernity: Embodying Disability Theory*. New York: Continuum, pp. 213–227.

Vandenbark, R. T. 2010. "Tending a Wild Garden: Library Web Design for Persons with Disabilities. *Information Technology and Libraries* 29, 1: 23–29.

Vanderheiden, G. C. 2003. "Opening Comments." Presented at the 2003 Voice over Internet Protocol Services Forum, Madison, Wisconsin. http://www.fcc.gov/voip/voipforum.html.

Van Sant, W. 2009. "Librarians Now Add Social Work to Their Resumes." *St. Petersburg Times*, June 8. http://www.tampabay.com.

Vash, C. L., and N. M. Crewe. 2004. *Psychology of Disability*. New York: Springer.

Wagenaar, A. C., E. M. Harwood, C. Silianoff, and T. L. Toomey. 2005. "Measuring Public Policy: The Case of Beer Keg Registration Laws." *Evaluation and Program Planning* 28: 359–367.

Wagner, M., L. Newman, R. Cameto, N. Garza, and P. Levine. 2005. *After High School: A First Look at Postschool Experiences of Youth with Disabilities: A Report from the National Longitudinal Transition Study-2 (NLTS2)*. Menlo Park, CA: SRI International.

Wakefield, D. 1998. *Disabilities Information Resources*. Cited in L. McLawhorn (2001), "Leveling the Accessibility Playing Field: Section 508 of the Rehabilitation Act." *North Carolina Journal of Law and Technology* 3: 63–100.

Wall, P. S., and L. Sarver. 2002. "Disabled Students in an Era of Technology." *Internet and Higher Education* 6: 277–284.

Wallace, D. P. 2001. "The Nature of Evaluation." In D. P. Wallace and C. V. Fleet (eds.), *Library Evaluation: A Casebook and Can-Do Guide*. Westport, CT: Libraries Unlimited, pp. 209–220.

Walling, L. L. 2004. "Educating Students to Serve Information Seekers with Disabilities." *Journal of Education for Library and Information Science* 45: 137–148.

Wang, J., and J. Mankoff. 2003. "Theoretical and Architectural Support for Input Device Adaptation." *Proceedings of ACM Conference on Universal Usability 2003*, pp. 85–92.

Ware, L. P. 2002. "A Moral Conversation on Disability: Risking the Personal in Educational Contexts." *Hypatia* 17, 3: 143–172.

Warkany, J. 1959. "Congenital Malformations in the Past." *Journal of Chronic Disabilities* 10: 84–96.

Warschauer, M. 2003a. "Demystifying the Digital Divide." *Scientific American* 289, 2: 42–48.

———. 2003b. *Technology and Social Inclusion: Rethinking the Digital Divide*. Cambridge: MIT Press.

Wattenberg, T. 2004. "Beyond Legal Compliance: Communities of Advocacy That Support Accessible Online Learning." *Internet and Higher Education* 7: 123–139.

Weimar, M. 1990. *Improving College Teaching: Strategies for Developing Instructional Effectiveness*. San Francisco: Jossey-Bass.

Wendell, S. 1996. *The Rejected Body: Feminist Political Interpretations on Disability*. New York: Routledge.

Wentz, B., and J. L. Lazar. 2011. "Are Separate Interfaces Inherently Unequal? An Evaluation with Blind Users of the Usability of Two Interfaces for a Social Networking Platform." Paper presented at *iConference 2011*, Seattle.

West, D. M. 2003. *Achieving E-government for All: Highlights from a National Survey.* Washington, DC: Benton Foundation/Rockefeller Institute of Government. http://www.benton.org/publibrary/egov /access2003.doc.

———. 2004. *State and Federal E-government in the United States, 2004.* Providence, RI: Brown University Press.

Westbrook, M. T., V. Legge, and M. Pennay. 1970. "Attitudes Toward Disability in a Multicultural Society. *Social Science and Medicine* 36: 615–623.

Whittle, S. 2007. "Social Networking: Not as Inclusive as You Might Think." *ZDNet,* November 5. http://www.zdnet.co.uk.

Will, B. H. 2005. "Library Services for All." *Library Journal* 130, 19: 47.

Williamson, K., and J. Roberts. 2010. "Developing and Sustaining a Sense of Place: The Role of Social Information." *Library and Information Science Research* 32: 281–287.

Winzer, M. A. 1993. *The History of Special Education: From Isolation to Integration.* Washington, DC: Gallaudet University Press.

———. 1997. "Disability and Society Before the Eighteenth Century: Dread and Despair." In L. J. Davis (ed.), *The Disability Studies Reader.* New York: Routledge, pp. 75–109.

Witt, N., and A. McDermott. 2004. "Web Site Accessibility: What Logo Will We Use Today?" *British Journal of Educational Technology* 35: 45–56.

Wolanin, T. R., and P. E. Steele. 2004. *Higher Education Opportunities for Students with Disabilities: A Primer for Policymakers.* Washington, DC: Institute for Higher Education Policy.

Woolfson, M. 2004. "E-government Needs to Be Truly Representative of the People. *New Media Age,* November 4, p. 18.

World Markets Research Centre. 2001. *Global E-government Survey.* Providence, RI: World Markets Research Centre.

Wright, K. B. 2000. "Computer-mediated Social Support, Older Adults, and Coping. *Journal of Communication* 50: 100–118.

Wu, M., R. Baecker, and B. Richards. 2005. "Participatory Design of an Orientation Aid for Amnesiacs." *Proceedings of ACM Conference on Universal Usability 2005,* pp. 511–520.

Xie, B. 2003. "Older Adults, Computers, and the Internet: Future Directions." *Gerontechnology* 2, 4: 289–305.

———. 2006. "Growing Older in the Information Age: Civic Engagement, Social Relationships, and Well-being of Older Internet Users in China and the United States." PhD diss., Rensselaer Polytechnic Institute, Troy, New York.

———. 2007. "Older Chinese, the Internet, and Well-being." *Care Management Journals: Journal of Long Term Home Health Care* 8, 1: 33–38.

Yang, C.-S., C.-H. Yang, L.-Y. Chuang, and C.-H. Yang. 2009. "A Wireless Internet Interface for Persons with Physical Disability." *Mathematical and Computer Modeling* 50: 72–80.

Yesilada, Y., R. Stevens, S. Harper, and C. Goble. 2007. "Evaluating

DANTE: Semantic Transcoding for Visually Disabled Users." *ACM Transactions on Computer-Human Interaction* 14: Article 14.

Young, J. M. 2010. *Americans with Disabilities Act at 20—Celebrating Our Progress, Affirming Our Commitment.* Washington, DC: National Council on Disability.

Yu, H. 2002. "Web Accessibility and the Law: Recommendation for Implementation." *Library Hi Tech* 20, 4: 406–419.

Yu, P. K. 2002. "Bridging the Digital Divide: Equality in the Information Age." *Cardozo Art and Entertainment Law Journal* 20: 1–52.

Zeff, R. 2007. "Universal Design Across the Curriculum." *New Directions for Higher Education* 137: 27–44.

Ziporyn, T. 1992. *Nameless Diseases.* New Brunswick, NJ: Rutgers University Press.

Zola, I. K. 1993. "Disability Statistics, What We Count and What It Tells Us: A Personal and Political Analysis." *Journal of Disability Policy Studies* 4, 2: 9–39.

———. 1994. "Towards Inclusion: The Role of People with Disabilities in Policy and Research Issues in the United States—a Historical and Political Analysis." In M. H. Rioux and J. M. Bach (eds.), *Disability Is Not Measles.* North York, ON: Roeher Institute, p. 49–66.

Index

About the Book

From websites to mobile devices, cyberspace has revolutionized the lived experience of disability—frequently for better, but sometimes for worse.

Paul Jaeger offers a sweeping examination of the complex and often contradictory relationships between people with disabilities and the Internet. Tracing the historical and legal evolution of the digital disability divide in the realms of education, work, social life, and culture, and also exploring avenues of policy reform and technology development, Jaeger connects individual experiences with the larger story of technology's promise and limitations for providing equal access online.

Paul T. Jaeger is assistant professor of information studies and codirector of the Information Policy and Access Center at the University of Maryland.